STILWELL'S
Personal File

CHINA · BURMA · INDIA
1942–1944

STILWELL'S
Personal File

CHINA · BURMA · INDIA
1942-1944

Edited by:
Riley Sunderland and
Charles F. Romanus

Volume 3

 Scholarly Resources Inc.
1508 Pennsylvania Avenue · Wilmington, Delaware 19806

PUBLISHER'S NOTE

Every effort has been made to present faithful facsimiles of the original documents. It should be noted, however, that some of the documents were in very poor condition, and consequently their reproductions are not of the highest quality which we strive for. A small number of documents which were so poor that legible reproductions were impossible have been transcribed and marked with asterisks adjoining the page numbers.

O,
D
767
.S76
1976
v.3

Library of Congress Catalog Card Number: 74-24967
International Standard Book Number: 0-8420-1799-2

Printed in the United States of America

Published by
SCHOLARLY RESOURCES, INC.
1508 Pennsylvania Avenue
Wilmington, Delaware 19806

TABLE OF CONTENTS

LIST OF MAPS, TABLES, CHARTS

MAPS

TABLES

CHARTS

Chapter XII
PLANS AND EVENTS, FALL, 1943

August, September, October and November 1943 were filled with a succession of conferences on plans for the re-taking of Burma. The policy for the coming dry season, in this theater, could be summarized as follows:

1. Strategic air offensive to be intensified as soon as the weather permits against bases and LOC in Burma.

2. Possible amphibious operations against the Andaman Islands and Ramree Island off Akyab.

3. Preparation for a full-scale operation against the Arakan, using two and two-thirds divisions with one additional division in reserve, to be completed by early January. If the amphibious operation against Akyab is not carried out, the Arakan offensive would be limited to securing the line Indin-Rathedaung-Kyauktaw. It would start in mid-January 1944.

4. Three divisions of the British IV Corps to seize Kalemyo and Kalewa. An all-weather road to be pushed to the Chindwin. This offensive was to start in February 1944.

5. Continued offensive on IV Corps front to seize bridgehead on Chindwin in Kalewa area, and advance to Yeu. Yeu to be retained during the monsoon with a force of three divisions and one in reserve which would come from the Arakan front in late April 1944.

6. One Chinese division to move forward to the Chindwin in October 1943 to cover the advance of the Ledo Road eastward. Another Chinese division to move forward to Shaduzup area in mid-January, while one regiment from another Chinese division, flown from Fort Hertz, moves south to Bumrang area. These two divisons, with one in reserve, to move on Kamaing and Myitkyina beginning in March, and continue against the Katha-Bhamo area in May. Chinese armies in Yunnan to move on Bhamo-Lashio in February.

7. In mid-January, one LRPG (Long Range Penetration Group) to operate from Homalin toward Katha to assist the Chinese advance.

8. One LRPG to begin operations in February and another in March from Chittagong area toward Haka-Gangaw-Pakokku.

Stilwell felt that the plan made at the Delhi conference for the re-taking of Burma was piecemeal and uncoordinated, that there were losses in timing which gave the Japanese a chance to jump around and that the plan prescribed too much in detail.

The CBI Theater Commander's chief task was to steer a course through this sea of planning which would nourish his own plans for a land route to China across north Burma, and for increased air lift into China. Not only CBI but SEAC as well had been given this directive at Quebec. Although the recapture of all of Burma was greatly desired, the operations had to be executed with the limited means at hand. There was constantly the danger of committing men and materiel to widespread operations which might jeopardize the immediate objectives. The more extended

LRPG's became, the broader the combined fronts became; and more aircraft would consequently have to be diverted from the Hump to support such operations.

President Roosevelt had directed that the tonnage lifted into China reach 10,000 tons monthly by the fall of 1943. (Chart 6.) He had definitely committed himself to the Generalissimo on this point. Moreover, the Ledo Base had to be stocked against the impending operations to clear north Burma. The achievement of these objectives could not be jeopardized by diverting aircraft equipment or tonnage to other more ambitious operations however desirable they might appear. Any plan had to be based logistically upon the means at hand. The employment of those means depended upon the strategic conceptions of the nations involved.

The British thought to by-pass Burma in favor of an attack on Sumatra and Malaya formally appeared in JPS (Joint Planning Staff) Paper No. 81, September 1943. This strategic concept might have crystallized had not the Combined Chiefs of Staff issued directions placing initial efforts elsewhere.

Stilwell's estimate of the value of amphibious operations was that they would be useful in persuading the Generalissimo to move the Y-Force troops into action.

In point of fact, several objectives had to be accomplished simultaneously, not as alternatives, and one of three courses must, therefore, predominate:

1.   Concentrate on the ferry route to China.

2.   Concentrate on the ground offensive against Burma.

3.   Start a long-term project to improve the Assam LOC.

Stilwell's attitude was that the Assam LOC must be improved in order that the offensive in north Burma could go through on schedule, and the Hump tonnage be raised to 10,000 tons per month concurrently with the North Burma Campaign. These were not alternatives to him, but the conjunction of three compatibles.

Actually, events and decisions outside the theater largely settled the strategy for the 1943-1944 dry season. The Cairo Conference (SEXTANT) in December was destined to reduce the contemplated amphibious operations.

Land operations against the Arakan area were begun, but were unsuccessful inasmuch as they fell short of the capture of Akyab. The plans for British operations in the Chindwin area were turned from offensive to defensive by the Japanese attack on Tiddim and Fort White and the consequent thrust towards Imphal and the Manipur Road in the spring of 1944. The valley campaign in north Burma was launched.

However, one decision of the Quebec Conference had materialized with the arrival of CBI of the 5307th Composite Unit (Merrill's Marauders). The 29th, 30th, and 31st of October 1943 witnessed the debarkation of the first American infantry troops in the theater: the three battalions of the 5307th.

A proposal had been made at the Quebec Conference in August 1943 that the United States should furnish a force similar to the Wingate Expedition of spring 1943 in order that they might engage in long-range penetration operations. Accordingly, on 1 September the Chief of Staff, General Marshall, directed that approximately 3,000 officers and men be shipped at once to the Asiatic theater to form three special units for employment in Burma. He further directed that these troops be selected from volunteers, in excellent physical condition, who were informed that they were to engage in a hazardous mission within a few months.

CHART 6—HUMP TONNAGE CARRIED BY ALL CARRIERS IN
INDIA–CHINA: 1943

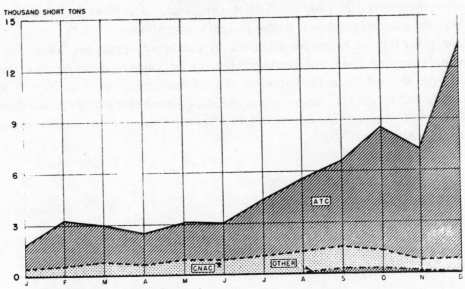

* China National Aviation Corporation.

A letter was dispatched 7 September to Stilwell, acquainting him with the action taken and outlining the proposed use of the force:

"It is visualized that three battalions will be employed separately—probably two in Assam and one from Yunnan, and that they will operate in front of main efforts. They will have pack transport and will be resupplied by air. Although operating separately the three efforts should be coordinated by one 'Group' Headquarters, composed of personnel who will train with the battalions and thus become familiar with their capabilities, personalities, communications and supply problems, and other vital factors, as well as to maintain liaison and coordinate with other friendly troops in the area."

In accordance with the Chief of Staff's 1 September directive, various command headquarters received radio instructions regarding the recruitment of personnel for the new force. Nine hundred and fifty troops who had served on Trinidad were secured through the Caribbean Defense Command; another 950 were found among the veterans of Guadalcanal and other South Sea operations; and a similar number, many with tropical service behind them, volunteered from the United States.

Soon after their arrival in CBI, the 5307th Composite Unit went into intensive training at Deogarh. Naturally, great emphasis was placed on jungle operations.

When the plans for the recapture of Burma by combined operations failed to materialize in November and December 1943, the contemplated use of long-range penetration troops now in training had to be shelved. With the approach of the offensive to open up the way for the Ledo Road, Stilwell desired to use this regiment in a modified form of long-range penetration operations in the North Burma Campaign. The Supreme Allied Commander approved and the organization was transferred to Stilwell.

Agwar   for the eyes of Gen. Marshall alone.

CK-36   WAVELL   AUG 30

Reurad 2391.

X-ray force of two divisions and corps troops
is ready now, except for four thousand infantry fillers. These
can be absorbed quickly when received. This force,
as British know, is well trained and in good shape.
If materiel arrives, we will have two light tank
battalions and a 4.2 mortar regiment to back
us up. Mortar unit will be thoroughly trained tank
units partially trained but enough to operate.
Training of x-ray force has been thorough and continuous, with emphasis on basic principles, marks-
manship, tactics, and special methods of jungle
warfare. Y-force re-organization
ordered completed by September one. This means
inactivation of one division in three to fill up
other two. Chen Cheng now back in Kunming.
I believe he will push this. It will give effective strength of eight thousand per division.
Replacements coming in slowly. By November
divisions may be up to ten thousand each
This depends on war ministry who now
appear to be

quarter. It would

769

be simple if they were willing to break up useless existing units as I have frequently recommended. Now in Yunnan eight corps and
one division, one corps on march in, two corps
held outside province for emergencies. After
reorganization, we will have on Paoshan front
nine divisions, on Mengtze front eight divisions, in Kunming area five divisions. These
troops have light weapons and mortars. With
even very meager tonnage we can give them
five battalions of seventy-five hows and some, sixty
mm. mortars, Boys rifles, bazookas thirty-
sevens, and tommies, with ammo. The
services will be sketchy but adequate. Two
classes of senior officers, corps, division and
regimental commanders, have already taken
course at Ramgarh. More coming. All
other officers going to Kunming schools. Unit
training being started in divisions. Instructor liaison groups starting off on August
twenty. It is only the lack of weapons and
ammo that breaks our hearts. Two thous-

(769)

We will build jeep road backward from TAGAP GA to meet road construction. Next fifty miles from road-head at mile fifty-one very difficult. Best estimate is possible junction with jeep road by end of year. Di-versions for air field construction have been serious, but Wheeler confident we can get through.

and tons a month would set it up. In gen-eral the Y-force, if it gets some weapons and signal material and if replacements come as promised, will be three times as good as it was before we took hold. It will still be far below the Ramgarh standard, but with Chen Cheng in command, I believe it is capable of a seri-ous effort, and in view of numerical superi-ority has better than a fair chance of success. If the G-mo should really get behind the ef-fort, the chances would greatly improve.

The Ledo road has been at a stand still for two months. Progress is picking up again. Our advanced posts now with in thirty miles of Shinbwiyang. We plan to take that place & build an air-field first thing to assure supply of one division that will push toward Mogaung. We can sup-ply that division until the road gets through to Shinbwiyang. Thereafter supply will be easy. With an air field at Shin, it is only a question of number of planes available

(76)

to support two divisions south of Shin. With any luck road should be there by end of year. — Unless japs reinforce materially in Myitkyina and Paoshan area our attack has very reasonable prospect of success and if British put on pressure, japs cannot afford to do it. British objections based on difficulty of supply, which could have been largely solved had they gone to work on the problem. They intend to limit their advance to the Chindwin, because they have no roads connecting with the net around Mandalay. If they stop at Chindwin, japs can divert forces to oppose Chinese attack. If British take Kalewa promptly, they can push towards Shwebo over road they used on way out. This line should be capable of sufficient improvement to maintain them, and they will have the Chindwin to use as well. The attacks must be co-ordinated to keep the japs from concentrating. They must be

(769)

vigorous to get the depth required. Energy is needed to solve the supply problem. Otherwise the means are available to do the job. The malaria bugaboo has not developed. Our American rate at Ledo is one per cent. The Chinese rate averages five per cent. The British have been warning me of a twenty-five per cent rate. I discount a serious jap effort in the air. I do not believe they will materially increase the Burma garrison. I believe delay until the fall of next year will be dangerous. I believe the air effort in China will not pay dividends. Last month the japs knocked off just as Chennault was about to give up his forward line. All the effort and tonnage that goes to the air offensive merely delays the creation of a dependable ground force. In another year, China may crack up and be lost. If that happens, not only do we lose our foot hold, but the japs may be able to use the man-power we want. (769)

¶. Difficulties of operation are appreciated. Danger of jap attack on Kunming has been foreseen, but reasonable protection is in sight. Delay gives japs further opportunity to mount the operation, whereas successful operation in Burma makes that area safe and allows us to retain base needed to prepare for action in central and east China. I cannot see how delay can help us, and but I can see how it would hurt us. British fearful of results of unsuccessful attempt. Failure to try at all may be much worse. In present mental attitude of British and Chinese, strong push needed to keep them to their commitments.

¶. Above written in haste and with apologies. Will amplify on your call any points I have missed or under-emphasized.

Stilwell

76.9

OFFICE OF THE COMMANDING GENERAL

UNITED STATES ARMED FORCES

CHINA BURMA INDIA

713

Agwar for the eyes of Gen. Marshall alone —

Rerrads 3243 and 3259, we need fresh air, and Mountbatten will be welcome. We also need real co-operation, and I am glad to know you made that point very clear to T. V. New subject. Yesterday I finally got from Ho Ying chin a list of the second thirty divisions. It is subject to change, but it commits them to the training program and recognizes our insistence on reorganization. Fifteen divisions are included as replacement and training units behind the thirty. On return of Pai Chung Hsi on the fourth believe we can decide on set-up for schools. If so, it may be possible to start training them on November first.

Stilwell.

Rcd
020130.

Send
020230.

775

Eyes alone

INCOMING RADIO   PRIORITY

RECEIVED : 02 SEPT 0855 GCT

FROM   : WAR

TO   : AMMISCA (FOR GEN STILWELLS EYES ONLY)

NR   : 3283   FILED: 01 SEPT 2037 GCT.

AMERICAN TROOPS WILL BE ASSEMBLED (FROM MARSHALL FOR STILWELLS EYS ONLY) IN INDIA IN EARLY NOVEMBER FOR ORGANIZATION, TRAINING, AND EMPLOYMENT IN BURMA FOR DEEP PENETRATIONS UNDER WINGATE IN FEBRUARY 1944. MESSAGES HAVE JUST BEEN DISPATCHED TO MACARTHUR AND HARMON CALLING UPON THEM TO PROVIDE 1000 RUGGED JUNGLE BATTLE TESTED VOLUNTEERS. 2000 MORE WILL BE PROVIDED FROM JUNGLE TRAINED UNITS OF THE CARIBBEAN DEFENSE COMMAND AND CONTINENTAL U S. THE THOUGHT OCCURRED TO ME THAT BRINK WITH A CADRE OF OFFICERS AND MEN WHO ARE FAMILIAR WITH WINGATES WORK IN THE THEATER COULD ORGANIZE THE INSTALLATION AND SUPERVISE THIS TRAINING.

THE GENERAL PLAN IS TO PREPARE THREE AMERICAN LONG RANGE PENETRATION GROUPS (BATTALIONS), TWO OF THESE PERHAPS TO OPERATE AHEAD OF LEDO FORCES AND *THE OTHER?* ORHESROM IN YUNNANN IN COOPERATION WITH SIMILAR BRITISH COLUMNS OPERATING TO THE SOUTH. DETAILS AS TO OUR SUGGESTED ORGANIZATIONS INTO THREE INDEPENDENT BATTALIONS, EQUIPMENT AND SUPPLY ARRANGEMENTS ARE BEING PREPARED BY THE STAFF AND WILL IMMEDIATELY FOLLOW. WEDEMEYER WHO WILL BE WITH MOUNTBATTEN IS WORKING THIS MATTER UP.

SEP 18 43 PM

INCOMING RADIO
RECEIVED: 2 ~~AUGUST~~ SEPT. 0855 GCT

FROM : AMMDEL

TO : AMMISCA

NO : AM 1425   FILED: 2 SEPTEMBER   0315 GCT

DECLASSIFIED
DOD Dir. 5200.9 Sept. 27, 1958
NCWN by _____ date 3-2-4-72

RECEIVED
WAR DEPARTMENT
U.S. MILITARY MISSION TO CHINA
CHUNGKING, CHINA

EYES ALONE GENERAL STILWELL. LATEST BRITISH PLANNING PAPER
WHICH I DISCUSSED TODAY WITH AUCHINLECK (FROM FERRIS) RECOMMENDS
ADOPTION SECOND PLAN MENTIONED IN MY 1388 WITH FOLLOWING TIMINGS:
FOURTH CORPS WITH THREE DIVISIONS STARTS GRADUAL MOVE TOWARDS
CHINDWIN IN NOVEMBER, WITH MINOR ACTIVITY ONLY UP TO FEBRUARY AND
A SERIOUS OFFENSIVE NOT STARTING UNTIL APRIL, IN MID APRIL (WITH
ONE ADDITIONAL DIVISION COMING FROM ARAKAN) TO SEIZE A BRIDGEHEAD
OVER CHINDWIN IN THE KALEWA AREA CONTINUE ADVANCE TO YEU AND HOLD
IT THRU MONSOON. ONE LONG RANGE PENETRATION GROUP TO START IN MID
JANUARY FROM HOMALIN TOWARDS KATHA TO ASSIST CHINESE ADVANCE. ONE
CHINESE DIVISION TO ADVANCE FROM LEDO TO CHINDWIN IN MID OCTOBER,
IN MID JANUARY THIS DIVISION TO ADVANCE TO SHADUZUP AREA WHILE ONE
CHINESE REGIMENT MOVES SOUTH FROM HERTZ TO BUMRANG AREA, IN MARCH
TWO CHINESE DIVISIONS WITH ONE RESERVE MOVE ON TO MYITKYINA AND IN
MAY SAME FORCE GOES TO BHAMO-KATHA AREA. YUNNAN FORCE JUMPS OFF IN
FEBRUARY WITH OBJECTIVE LASHIO-BHAMO AREA. WOULD GREATLY APPRECIATE
YOUR GENERAL THOUGHT ON THIS AS A GUIDE IN FUTURE DISCUSSIONS. UNDER
THIS PLAN DAILY TONNAGE INTO ASSAM FOR ATC, HUMP TONNAGE AND 10TH AND
14TH AIR FORCES WOULD BE 440 A DAY FROM OCTOBER THRU DECEMBER, 390
FROM JANUARY THRU MARCH AND 380 FROM APRIL THRU MAY. WE WOULD GET
ABOUT 700 TONS A DAY FOR OPERATIONS BASED ON LEDO IN ADDITION. IF

~~GRADED CONFIDENTIAL PARAPHRASED~~
~~VERSIONS REGRADED UNCLASSIFIED~~
~~ORDER SEC ARMY BY TAG/TW 254~~
7236   (780)

the ALTERNATE PLAN OF PUTTING THE MAIN EFFORT TOWARDS KATHA (FIRST
PLAN IN MY 1388 MESSAGE) WAS ADOPTED CORRESPONDING TONNAGES AVAILABLE
FOR SAME PURPOSES FOR SAME PERIODS WOULD BE FIVE TWO ZERO, 620 AND
850. SOME INDICATION YOUR OPINION RELATIVE MERITS THESE TWO PLANS
WOULD BE HELPFUL. ((CONFERENCE CLEARLY INDICATED LAND OPERATIONS HAVE
FIRST PRIORITY AND HUMP OPERATIONS SECOND IN BRITISH MINDS.)) THEY
PROPOSE TO CURTAIL WORK ON AIRFIELDS AND CARRY OUT A PROGRAM DESIGNED
TO SUPPORT LAND OPERATIONS. HAVE YOU ANY DEFINITE INFORMATION ON
WHETHER THESE MATTERS OF RELATIVE PRIORITY ARE CORRECT QUERY IN ORDER
TO PERMIT BRITISH TO CONCENTRATE TROOPS AND SUPPLIES THIS PRIORITY IF
CORRECT MUST START IMMEDIATELY OR THE ALREADY LATE LAND OPERATIONS
WILL BE FURTHER DELAYED. WILL YOU OR MAY I APPROACH WAR DEPARTMENT ON
THEIR UNDERSTANDING OF THE DECISIONS AT QUEBEC RELATING TO THIS QUERY
IT WOULD ALSO BE WISE TO ASK IF THE FORCY 700 TON FIRST PRIORITY FOR
AIR FORCES WILL BE CHANGED. WITH REDUCED TONNAGES TO MAKE MAXIMUM USE
OF WHAT WE GET INTO ASSAM ABOUT FIFTY PERCENT OF ALL HUMP CARGO SHOULD
BE YOKE SUPPLIES ALREADY IN ASSAM STARTING NOW. THIS IS A ROUGH FIGURE
AND I WILL SEND DETAILS LATER

SEP 4 '43 AM

RECEIVED
WAR DEPARTMENT
U. S. MILITARY MISSION TO CHINA
CHUNGKING, CHINA

789

17236

Agwar   for the eyes of Gen. Marshall alone.

Rewrad 3283.   The troops mentioned
will be most welcome and can be of
great use. I trust that the provision
for their use quote under Wingate un-
quote is ~~a mistake~~ NOT A FINAL DECISION. The command business
is complicated enough already. Brink can
be used to advantage in training and
supervision.

Stilwell.

Received   ~~Sent~~
030345.   030430.

1879

Arundel for Ferris - Eyes alone -

Reurad AM 1425. You can assume
that land operations will get priority, but
by no means exclusive priority. Do not repeat not approach W.D. on Quebec decisions.
In all probability the forty seven hundred ton
plan will be changed. My information indicates we cannot do a great deal before Lord
Louis gets here. All the factors are not visible
yet. As to your query on general plan, I do
not like it. It is piece-meal and un-coordin-
ated. The lapses in timing give the japs a
chance to jump around. The good weather
is not used to advantage. It prescribes too
much in detail. It begins to look to me
as if G-4, G.H.Q. is going to run the
war. You had better tip off Louis so
he wont make any bad blunders -

                                    Stilwell -

Recd my cntr 0431

Sent 030530

(775)

OFFICE OF THE COMMANDING GENERAL

UNITED STATES ARMED FORCES

CHINA BURMA INDIA

Agwar – for the eyes of Gen. Marshall alone

High circles here have been stung by the recent criticism in the U.S. of their methods and aims. The truth hurts. There are rumors that TAI LI the gestapo chief may be on the way out. If this occurs, it will prove how sensitive to American opinion this regime really is. The indications are that the tribal chieftain technique is applicable. If T.V.'s departure could be expedited, it would help.

Stilwell.

SECRET UNCLASSIFIED RESTRICTED CONFIDENTIAL
REGRADED ORDER SEC ARMY BY TAG PER 723058

SEP 4 '43 AM
RECEIVED

Received 040352

Sent 04445.

REGRADED CONFIDENTIAL
ORDER SEC ARMY BY TAG/BW-350

09161

778

885

RECEIVED IN ~~SECRET CODE~~

RECEIVED   : 4 SEPTEMBER 0540 GCT

FROM   : WAR   PRIORITY

TO   : AMMISCA

NR   : 3286   FILED : 1 SEPTEMBER 2349 GCT

FURTHER INFORMATION PERTAINING TO THREE AMERICAN LONG RANGE PEN-
ETRATION GROUPS FOLLOWS: (FOR PERSONAL ATTENTION STILWELL FROM MARSHALL)
TOTAL OF APPROXIMATELY TWO THOUSAND EIGHT FIFTY OFFICERS AND MEN ORGANIZED
INTO CASUAL DETACHMENTS WILL ARRIVE INDIA IN EARLY NOVEMBER. THEY WILL/BE
ALL
VOLUNTEERS. NINE FIFTY WILL BE BATTLE TESTED TROOPS IN JUNGLE FIGHTING
FROM THE SOUTH AND SOUTHWEST PACIFIC. NINETEEN HUNDRED WILL BE FROM JUNGLE
TRAINED TROOPS FROM THE CARIBBEAN DEFENSE COMMAND AND THE CONTINENTAL UNCLE
SUGAR. ALL WILL BE OF A HIGH STATE OF PHYSICAL RUGGEDNESS.

ABOVE VOLUNTEERS HAVE BEEN CALLED FOR WITH REQUISITE QUALIFICATIONS
AND COMMENSURATE GRADES AND RATINGS CONFORM INDEPENDENT BATTALIONS AFTER THEIR
ARRIVAL IN THE THEATER. THEY MUST THEN BE INTENSIVELY TRAINED IN JUNGLE WAR-
FARE, ANIMAL TRANSPORTATION AND AIR SUPPLY IN A SUITABLE JUNGLE AREA IN
PREPARATION FOR COMBAT IN PREPARATION FOR COMBAT IN FEBRUARY. THESE UNITS
SHOULD BE SUPPLEMENTED BY SUCH NATIVE GUIDES AND INTERPRETERS AND EITHER
BRITISH, INDIAN OR CHINESE LIAISON GROUPS AS MAY BE NECESSARY.

A FEW SELECTED OFFICERS AND NONCOMS FROM YOUR FORWARD AREA SHOULD
BE PROVIDED FOR ABSORPTION IN THE UNITS, AND TO SET UP BIVOUAC AND TRAINING
AREAS PRIOR TO THEIR ARRIVAL.

Training

IN ORDER TO COORDINATE RAWYHING WITH AIR SUPPLY, IT IS
CONSIDERED DESIREABLE THAT YOU SELECT A TOTAL OF ABOUT FIFTEEN COMPANY
GRADE AIRCORPS LIAISON OFFICERS WITH EXPERIENCE ON AIR SUPPLY LIAISON
FOR TRAINING WITH AND ASSIGNMENT TO THEIR UNITS.

INFORMATION IS DESIRED AS TO THE TRAINING AREA YOU PLAN FOR USE
OF THESE UNITS, AND ANYTHING WE CAN DO TO ASSIST.

PROPOSED WILLIAM DOG TABLE OF ORGANIZATION AND TABLE OF EQUIPMENT
WILL BE DISPATCHED BY AIR TO YOUR REAR ECHELON HOW QUEEN DELHI TO ASSIST
YOU IN ORGANIZING THESE UNITS. TWO COMPLETE SETS OF OF ORGANIZATIONAL
EQUIPMENT AND SPECIAL INDIVIDUAL JUNGLE EQUIPMENT IN ACCORDANCE WITH THIS
PROPOSED TABLE OF EQUIPMENT WILL BE SHIPPED IN AT LEAST TWO SEPERATE LOADINGS
TO CALCUTTA THE FIRST LEAVING UNCLE SUGAR ABOUT TWENTIETH SEPTEMBER. UPON
TABLES
RECEIPT OF KYYLES TAKE SUCH ACTION AS NECESSARY TO EAR MARK CHINESE LEND
LEASE EQUIPMENT FOR USE THESE TROOPS IN FIRST PHASE TRAINING TO PROVIDE FOR
ANY POSSIBLE LAG IN ARRIVAL EQUIPMENT FROM UNCLE SUGAR.

DESIRED THAT YOU TAKE STEPS TO PROCURE FOUR FIFTY PACK MULES AND
PACK EQUIPMENT WHICH WILL BE SUITABLE FOR JUNGLE OPERATIONS WITH THESE UNITS.
MEANWHILE, TWO QUARTERMASTER PACK TROOPS (ABOUT EIGHTY OFFICERS AND MEN EACH)
WITH A TOTAL OF FOUR FIFTY PACK MULES WILL BE SHIPPED FROM UNCLE SUGAR ABOUT
MID OCTOBER. RECONDITIONING PERIOD OF THESE ANIMALS UPON ARRIVAL INDIA
AFTER LONG SEA VOYAGE WILL PROBABLY REQUIRE YOUR USING THE ANIMALS PROCURED
IN INDIA FOR THE OPERATIONS.

PLEASE ADVISE WAR DEPARTMENT OF ANY ADDITIONAL REQUIREMENTS IN
CONNECTION WITH THE ABOVE PLAN

17,292

(783)

INCOMING RADIO

RECEIVED: 4 SEPTEMBER 0900 GCT

FROM : AGWAR   PRIORITY

TO   : AMMISCA   AMMDEL   **PRIORITY**

NO   : 3300   2304 FILED: 03 SEPT 1656 GCT

SUBSEQUENT TO YOUR COMMENTS (IN AG 1408 AMMDEL 19TH
AUGUST)REGARDING PROPOSED COMBINED LIAISON COMMITTEE IN INDIA,
THE SOUTHEAST ASIA COMMAND WAS ESTABLISHED UNDER LORD MOUNTBATTEN.
(FROM MARSHALL TO STILWELL EYES ONLY INFORMATIONAL FERRIS)
DECISION WAS ALSO REACHED BY COMBINED CHIEFS OF STAFF AND
APPROVED BY PRESIDENT AND PRIME MINISTER TO SET UP A COMBINED
LIAISON COMMITTEE IN NEW DELHI AS SET FORTH IN COMBINED CHIEFS
OF STAFF FINAL REPORT PARAGRAPHS 59 AND 60 (CCS 319/5) EN
ROUTE TO YOU BY COURIER AND PARAPHRASE OF WHICH FOLLOWS.

BEGINS PARAPHRASE: A COMBINED LIAISON COMMITTEE IS TO BE SET
UP IN NEW DELHI TO PROVIDE COORDINATION AND FACILITATE FREE
EXCHANGE OF INFORMATION BETWEEN BRITISH AND US QUASI MILITARY
AGENCIES IN INDIA AND THE SOUTHEAST ASIA COMMAND. BEFORE ANY
QUASI MILITARY ACTIVITIES INVOLVING OPERATIONS IN SOUTHEAST
ASIA THEATER OR IN INDIA ARE UNDERTAKEN THERE IS TO BE FULL
AND OPEN DISCUSSION IN COMBINED LIAISON COMMITTEE. BEFORE PLANS
FOR SUCH OPERATIONS IN THESE AREAS ARE PLACED IN EFFECT BY US
AGENCIES, CONCURRENCE OF SUPREME COMMANDER SOUTHEAST ASIA
THEATER, THE GOVERNMENT OF INDIA, OR THE COMMANDER IN CHIEF
INDIA MUST BE OBTAINED AS APPLICABLE. END PARAPHRASE.

THIS CCS DECISION FOLLOWS SUBSTANTIALLY THE PLAN FOR THE
COMBINED LIAISON COMMITTEE OUTLINED IN OURAD AMMISCA 2989

REGRADED CONFIDENTIAL
ORDER SEC/ARMY BY TAG/3W-350

AMMDEL 2006 EXCEPT FOR TWO CHANGES AS FOLLOWS:

    (A)   BEFORE OPERATIONS OF QUASI MILITARY AGENCIES IN AREA DESIGNATED ARE PLACED IN EFFECT CONCURRENCES AS INDICATED MUST BE OBTAINED;

    (B) THE SOUTHEAST ASIA COMMAND IS INTRODUCED.

THESE TWO CHANGES CAN BE INCORPORATED IN THE PROPOSED INSTRUCTIONS SUBMITTED TO YOU IN OURAD AMMISCA 2989 AMMDEL 2006, TO THE END THAT THE COMMITTEE WILL BE CONSTITUTED AS ORIGINALLY PLANNED EXCEPT: (1) THAT THESE AGENCIES(OSS, OEW, OWI, AND FCC) WILL HAVE TO OBTAIN CONCURRENCES BEFORE CARRYING OUT OPERATIONS IN AREA DESCRIBED, AND, ALTHOUGH CCS 319/5 DOES NOT SO SPECIFY, IT IS PRESUMED THE COMBINED LIAISON COMMITTEE WILL BE INSTRUMENTAL IN OBTAINING SUCH CONCURRENCES ; (2) THE COMBINED LIAISON COMMITTEE SHOULD FACILITATE EXCHANGE OF INFORMATION BETWEEN YOUR HEADQUARTERS AND GHQ AND WITH THE SOUTHEASTERN ASIA COMMAND.

PRIOR TO DISCUSSING MATTER ALONG THESE LINES WITH THE BRITISH CHIEFS OF STAFF YOUR COMMENTS ARE DESIRED.

THE COMBINED LIAISON COMMITTEE WAS HIT UPON FOR TWO MAIN REASONS, FIRSTLY AS AN ALTERNATIVE TO INTEGRATION OF COMMITTEES AND AGENCIES WHICH THE BRITISH ENDEAVORED TO OBTAIN FOR SO MANY MONTHS; AND SECONDLY TO PROVIDE A FORUM FOR HANDLING US QUASI MILITARY AGENCY ACTIVITIES WITHIN THE INDIAN GOVERNMENT WHICH THE BRITISH FELT THEY WERE ENTITLED TO EXERCISE SOME CONTROL OVER OR KNOW MORE ABOUT, BUT WERE UNSUCCESSFUL IN THEIR ATTEMPT TO DO SO.

THE US CHIEFS OF STAFF HAVE INFORMED THE BRITISH CHIEFS OF STAFF THAT THEY DISAPPROVE INTEGRATION OF BRITISH AND US IN- 784

1.7302

TELLIGENCE STAFF OFFICERS (EXCEPT IN CASE OF SUPREME COMMAND COMBINED STAFFS). THE AVOIDANCE OF THIS LONG-STANDING BRITISH PROPOSAL TO OBTAIN INTEGRATION AND INTERMIXTURE OF BRITISH AND US MEMBERS OF INTELLIGENCE COMMITTEES, AND OF QUASI MILITARY AGENCIES, IS CONSIDERED ADVANTAGEOUS.

THE WAR DEPARTMENT INTENDS THAT YOUR CHINESE SOURCES ARE NOT TO BE AFFECTED BY THIS SETUP. HOWEVER, IT IS BELIEVED THAT THE INTRODUCTION OF MOUNTBATTEN WITH A COMBINED STAFF WILL PERMIT A MUCH MORE HARMONIOUS AND TRUSTFUL ATTITUDE ON THE PART OF ALL, ESPECIALLY THE CHINESE

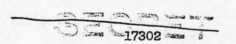

17302

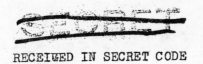

RECEIVED IN SECRET CODE

INCOMING RADIO:

PRIORITY

RECEIVED : 05 SEPT 0300

FROM : AMMDEL

TO : AMMISCA (FOR THE EYES OF GEN STILWELL ONLY)

NR : AM 1441   FILED: 04 SEPT 1014.

HEAVY BOMBER QUESTION HAS BEEN PRESENTED TO LOCAL BRITISH
(FOR EYES ALONE STILWELL FROM FERRIS) BY THEIR PEOPLE INDICATING
CONSIDERATION OF THIS QUESTION BY COMBINED CHIEFS STAFF ON
SEPTEMBER FIFTEEN. CONCENSUS OPINION HERE THAT IT WOULD HELP
OUR CAUSE MATERIALLY TO SEND OLIVER TO AGWAR TO REPRESENT
THEATER ON WHOLE QUESTION. TO DO SO MEANS SPEED UP ON COMPLETION
OF FINAL RADIO TO AGWAR. WOULD YOU BE AGREEABLE TO COME HERE
BY SEPTEMBER EIGHT TO OKAY FINAL RADIO AND BRING CHENNAULT OR
HIS REPRESENTATIVE AND CHENNAULTS PLAN. POSSIBLY YOU WOULD
PREFER KUNMING BUT DELHI WOULD SPEED MATTERS MORE. GENERAL
GEORGE HERE SAYS HE CAN PROVIDE PLANE TO RETURN OUR REPRESENTATIVE
TO STATES. CAN WE HELP YOU BY PLANE FROM HERE. WILL YOU PLEASE
INDICATE YOUR WISHES TO ME. STRATEMEYER CONCURS IN THIS RADIO

SEP 5 43 AM

17,3 29.

Agwar 725 for eyes of Gen. Marshall alone.

Reurad 3300. Comment on changes. Concurrence of liaison committee now necessary. Does this mean that if for instance I want to operate in Thailand I cannot arrange to do so with Mountbatten, but must ask the liaison committee? I still do not like this liaison committee, but it is better than integration, and for that reason is welcome. We will do our best to make it work.

Stilwell —

Received
05 0430

Sent
06 0530

for info 9/5

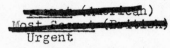

NEW DELHI

the 7th September, 1943.

My dear General,

General Stratemeyer tells me that he hopes to go to Chungking tomorrow to meet you.

2. We have recently been discussing the course of operations in Upper Burma during the coming winter and have already had a preliminary meeting with General Ferris and Colonel Merrill, at which we exchanged ideas and discussed possibilities generally, without of course coming to any definite conclusion in view of the fact that you were not present. Since, I have further examined the whole subject with my Chiefs of Staff here with the results embodied in the enclosed telegram which I am sending to the Chiefs of Staff in London. I think the telegram is self explanatory. As you will see, we have defined as our aim the giving of all possible assistance to the Chinese forces from Ledo and Yunnan so as to facilitate their advance to the utmost possible extent, as it is these forces which will have to secure actual physical possession of the road to China. The telegram shows clearly, I think, that there are two possible courses open to our troops on the Assam front, and also sets out the reasons why I think it is preferable to advance towards Mandalay rather than towards ~~Bhamo~~ The telegram also gives our estimates of the probable effect that our operations will have on the air ferry lift to China.

Bhamo/

3. If these operations are to be carried out, it will entail a drastic turn over of available tonnage on the Assam L. of C. from one purpose to another, and it will also mean a considerable re-distribution of Engineer resources. Both these processes are bound to take a certain amount of time and cannot be carried out in a few days. We are now nearing the end of the monsoon and I feel that it is a matter of great urgency to decide on what we are going to do during the coming dry season, for, if we do not so decide at an early date, we may find ourselves overtaken by the next monsoon before we have achieved our objects. I do not expect Admiral Mountbatten to arrive in Delhi until the end of September and I feel that when he does arrive it will take him some weeks before he can acquaint himself fully with the situation and the possibilities of future action.

4. I shall be very grateful, therefore, if you will let me know whether you can give me a definite opinion now regarding the proposals contained in my telegram to the Chiefs of Staff in London. You will, I am sure, believe me when I say that I am not trying to hurry you in any way, because I know that there are many other considerations which you have to balance before you can come to any definite conclusion regarding land operations in Upper Burma. I do however feel that the matter is one of great urgency

in view of the length of time that it takes to give effect to a decision owing to the great physical difficulties and lack of communications in the theatre in question.

I hope you are very well and that I shall have the pleasure of soon seeing you again in Delhi

yours sincerely

Lieut.-General J.W. Stilwell, U.S.A.,
    Theatre Commander,
        U.S. Army Forces, China Burma India,
        Chungking.

INCOMING RADIO:

RECEIVED: 08 SEPT 0300 Z.

FROM   : WAR

TO   : AMMISCA (FOR THE EYES OF GENERAL STILWELL ONLY)

NR   : 3318   FILED: 06 SEPT 2345 Z.

FROM THE PRESIDENT TO GENERAL STILWELL FOR DELIVERY TO
THE GENERALISSIMO PD THANK YOU VERY MUCH FOR YOUR MESSAGE. EYE
HAVE ASKED MOUNTBATTAN TO GO TO SEE YOU IN CHUNGKING AS SOON AS
POSSIBLE AFTER HE GETS TO BURMA. EYE UNDERSTAND HE WILL BE
THERE BEFORE THE END OF THE MONTH. THERE IS NOTHING LIKE A
FIRST HAND PICTURE AND EYE KNOW YOU WILL REALIZE THE DIFFICULTY
OF MAKING FINAL DECISIONS WHEN WE ARE AS FAR AWAY AS QUEBEC
AND WASHINGTON.

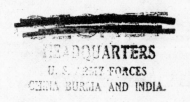

HEADQUARTERS
U. S. ARMY FORCES
CHINA BURMA AND INDIA

No. 55

Chungking, China
September 8, 1943

MEMORANDUM for, His Excellency, The Generalissimo.

The following message has just been received from the President for The Generalissimo:

"Thank you very much for your message. I have asked Mountbatten to go to see you in Chungking as soon as possible after he gets to India. I understand he will be there before the end of the month. There is nothing like a first hand picture and I know you will realize the difficulty of making final decisions when we are as far away as Quebec and Washington."

JOSEPH W. STILWELL
Lieutenant General, U. S. Army
Commanding

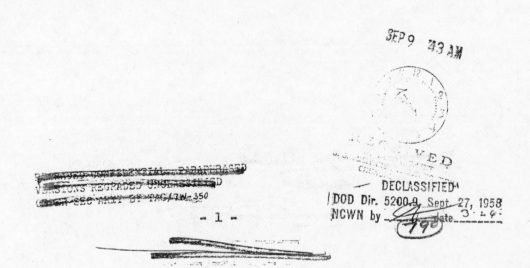

- 1 -

896

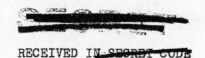

RECEIVED IN SECRET CODE

INCOMING RADIO

RECEIVED: 09 SEPTEMBER 0945 GCT

FROM   : AMMDEL

TO   : AMMISCA

NO   : AM 1476   FILED: 08 SEPTEMBER 1011 GCT

SAW ABBREVIATED LONDON RADIO (FOR EYES ALONE HEARN
FROM FERRIS) TO LOCAL BRITISH WHICH GAVE LORD LOUIS PRIN-
CIPAL STAFF. CHIEF STAFF BRITISH. TWO DEPUTY CHIEF STAFFS,
ONE US MAJOR GENERAL AND AIR MARSHALL. ASSISTANT CHIEFS
STAFF US REAR ADMIRAL, BRITISH GENERAL, AIR MARSHALL AND
US BRIGADIER AIR. ADMINISTRATIVE SECTION WITH BRITISH OR
AMERICAN HEAD. INTELLIGENCE SECTION USING PRESENT FACILITIES.
LOCATION NEW DELHI FOR PRESENT. WE HAVE RECEIVED NO REPEAT
NONE WORD HERE ABOUT ANY OF THIS PLAN FROM AGWAR. SENDING
THIS TO YOU WHILE BOSS IS SOUTH. IF YOU GET ANY DOPE LET
ME HAVE IT. BRITISH NOW MAKING PLANS FOR HOUSING AND CAR=
ING FOR LORD LOUIS AND STAFF,

SEP 10 43 PM

RECEIVED
WAR DEPARTMENT
U. S. MILITARY MISSION TO CHINA
CHUNGKING, CHINA

DECLASSIFIED
DOD Dir. 5200.9, Sept. 27, 1958
NCWN by ___ date 3-24-22

PREPARED CONFIDENTIAL PARAPHRASED
VERSIONS REGRADED UNCLASSIFIED
ORDER SEC ARMY BY TAG/7W-350

17538

(791)

RECEIVED

INCOMING RADIO

RECEIVED: 10 SEPTEMBER 0705 GCT

FROM   : AQUILA

TO   : AMMISCA CGAAF MILID W 2083 TE

NR   : S 22 TE   FILED: 09 SEPTEMBER 1035 GCT

PRIORITY

RECEIVED
U.S. MILITARY ... TO CHINA
CHUNGKING ....

SPECIAL OPERATIONS REPORT FOR SEPTEMBER 7TH: 8 B 24S FROM
100 TO 300 FEET DROPPED 31 MARK 13, 2 LOOK REPEAT 2 LOOK, 1,000
MINES IN CHANNEL SOUTHWEST OF ELEPHANT POINT IN RANGOON ESTUARY.
ACCURATE AUTS WEAPON FIRE OF MODERATE INTENSITY ENCOUNTERED FROM
GROVE POINT, ELEPHANT POINT AND ALONG COAST TO 4 MILES SOUTHWEST
OF ELEPHANT POINT. FLIGHT EXPENDED 750 ROUNDS CALIBER 50 AMMUNI-
TION STRAFING GUN POSITIONS AT ELEPHANT POINT. ENEMY HAD NO WARNING.
(CGAAF FROM DAVIDSON INFO AFABI$ AFDIS MILID AMMISCA) OBSERVED 1
SUNKEN 2 MASTED VESSEL WITH 1 STACK IN CHANNEL 5 MILES SOUTHWEST
OF ELEPHANT POINT. 1 X 100 FOOT RIVER CRAFT SIGHTED AT 16
DEGREES 15 MINUTES NORTH SIDE 6 DEGREES 05 MINUTES EAST HEADED
NORTHEAST UP CHANNEL

air of Intel.
G-2
C/5

Eyes Alone

REGRADED CONFIDENTIAL PARAPHRASED
VERSIONS REGRADED UNCLASSIFIED
ORDER SEC ARMY BY TAG 7N 350

DECLASSIFIED
DOD Dir. 5200.9, Sept. 27, 1958
NCWN by _____ date 3-24-72

79 2

CHUNGKING, CHINA,
16 September 1943.

His Excellency,
General Sir Claude J. E. Auchinleck,
G.C.I.E., C.B., C.S.I., D.S.O., O.B.E.,
GHQ in India,
New Delhi, India.

My dear General:

In answer to your letter I intended to get off
a preliminary radio, but apparently we had some bad staff
work and it did not go. I have since sent one which I
trust got through.

As to the plans, there is little choice for us.
We have to follow an obvious route from Ledo, and we have
to push down the Burma Road to the Lashio area. It is the
timing I am concerned about. In general, I believe that
as set-up, the steps are unnecessarily delayed. If we are
going to jump on the Japs, we should do it, as far as
possible, all together. Also the advance from Ledo seems
to be so rigidly prescribed that little initiative is left
to the commander. ("One regiment, on such a date, will
go to such an area".) Also, I understood the orders to
call for "vigorous and aggressive" action, and I don't
find a hell of a lot of it in the plan. However, we will
proceed as indicated, and perhaps our doubts will be
resolved when Admiral Mountbatten arrives.

Best wishes.

Sincerely yours,

JOSEPH W. STILWELL,
Lt. General, U.S. Army.

899

Memorandum for Her Excellency Madame Chiang

with five (5) attachments, unnumbered

classified memorandum.

[227]

CHUNGKING, CHINA,
16 September 1943.

MEMORANDUM FOR HER EXCELLENCY MADAME CHIANG:

Time does not now allow of further delays in preparation for the offensive which the Generalissimo has sanctioned. Only the most energetic action can put the troops into condition to carry it out. Failure to do this will put China in a bad light and jeopardize our chances of opening a road of supply. The following action is recommended as necessary to accomplish the result desired.

1. General Directive to War Ministry, covering details that otherwise have to be taken to the Generalissimo, to cover both X and Y force and training program.

2. Directives to Ch'en Ch'eng, Hou Ch'in Pu, Chiao T'ung Pu, and Ts'ai Cheng Pu.

3. Specific Orders on command, S.O.S. set-up, trucks, road repair, replacements, extra units for Kwangsi and Yunnan, ten more divisions for first thirty, rations, my status, training in second thirty divisions, assignment of a commander for the second thirty, and reorganization of both first and second thirty.

JOSEPH W. STILWELL,
Lt. General, U.S. Army.

DIRECTIVE TO WAR MINISTRY:

First priority will be given to the reorganization, equipment and training of the first thirty divisions. Consistent with the security of Szechuan and Yunnan provinces, all available resources will be devoted to this project. The reorganization and training of the second thirty divisions will start at once. The command of all troops in Yunnan and Kwangsi will be unified under General Ch'en Ch'eng, who will operate under a general strategic plan of defense along the Indo-China and Siam borders and offense along the Burma border. Every effort will be made to prepare the Yunnan troops for action by December 1. The Minister of War will coordinate with General Stilwell all matters of supply and training incidental to these preparations.

CHUNGKING, CHINA,
16 September 1943.

DIRECTIVE TO CH'EN CH'ENG:

You are designated to command all troops in Yunnan
and Kwangsi Provinces. You will proceed with the
reorganization already agreed upon and begin a
comprehensive training program, with U.S. assistance and
supervision. You will unify the service of supply in
Yunnan province forward of the general depots of the
Hou Ch'in Pu, who will deliver to you at Kunming all
needed supplies that are available. Weapons, munitions,
equipment and medical personnel will be delivered to you
by the Americans as they can be transported from India.
You will be responsible for repair of roads and installation
of communications and medical service. Necessary trucks
and labor may be requisitioned. You will maintain a
defensive attitude along the southern borders, and be
ready to attack into Burma by December 1. Further
instructions for this offensive will reach you later.

DIRECTIVES to Hou Ch'in Pu, Chiao T'ung Pu, and Ts'ai
Cheng Pu should authorize necessary expenditure of
materiel and funds to carry out the mission, and should
direct full cooperation and prompt action.

DIRECTIVE to Lung Yün should direct him to furnish General
Ch'en Ch'eng any labor and materiel procurable locally that
he needs.

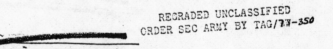

904

CHUNGKING, CHINA,
16 September 1943.

SPECIFIC ORDERS:

1. General Ch'en Ch'eng is designated as commander of all troops in Yunnan and Kwangsi provinces.

2. The C. E. F., S. O. S. will embrace all supply activities forward of Hou Ch'in Pu depots in Kunming.

3. Extra divisions will be designated at once to fill the list of the first thirty divisions.

4.   is designated to command the second thirty divisions. He will confer with General Ho Ying Chin and General Stilwell on reorganization and training, which will start at once.

5. Every effort will be made to bring all units to strength as soon as possible. For this purpose complete units may be transferred from other war zones.

6. Two more armies will be furnished as general reserve in the Yunnan area.

7. The necessary trucks will be furnished at once — civilian trucks may be requisitioned, under a plan to replace them later.

8. The program of road repair will be pushed energetically. Labor may be forced where necessary.

9. The ration for the Yunnan troops will be improved.

10. General Stilwell is directed as joint Chief of Staff to report direct to the Generalissimo on the progress of preparations.

905

PLAN OF OPERATIONS

1. It is vitally important to re-open communications between India and China. This can be done only if the Chinese attack towards Lashio, in conjunction with a Chinese-British attack from Ledo and Imphal. The Generalissimo has sanctioned the general plan.

2. Such an attack should be strong and should be pushed energetically. The obvious counter to it is an attack by the Japs from Indo-China towards Kunming. The Indo-China frontier must therefore be made safe so that operations on the Paoshan front can proceed without anxiety for the rear.

3. At present, and as planned, there will be on the Mengtze front, the 52nd Army, the 8th Army, both dependable, and the 60th Army, Yunnan provincial troops, entirely undependable. There are in addition about five brigades of Yunnan troops, which, like the 60th Army, cannot be depended on. In Kwangsi is the 31st Army of two divisions. In reserve, in the Kunming area, will be the 5th Army. In case of a Jap attack from Indo-China, it must be used there and so cannot be counted on for use at Paoshan. This leaves only 9 divisions for the Paoshan attack, which should be very strong.

4. If the Paoshan divisions are filled up and trained, and if further replacements for battle losses are provided, they should be able to carry out their mission. But the Kunming base must be so strongly held that the Japs will not attempt an attack there. At present the force is not sufficient. Three more diam should be provided, -- one to replace the 60th Army, and two to reinforce Kwangsi.

5. If this is done, a Jap attack towards Mengtze, which is the greatest danger, can be taken in flank by an advance towards Hanoi from Kwangsi. This is the best answer to the Jap threat; they could not afford to continue towards Kunming with a strong force threatening their communications. They would have to fight on diverging lines, and neither group could be strong enough to get a decision.

6. Success in Burma is thus intimately related to the strength of the Indo-China border garrison.

CHUNGKING, CHINA,
16 September 1943

PRINCIPLES OF WAR

No one knows whether war is an art or a science.
However, there are certain principles which have been
proved up to now to be unchanging. The most important
of these principles are the offensive, the objective,
economy of force, mass, surprise and mobility.

To win it is necessary to take the offensive. A
defensive attitude allows the enemy to choose the point of
attack and concentrate superior forces against it. The
initiative passes to the enemy in defensive warfare.

The objective is the goal chosen as being decisive
if reached. It may be geographical, or political, or
psychological, but usually is the opposing armed force.

Economy of force means that a minimum of strength
must be used at unimportant points to allow of maximum
concentration at important ones.

Mass means the assembling of the greatest possible
strength in men and weapons and supplies at the point
chosen as decisive.

Surprise has a double value in bringing superior force
to bear at a given point before the enemy can readjust to
meet it, and in producing a psychological effect out of all
proportion to the means used.

Mobility increases the relative strength of the side
which is superior in this respect. To be able to move twice
as fast as the enemy is the same as having twice the number
of men. Speed of execution is possible only when we have
mobility.

There are other principles, but the above are the
essential ones. Success comes from taking the offensive
against an objective carefully selected, massing all
available means at that point at the expense of others,
making the preparations secretly so as to get surprise, and
then pushing the action through at high speed. This applies
to campaigns as well as separate engagements.

These principles have remained unchanged in spite of
the development of many new weapons. They seem to be
applicable to any conceivable type of warfare. They were
as true in Hannibal's time as in Napoleon's, and they are
true today.

907

UNITY OF COMMAND

1. In any theater of operations one man alone must
be in charge. If there are two, each will inevitably
believe his mission to be the important one, and he will
not release reserves to assist the other. Ch'en Ch'eng
commands the Paoshan front; Lung Yün the Mengtze front.
Each will want to use the general reserve. Each will
claim he cannot accomplish his mission without it. They
will appeal, and the Generalissimo will have to decide.
This forces unity of command on us, even where there is
none contemplated. But it causes delay and uncertainty,
and the decision has to be made by a man who is not on
the ground. Such conditions have been fatal so many
times that there is no argument about it. The only way
to get two forces coordinated is to put them under the
command of one man. He is then responsible for both
fronts and will use his resources to the best advantage.
In this case, Ch'en Ch'eng should be in command of all
troops in Yunnan and Kwangsi.

Besides the tactical use of troops, another
strong reason for unity of command is the question of
supply. At present, Ch'en Ch'eng controls the supply of
the Paoshan front, and Lung Yün of the Mengtze front.
The Hou Ch'in Pu has general depots at Kunming for
distribution of supplies to both. The same demands will
arise for supplies as for reserves of troops, and there
will be no one to establish priorities. This again will
necessitate an appeal to Chungking for a decision. The
same problem will arise in connection with trucks, labor,
funds for road repair, medical service, air support,
etc. etc.

If there is to be, as there should be, a strong
force in Kwangsi, the argument for a unified command
becomes stronger. As the number of factors that may
cause complications increases, the need for a responsible
coordinating head increases in the same ratio.

This matter is of vital importance to the success
of the campaign.

CHUNGKING, CHINA
16 September 1943.

COMBAT

I. Infantry is the basic arm. Ground can be held only
when troops stand on it or cover it with fire. This is the
reason that all other arms are auxiliary, - aviation,
artillery, engineers, tanks, etc. etc. Their sole purpose
is to help the Infantry forward. Aviation can do great
damage, but it cannot hold ground. Artillery can do great
damage, but it cannot hold ground. The Infantry man must
go and stand on it in order to get a decision. With the
growing power of aviation, it is possible that a nation may
be so paralyzed in its industry that it will quit, but this
has yet to be proven. So far as we know, we must still
build our army around the Infantry.

II. Infantry acts by fire and movement. Fire is
brought on the enemy position by one element, while another
element maneuvers to close on the position and take it.
This is the essence of combat, and this rule applies to
units of any size, from a squad up. The supporting weapons --
machine guns, mortars, artillery, etc. - keep the enemy down
and fixed in position, while a maneuver detachment closes
in on him, usually, and preferably, from a flank.

III. The general progress of a fight when two opposing
forces meet is as follows:-

Reconnaissance continues till the enemy's position,
strength, and dispositions are determined. Then a part of
the force is used to pin him down. Then the point of attack
is chosen, and all possible force is concentrated against it.
The bulk of the fire-power is put on this point and the
Infantry attack is then made. If successful, the pursuit
begins at once and is continued to the limit of endurance.

There is a rule of thumb for this procedure which
is called the five F's, - FIND the enemy, FIX him in position,
FIGHT him till he gives way, and then FINISH him, FENDING
at all times. ("Fending" means to keep up reconnaissance
so that he cannot surprise us.)

909

CHUNGKING, CHINA,
16 September 1943.

ORGANIZATION

1. Organization is based on the weapons available.

2. There are really only 3 combat echelons, – the platoon, the battalion, and the division. Other echelons are commonly inserted for administrative purposes and ease of command.

3. The platoon is the smallest unit commanded by an officer. It has flat trajectory weapons, – rifles and light machine gun; and high trajectory weapons, – the 60mm mortar.

4. The battalion is the next combat echelon. It has flat trajectory weapons, – the heavy machine gun; and high trajectory weapons, – the 81 or 82mm mortar.

5. The division is the third combat echelon. It is the smallest unit capable of independent action. It has up to now had flat trajectory weapons, – the 75mm gun, and high trajectory weapons, the 155mm howitzer. Modern practice is to use a compromise, – 75mm and 105mm howitzers, and put anything heavier in the corps artillery.

6. Between the platoon and the battalion is the company, which has no extra weapons, and between the battalion and the division is the regiment. Usually there are anti-tank weapons in the regiment.

CHUNGKING, CHINA,
16 September 1943.

UNITS

SQUAD   — 12 men commanded by a corporal.

PLATOON   — 3 squads commanded by a Lieutenant.

COMPANY   — 3 platoons commanded by a Captain.

BATTALION   — 3 rifle companies and 1 machine gun company
                 commanded by a Major or Lt. Colonel.

REGIMENT   — 3 battalions and 1 anti-tank company
                 commanded by a Colonel.

(BRIGADE   — Now discontinued in most armies)

DIVISION   — 3 regiments of Infantry and several battalions
                 of Artillery commanded by a Major General.

CORPS   — 2 or 3 divisions. (The Chinese chün)

ARMY   — 2 or more corps. (The Chinese chit'uan chün)

(N.B. The Chinese "chün" has been erroneously called an
       Army. It is really a Corps.)

GROUP OF ARMIES — 2 or more armies. (No equivalent in the
                    Chinese service.)

Special units, such as medical, signal, engineer, chemical,
motor transport, etc. are organized into companies,
battalions, and regiments.

CHUNGKING, CHINA
16 September 1943.

FORMATIONS

COLUMN   LINE   ECHELON

When we are not sure of the enemy's position, we stay in column. We can then quickly form line to the right, to the left, or to the front.

When we know where the enemy is, we form line, because in that way we can bring all our fire power to bear on him.

When we do not know where he is, but expect him to the right or left, we echelon to the right or left, because in that way we are still safely in column, and can also quickly form line.

The column formation has depth. It allows of successive impulses but each impulse is weak. The line formation has no depth. It allows of one impulse, but a very strong one. Committing units one by one is called piece-meal action. It is much better to concentrate and deliver a telling blow. The enemy has a much better chance of beating off three weak attacks than of repelling one very strong one, since he can use all of his supporting weapons against each weak attack in turn. (The principle of mass.)

Weapons

Weapons are classified in many ways. One way is to classify them according to the trajectory of the projectile, as flat or curved trajectory weapons. The rifle, machine gun, and, in the artillery, the gun are all flat trajectory weapons. The mortars are high trajectory weapons. The howitzers are curved trajectory weapons between the two.

In flat ground the flat trajectory weapon is more effective; on broken ground the high trajectory. High trajectory weapons can reach ground inaccessible to flat trajectory weapons.

Diagram

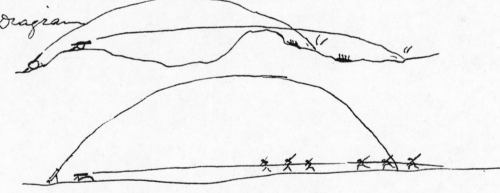

CHUNGKING, CHINA,
16 September 1943.

WEAPONS

Weapons are classified in many ways. One way is to classify them according to the Trajectory of the projectile, as flat or curved trajectory weapons. The rifle, machine-gun, and, in the artillery, the gun, are all flat trajectory weapons. The mortars are high trajectory weapons. The howitzers are curved trajectory weapons between the two.

On flat ground the flat trajectory weapon is more effective; on broken ground the high trajectory. High trajectory weapons can reach ground inaccessible to flat trajectory weapons.

CHUNGKING, CHINA,
16 September 1943.

ARTILLERY WEAPONS

1. 75mm pack howitzer. Ranges up to 9,000 yards. A very effective weapon. One battalion of three batteries, (4 guns to a battery) are contemplated in each division. Later, 2 battalions. The piece breaks down into six mule-loads. It can be set up and fired in three minutes. We have improvised a mount so that the piece can be hauled behind a truck, assembled.

2. 105mm howitzer. Hauled by a truck, which carries its crew. A very effective and accurate weapon, with long range. We plan on one battalion per division, with extra battalions in the corps.

3. 155mm howitzer. Hauled by a heavy truck or a tractor. A very effective weapon, but heavy and harder to move around than the others. Its ammunition supply makes it a problem. We have about 50 of these in India.

4. Heavier artillery than the types mentioned is not suitable for use in China.

CHUNGKING, CHINA,
16 September 1943.

INFANTRY WEAPONS

1. Rifle and Bayonet — (7.92mm   Basic weapon —
(or about .30 cal.   Single shot

2. Thompson Sub-Machine Gun. Cal. .45 (Fires pistol ammunition,
in clips. Automatic and semi-automatic fire. Latter term means trigger
must be pulled for each shot, but ejection and loading are automatic.
The Tommy gun is good in the jungle, at night, at close quarters, etc.
It has not sufficient range to be an all-purpose weapon. We have one in
each squad of 12 men.)

3. Light Machine Gun, air-cooled, on a bipod mount. There are many
types. We have the BREN, one of the best. Shoots .303 caliber, British
ammunition, from magazines that are slipped in on top of the barrel. We
have one in each squad. We have on order a new type that fires 7.92
ammunition.

4. Heavy Machine Gun, water-cooled, on heavy tripod mount. We have
the Maxim and Browning, which are very similar. Fed by belts carrying
250 rounds each. Very accurate and effective. Usually there is a company
of 8 to 12 guns in each battalion. (3 rifle companies and 1 machine gun
company.)

5. 60mm Mortar, carried by one man. Projectile weighs about 4 pounds.
Effective range, 1,000 yards. We will have two, and ultimately three, to
a company.

6. 81mm (U.S.) and 82mm (Chinese) Mortar. A heavier mortar, with an
effective range of about 2,000 yards. We will have 2 or 3 per battalion,
and ultimately 4.

7. 4.2 inch Mortar. Very effective weapon, which can take the place
of light artillery at need. We will have 120 of these, all in India,
organized in a regiment.

8. 37mm Gun. A flat-trajectory anti-tank weapon, on a wheeled mount.
Usually 6 to 12 to a regiment. Very effective at 1,000 yards.

9. Boys Anti-Tank Rifle. A powerful, .50 caliber, single-shot rifle,
effective at close ranges — served by two men. We will have two to a company.

10. Bazooka. A new weapon, served by two men, which fires a rocket,
effective at 200 yards. Will knock out any but heavy tanks.

11. Hand Grenades. For close-in fighting. All infantry-men are
armed with them. Effective at 25 yards.

12. Flame-Thrower. Two types, — one-man and two-man sets. The two-man
set can be mounted on a light tank; it shoots a flame 200 feet.

916

CHUNGKING, CHINA,
16 September 1943.

TANKS AND TRUCKS

1. Light Tank -- Weight about 11 tons. Armed with one 37mm gun and 2 machine guns. Speed about 25 miles per hour. We have 1,000 on order, and will begin by organizing two battalions of about 75 tanks each. Heavier tanks are not suitable for use in China on account of the bridges, which are not designed for heavy weights. This tank can be run over fairly rough ground.

2. Scout Car -- An armored motor car, on wheels. Armed with machine guns. For scouting purposes. Considerable mobility off the road.

3. Bren Carrier -- A small, two-man, track vehicle. (No wheels) Carries one machine gun. Used for many purposes, such as carrying ammunition and supplies over rough ground. We will have several hundred of them.

4. Trucks -- Three types will be used, -- the 2-1/2 tonner, the 1-1/2 tonner, and the 3/4 tonner. The 1/4 tonner, or jeep, is used for many purposes. We will have a small number of amphibious trucks and jeeps.

RECEIVED IN SECRET CODE

INCOMING RADIO

RECEIVED : 16 SEPT. 1716 GCT

FROM : WAR

TO : AMMISCA AMMDEL

NR : 3378 3019 FILED: 16 SEPTEMBER 0000 GCT

RECEIVED
WAR DEPARTMENT
U. S. MILITARY MISSION TO CHINA
CHUNGKING, CHINA

CODE NAME FOR PROJECT (MARSHALL FOR STILWELL AND FERRIS)

REFERRED TO IN OUR 3367 TO AMMISCA 2993 TO AMMDEL 14TH SEPT IS GALAHAD

RPT GALAHAD

This is Long Range Penetration Brigade groups
Shipment #1688
See also —

17078	*17785*
17236	*17787*
17292	
17235	

C/S _____

G-3 _____

G-1 _____

1005

SEP 17 43 PM

RECEIVED
WAR DEPT.

REGRADED CONFIDENTIAL PARAPHRASED
V... ...S REGRADED UNCLASSIFIED
ORDER SEC ARMY BY TAG/7W-350

DECLASSIFIED
DOD Dir. 5200.9, Sept. 27, 1958
HCWN by _____ date 3-28-72

17866

918

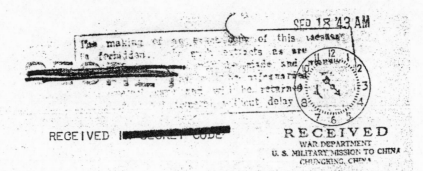

The making of ~~additional copy of this message~~
is forbidden. ~~Only such extracts as are~~
~~...~~ made and ~~...~~
~~...~~ paraphrased ~~...~~
~~...~~ and will be returned
~~...~~ without delay

RECEIVED I ~~SECRET CODE~~

R E C E I V E D
WAR DEPARTMENT
U. S. MILITARY MISSION TO CHINA
CHUNGKING, CHINA

INCOMING RADIO

PRIORITY

RECEIVED : 17 SEPT 0521 GCT

FROM : AQUILA

TO : AMMISCA, CGAAF (W 2196 TB)

NO. : S 40 TB   FILED 17 SEPT 0406 GCT

BEEBES OPERATIONAL INTELLIGENCE AND BOMBARDMENT
EXPERIENCE NEEDED BY CHENNAULT (PAREN ARNOLD FROM STILWELL PAREN)
DESIRE BEEBE REMAIN WITH FOURTEENTH AIR FORCE AS BOMBER COMMANDER
AND BE PROMOTED TO BRIGADIER GENERAL STOP AN OFFICER SHOULD BE
MADE AVAILABLE FOR ASSIGNMENT TO STAFF OF SOUTHEAST ASIA COMMAND
OR STRATEMEYER CAN DESIGNATE SUCH OFFICER.

Eyes alone

C/S H

F 18 ept

(10.1.1)

DECLASSIFIED
~~...~~ Dir. 5200.9, Sept. 27, 19~~..~~
~~...~~ by ~~...~~ date 3-22-~~..~~

REGRADED CONFIDENTIAL PARAPHRASED
~~...~~
~~...~~ /7W-350

RECEIVED IN SECRET CODE

INCOMING RADIO

RECIEVED: 17 SEPT 0732 GCT

FROM   : TIGAR

TO   : AMMISCA

NO   : MM 261   FILED: 17 SEPT. 0328 GCT

FOR EYES ALONE OF GENERAL STILWELL. I DO UNEQUIVOCABLY
SHARE YOUR HIGH OPINION OF FERRIS WHICH I BELIEVE YOU WILL
RECALL FROM OUR CONVERSATION SOME TIME AGO. FOR EYES ALONE
GENERAL STILWELL FROM WHEELER REPLYING URAD T 652 SEPTEMBER
16. YOU WILL BE INTERESTED TO KNOW THAT FOR SOME TIME I HAVE
CONTEMPLATING RECOMMENDING TO YOU THAT FERRIS BE ASSIGNED TO
SERVICE OF SUPPLY WITH VIEW TO CONSOLIDATING REAR ECHELON AND
SOS
SIS HEADQUARTERS INTO ONE HEADQUARTERS TO HANDLE YOUR AD-
MINISTRATION, SUPPLY, CONSTRUCTION, TRANSPORTATION ETC WHICH
DUTIES WERE CONCEIVED AS RESPONSIBILITIES OF SERVICE OF SUPPLY
WHEN IT WAS ORIGINALLY SET UP. WHETHER YOU WOULD BE WILLING
OR NOT TO CONSIDER SUCH REORGANIZATION, NEVERTHELESS I WOULD
ESPECIALLY DESIRE TO HAVE FERRIS. WOULD LIKE TO DISCUSS WITH
YOU WHEN BILL AND I VISIT CHUNGKING. HOLCOMBE SEEMS TO BE IN
BETTER HEALTH AND I AM AWAITING FURTHER REPORT BY MEDICOS BUT
THEY EXPECT THAT FUTURE CHECK WILL NOT BE FAVORABLE

SEP 20 23 PM

1016

SECRET   RECEIVED

RECEIVED I~~N SECRET CODE~~

INCOMING RADIO

RECEIVED: 18 SEPTEMBER 0745 GCT

FROM   : AQUILA   URGENT

TO   : AMMISCA

NO   : S 43 TA   FILED: 18 SEPTEMBER 0455 GCT

URGENT

HUSH FOR GENERAL STILWELLS EYES ALONE . AT COMMANDER
IN CHIEFS MEETING THIS MORNING GENERAL AUCHINLECK INFORMED
ME THAT LORD MOUNTBATTEN WOULD ARRIVE NEW DELHI SEPTEMBER
30 TH AND ASKED IF YOU WOULD BE PRESENT TO GREET HIM . I
STATED THAT I DID NOT KNOW . I RECOMMEND THAT YOU COME TO
DELHI IN ORDER TO BE PRESENT WHEN LORD MOUNTBATTEN ARRIVES

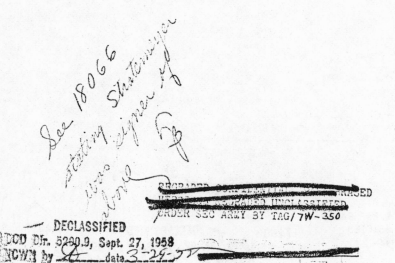

SEP 20 43 PM

RECEIVED
WAR DEPARTMENT
ARMY FORCES TO CHINA
CHUNGKING, CHINA

(1014)

17956

RECEIVED IN SECRET CODE

R E C E I V E D
WAR DEPARTMENT
U. S. MILITARY MISSION TO CHINA
CHUNGKING, CHINA

INCOMING RADIO

RECEIVED: 1110 GCT 18 SEPT

FROM   : AMMDEL

TO   : AMMISCA

NR   : AM 1552   FILED: 17 SEPT 0816 GCT

UNDERSTAND THAT AS RESULT OF VISIT GEORGE OF ATC HERE,
THAT STRATEMEYER IS TAKING OVER AIR FREIGHT AND WILL HANDLE ALL
PRIORITUES REPEAT PRIORITIES OF SHIPMENTS. STILWELL FROM FERRIS.
BELIEVE WE SHOULD CONTROL PRIORITIES OTHERWISE YOU KNOW WHO WILL
GET GRAVY. THIS TO YOU IN CASE OF PERSONAL APPROACH.

c/s A

Sec 17776

09549

17,963

SECRET  PRIORITY
PRIORITY

INCOMING RADIO:

RECEIVED: 18 SEPT 1110 Z.

FROM   :   AMMDEL

TO   :   AMMISCA (FOR THE EYES OF GENERAL STILWELL ONLY)

NR   :   AM 1564   FILED: 18 SEPT 0905 Z.

EYES ALONE GENERAL STILWELL. SELECTED AS MOST SUITABLE
FOR DISEMBARKING GALAHAD PROJECT PERSONNEL IS PORT OF BOMBAY.
(FROM FERRIS) WILL BE TRANSHIPPED FROM THERE BY RAIL TO ASSAM.
SUITABLE TRAINING AREA EXISTS TWO MILES WEST OF MARGHERITA BRIDGE
WITH DENSE JUNGLE HILLS AND RIVER AVAILABLE. PENDING ARRIVAL AND
RECONDITIONING OF PACK MULES FROM UNCLE SUGAR, 450 HORSES FROM
AUSTRALIAN SHIPMENT ARE BEING SELECTED AND EARMARKED FOR THIS
PROJECT. BRITISH PACK EQUIPMENT WILL BE PROCURED IF POSSIBLE.
WE HAVE STARTED ON ORGANIZATIONAL DETAILS SO AS TO CHECK AGWAR
DOPE ON ARRIVAL. STRONGLY RECOMMEND THAT BRINK START NOW ON
GETTING THIS UNIT CARED FOR, TRAIN IT AND COMMAND IT. HE WILL BE
TOPS. MAY HAVE TO GO TO AGWAR SO WE CAN USE HIM FOR THIS. YOUR
REACTION DESIRED SO EYE CAN INFORM HIM.
NEW SUBJECT: STILL WORKING IN DARK HERE ON NEW COMMAND SET UP.
HOPE YOU HAVE DIRECTION FROM AGWAR ON SUBJECT.

SEP 20 43 PM

RECEIVED

1018

OFFICE OF THE COMMANDING GENERAL
UNITED STATES ARMED FORCES
CHINA BURMA INDIA

ROUTINE

AD 2059

Ammdel for Ferris - EYES ALONE

Ref. Aquila 5 43 TA unsigned Was that message from you query. My presence here necessary on several counts. Cannot come down to meet Louis. Have been asked to remain here, but could meet him at Kunming when he comes up, if he wants preliminary talk. Please explain to him. New subject Rewrad N64. O.K. on Galahad preparations. Brink can be told to supervise training. I am not at all sure about command and want to go slow on that. New subject. No dope on new command set up that can be pushed out till Louis arrives.

Stilwell –

Recd 0351

Sent TB 0500

SEP 20 48 PM

1015

TIGAR   for eyes of Gen Wheeler alone —

T66H

Kenrad MM 268. There is urgent
need of trained investigators in an
important matter now pending. I
have ~~given~~ Cooper had to get help for
Cooper to get it done. Policy of prior
consultation is unchanged. There has
been a slip-up in staff work, which is
regretted, but we must have the services of these two officers for the present at
least.   Bear with us.

Stilwell —

recd 0350
Sent 7B 0430

See 17986

09575

(1020)

925

CANNON

RECEIVED IN SECRET CODE

SEP 20 '43 PM

INCOMING RADIO

RECEIVED   :   19 SEPTEMBER 2152 GCT

FROM   :   AMMDEL

TO   :   AMMISCA

NO   :   AM 1567   FILED 19 SEPT 0530 GCT

FOLLOWING MY RECOMMENDATION PAREN FOR EYES ALONE STILWELL FROM
FERRIS REURAD TWO ZERO FOUR SEVEN SEPTEMBER EIGHTEEN PRD LIEUT
COL HOWARD MIKE MEANS NOW WITH STRATEMEYER BUT ORIGINALLY WITH
US PRD HE IS SUPERIOR CMA AIR CORPS CMA CAME TO BE IN OUR AIR
SECTION OF HOW QUEEN PRD HE IS TOPS AND WOULD SATISFY YOU PRD
NEXT IS CANNON NOW WITH BOATNER PRD HE IS EXCELLENT OFFICER
CMA HARD WORKER THOROUGH AND WILL FILL THE BILL PRD BOATNER
IS RECEIVING OFFICERS TO REPLACE CANNON PRD IF YOU WANT TO
LEAVE CANNON CMA SUGGEST VAN NATTA WHO HAS FINE REPUTATION BUT
UNKNOWN BY ME PRD EASTERBROOK AND LINDSEY YOU KNOW BUT DESERVE
CONSIDERATION PRD WOULD LIKE TO SUGGEST THAT POWELL BE PULLED
FROM RAMGARH SINCE THAT WORK IS NOW WELL IN HAND AND HIS
EXPERIENCE THERE SHOWED BIG HELP PRD HE ALSO HAS THE STUFF NEW
SUBJECT ARNOLD PLANS TO LEAVE HERE TOMORROW FOR UNCLE SUGAR
NEW SUBJECT COLONEL PETER FLEMING CHIEF BRITISH DECEPTION
PLANNING SECTION DELHI LEFT LAST WEEK FOR CHUNGKING TO ARRANGE

REGRADED
ORDER SEC ARMY BY TAG/BW-350

(1019)

926

WITH CHINESE FOR CHANNELS TO ENEMY FOR PASSING HIS MATERIAL
AND TO CONFER BRITISH MILITARY ATTACHE RELATIVE DECEPTION
IMPLIMENTATION IN CHINA PRD HUNTER IS WORKING THIS END WITH
FLEMING PRD THOUGH YOU SHOULD KNOW.

18,036

1019

Amnnken   for Dorn - Eyes alone KING-1459

2° Reuzad c 524.   Am reluctant to
throw the J.A.'s around as recommended.
J.a. is legal adviser only and a change
will not cure the basic trouble. Any other
staff officer could * similarly influence
the situation. Let it ride for a while.
                                    Stilwell -

SEP 20 43 PM

Treat as urgnd c

red file nnn 0420
Scnt TB   05

TFD

19574

CONFIDENTIAL

7W-350

1022

INCOMING RADIO:

RECEIVED: 20 SEPT 1100 Z.

FROM   : AMMDEL

TO   : AMMISCA (FOR THE EYES OF GEN STILWELL ONLY)

NR   : AM 1574   FILED: 20 SEPT 0525 Z.

RECEIVED
AIR DEPARTMENT
U. S. MILITARY MISSION TO CHINA
CHUNGKING, CHINA

      ORIGINATED WITH STRATEMEYER MESSAGE REURAD 2059
(FOR EYES ALONE STILWELL FROM FERRIS). EYE SHALL CONVEY
YOUR INSTRUCTIONS TO LORD LOUIS AND INFORM YOU.
NEW SUBJECT: BELIEVE SOME ONE IN INDIA OR CHINA SHOULD BE
GIVEN DEFINITE RESPONSIBILITY FOR GALAHAD. ALL INFORMATION
ON PROJECT BEING WITHHELD EXCEPT TO GEORGE THREE AND FOUR,
AND SPECK. COMMANDER SHOULD BE APPOINTED TO LET HIM WORK INTO
THE PICTURE AND DEVELOP TRAINING IN ORDER TO HAVE BEST
ORGANIZATION. THERE IS LOTS TO BE DONE ON THIS PROBLEM.
NEW SUBJECT: STRATEMEYER HAS JUST PRESENTED REQUEST TO SPECK
FOR ADDITIONAL LIVING SPACE AT DELHI FOR TWO FIVE ZERO OFFICERS
AND FOUR FIVE ZERO ENLISTED WHICH STRAT SAYS HAS YOUR APPROVAL.
THIS IS CONSIDERABLE LOAD FOR DELHI WITH LORD LOUIS OUTFIT
TOO. TENTH AIR FORCE STILL HERE AND ONLY CRUMB IS MOVING
FORWARD. DECISION FROM YOU ON ADDITIONAL SPACE REQUESTED.

09615

1023

Ammdel for Ferris. – EYES. ALONE.
AD 2081

Reurad AM 1574. I told Strat that if Imperial were full, he could look for accommodations similar to what Milani and his gang have. His staff was to be kept small. What ~~is it~~ does this fantastic figure of two hundred and fifty include? I never heard of it. I will lay off of this matter and leave it to you to adjust to the best interests of all concerned. New subject. Tenth Air Force has been told to get closer to the troops. Tell ~~Davidson~~ Stratemeyer this is exactly what I meant. New subject. Brink can be tentatively named to handle Galahad. He will have to prove his case.

Stilwell.

Recd   0306
SENT   0436

SEP 21 43 PM

1024

930

Office of H.M.Military Attache,
British Embassy,
Chungking.
21st September 1943

Ref:M/100/12

Dear General Stilwell,

I have just received the following Most Immediate secret cipher message from the Commander-in-Chief in India addressed personally to you.

The message has NOT been paraphrased, but I am instructed to inform you that should it be essential for you to retransmit it in American cipher the text must first be paraphrased.

I should be grateful if you would acknowledge receipt of this letter.

1. "Have discussed today with Generals FERRIS and WHEELER various points arising from "quadrant" decisions and have reached measure of agreement with them on all points except the move of certain engineer units from airfield construction to IMPHAL-TAMU road.

2. My instructions from combined Chiefs of Staff are to put main effort into land and air operations even at expense of air lift to CHINA. Operations from IMPHAL forward of TAMU must be supported by road up to TAMU and I am convinced that I can only get this brought up to requisite standard by end of December if I give orders at once for the move of certain engineer units now employed on constructing airfields ferry route.

3. I believe that these airfields are already sufficiently advanced to permit of lifting up to 7000 tons a month over the hump and can also operate combat forces required for protection of airfields. Now that priority has been placed on land operations, we are NOT likely to be able during campaigning season to deliver along the ASSAM L of C stores sufficient to enable more than this quantity to be flown into CHINA. Work remaining unfinished is mainly improvement of taxi ways, completion of accomodation, etc. With resources which will remain after removal of engineer units in question it will still be possible to complete these remaining tasks by 1st May 1944, before onset of next monsoon.

4. General WHEELER explains that he has NOT officially received any intimation of the changes in priorities as result of "quadrant," and he is doubtful whether full implications can have been placed before combined Chiefs of Staff and President. He feels that it is uneconomical to remove resources from a task which is nearly complete and emphasises his conviction that we shall eventually need both for the ferry lift and for operational purposes all the airfields we can get in ASSAM.

5. I sympathise with his point of view but in view of my clear instructions and fact that British land operations from IMPHAL can only be successful if based on reliable road I consider I have NO option but to move engineering units from airfields. I feel however that in view of the fact that Generals WHEELER and FERRIS have NOT received official instructions regarding "quadrant" decisions you must be given the opportunity to approach WASHINGTON . I have therefore at General WHEELER's request delayed orders for moves. I cannot however delay longer than 23rd and propose to issue orders on that date. I am repeating this to Chiefs of Staff in LONDON and joint staff mission WASHINGTON".

Yours sincerely,

Lt.Gen.J.W.Stilwell, D.S.C.,
G.O.C. American Forces in India,
Burma and China,
Chungking.

RECEIVED IN SECRET

SEP 22

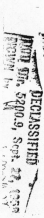

INCOMING RADIO

RECEIVED : 21 SEPT 1200 GCT

FROM : AMMDEL

TO : AMMISCA

NR : AM 1584   FILED: 21 SEPT 0945 GCT

URGENT

U.S. .... CHUNGKING, CHINA

EYES ALONE STILWELL FROM FERRIS. THIS SUMMARIZES CONFERENCE WITH
AUCKINLECK ON ALLOTMENT OF ASSAM TONNAGE FOR OCTOBER ALTHOUGH SAME
GENERAL SITUATION APPLIES FOR SEVERAL MONTHS THEREAFTER. (1). WE AGREED
TO REDUCTION TO MOVEMENT OF 13000 PERSONNEL, 700 ANIMALS AND 1000
VEHICLES. THIS WILL GIVE BOATNER ALL OF 38TH DIVISION, 22ND DIV LESS
1 ARTILLERY BATTALION, AND FOLLWOING CORPS UNITS: ENGINEBR REGIMENT,
MOTOR TRANSPORT REGIMENT, ANTI AIRCRAFT BATTALION, GUARD BATTALION,
SIGNAL BATTALION, AND SMALL MEDICAL UNITS. BOATNER WILL NOT GET CORPS
ANIMAL TRANSPORT REGIMENT IN OCTOBER. WE STILL HAVE BACKLOG OF
PERSONNEL FOR MOVEMENT TO ASSAM BUT BELIEVE WE GOT FAIR BREAK IN
FACE OF CONCENTRATION OF FOURTH CORPS. (TWO.) ON CRITICAL QUESTION OF
MOVEMENT OF SUPPLIES WE WERE SLATED FOR BIG CUT ON THEORY THAT
INCREASED DEMANDS OF HIGHER PRIORITY GROUND OPERATION SHOULD ONLY
BE MET AT EXPENSE OF AIR LIFT TO CHINA. FINAL RESULT WAS AN
ALLOTMENT TO US OF 1440 TONS PER DAY (INCLUDING HIG OCTANE
POL) SUBJECT TO POSSIBLE REDUCTION BY 180 LONG TONS BECAUSE
OF ACCIDENTS AND OTHER CONTINGENCIES. THIS FIGURE WILL ALLOW
SUPPORT OF LEDO ROAD AND CHINESE CORPS ON SCALE PREVIOUSLY
PLANNED. BY CLOSE MANAGEMENT AND MOVING YOKE STOCKS NOW IN ASSAM
WE CAN SUPPORT TENTH AIR FORCE AND ALSO EIGHT OR NINE THOUSAND
SHORT TONS OVER THE HUMP IF ATC CAN CARRY THAT MUCH, WHICH IS
DOUBTED HERE. WHAT WE SHALL LACK IS BUILDUP IF STOCKS

18,117   SECRET

PAGE 2.

IN ASSAM BEHIND LEDO ACTIVITIES AND EXTRA CAPACITY TO PREPARE FULLY

FOR ADDITIONAL SPECIAL FORCES ESPECIALLY GALAHAD WHICH QUADRANT

APPARENTLY SET UP FOR US. AUCHINLECK HAS NOT HEARD OF THESE SPECIAL

TROOPS FROM LONDON. IN SHORT WE SHALL EAT INTO STOCK PILES WE HAVE

FORTUNATELY AT LEDO, OTHERWISE THE TOTAL LIFT TO CHINA COULD BE ONLY

4000 TONS PER MONTH. (THREE) GENERAL COMMENTS. AUCHINLECK HAS

SPECIFIC WORD FROM LONDON THAT GROUND OPERATIONS HAVE FIRST PRIORITY

AND THAT AIR FERRY LIFT COMES SECOND. SINCE PRIMARY INTEREST IN

GROUND OPERATIONS MEANS FOURTH CORPS TO HIM HE FEELS OBLIGATED TO

MEET ESSENTIAL REQUIREMENTS FOURTH CORPS REGARDLESS OF EFFECT ON AIR

FERRY. WE LACK INFORMATION HERE ON SUBORDINATION OF AIR LIFT TO

THAT EXTENT. AUK WAS AS USUAL FAIR AND REASONABLE BUT TAKES THIS

PRIORITY MATTER VERY SERIOUSLY AND WILL USE IT TO THE LIMIT NECESSARY

TO GET FOURTH CORPS READY BY FEBRUARY. MY IMPRESSION IS THAT HE DOES

NOT SUFFICIENTLY APPRECIATE CONNECTION BETWEEN HIS GROUND OPERATIONS

AND EFFORTS OF YUNNAN FORCE AND FOURTEENTH AIR FORCE WHICH ARE

DEPENDENT ON AIR LIFT. BRITISH REQUIREMENTS FOR GROUND OPERATIONS

WILL EXPAND STEADILY AND UNLESS THERE IS MARKED EXPANSION OF ASSAM

LOC, SUPPORT FOR FOURTEENTH AIR FORCE AND YOKE FORCE OVER THE HUMP

WILL BE GRADULLY REDUCED TO NOTHING OR NEAR TO IT. FAILURE TO

DEVELOP ASSAM TONNAGE WILL MEAN LONG RANGE RESTRICTION ON AID TO

CHINA BECAUSE WE WONT BE ABLE TO GET SUPPLIES TO LEDO AREA. THE

PRESENT PICTURE BEING THAT TOTAL OF 4000 TONS PER MONTH IS THE ONLY

~~SECRET~~ URGENT

15,117

933

SURPLUS OVER OPERATIONAL NEEDS. THIS AMOUNTS TO NOTHIING IN
CONSIDERATION OF ROAD CAPABILITY AND AIR TRAFFIC WHICH WAS PLANNED TO
GO 20000 TONS. FROM LONG RANGE ANGLE THIS STINKS. BEGINNING NOW
WE MUST CONSIDER RESTRICTING MOVEMENT OF ATC PERSONNEL AND VEHICLES
TO ASSAM TO AVOID BUILDING UP ORGANIZATION FAR BEYOND THAT NEEDED
TO MOVE AVAILABLE TONNAGE. AUCHINLECK AND WHEELER HAVE REFERRED
TO YOU PROPOSAL TO WIRHDRAW CONSIDERABLE NUMBER BRITISH ENGINEERS
FROM AIR FIELDS TO USE IN IMPHAL ROAD. THERE WAS NO DIFFERENCE
ON GENERAL PRICIPLES OR TECHNICAL DETAILS, SINCE MATTER CAME TO MEET
ENTIRELY ON QUESTION OF PRIORITY . FOR A MOMENT IT LOOKED LIKE BRITISH
HAD DISCLOSED LARGE CIVIL TONNAGE MOVING TO ASSAM AS WE HAVE ALWAYS
EXPECTED BUT WHEN QUESTION CAME UP NEW SETS OF FIGURES WERE
PROVIDED. OUR STAFF BELIEVES THERE IS CLASH BETWEEN GHQ AND
CIVIL GOVERNMENT ON THIS AND THAT WE MIGHT HAVE TO GO THROUGH
WASHINGTON TO GET MILITARY PRIORITY. IF NEW COMMAND IS NOT
OPERATING BEFORE NOVEMBER ALLOTMENTS ARE MADE WE SHOULD TAKE
THIS UP. WAR DEPARTMENT HAS BEEN GIVEN NO INFORMATION ON THIS
CONFERENCE.

18,117.

SEP 22 '43 AM

URGENT

1028

BURSAM OT 11

Relot for Boatner. <u>EYES ALONE.</u>

Reurad G 208. Hold everything. If question arises, senior man on the ground will be it. I am having a battle on this matter with war ministry, who claim the boys do not like you. There is a whispering campaign on, and this may be attempt to get at me through you. We have made too much progress. Invidious comparisons have been made, & face has been lost. Congratulations on malaria record.

Stilwell.

recd 0322
Sent 0500

1027

OFFICE OF THE COMMANDING GENERAL

UNITED STATES ARMED FORCES

CHINA BURMA INDIA

~~████~~ *URGENT*

TORCH CH66 FOR WHEELER - EYES ALONE

Reurad X 3 - Baird can stay on the job
till you dig up a replacement for him If
you can't get one promptly, let me know and
I will produce someone who can run Hell
Gate. I would not ask you for Baird except
for exceptional qualifications he possesses for
a most important investigation now under
way. If you are skinned down to where one
major will make or break us, you should have
more help and I will dip into the C.T. and C.C.
to get it if you say so.

Stilwell -

Recd 0200
Sent 0313

(1033)

936

RECEIVED IN ~~SECRET~~ CODE

INCOMING RADIO

RECEIVED :   23 SEPT, 0930 GCT

FROM   : WASHINGTON

TO   : AMMSICA

NR   : 3430   FILED : 22 SEPT, 2316 GCT

PRIORITY

I GATHER FROM BISSELL AND OTHERS REPEAT OTHERS, THAT YOU HAVE CONSISTENTLY OVERWORKED AND ARE MUCH IN NEED OF A SHORT REST AND THAT YOU REFUSE TO SPARE YOURSELF IN ACCORDANCE WITH THE CONGENITAL AFFLICTION OF ALL HIGHER COMMANDERS. (PERSONAL TO STELWELL FROM MARSHALL)

I WANT YOU IMMEDIATELY TO TAKE TWO WEEKS REST. I THINK IT ESPECIALLY IMPORTANT THAT YOU DO THIS BEFORE MOUNTBATTEN GETS OUT THERE.

IN ACCORDANCE WITH THE ABOVE I HAVE GONE AHEAD THROUGH SIR JOHN DILL AND YOU WILL PROBABLY RECEIVE AN INVITATION FROM GENERAL AUCHINLECK FOR THE VALE OF KASHMIR OR SOME OTHER PLEASANT SPOT AND MY INSTRUCTIONS ARE TO YOU TO ACCEPT IT. YOUR EXPENSE ACCOUNT CAN BE INCREASED TO WHATEVER EXTENT YOU FEEL NECESSARY. PLEASE ACKNOWLEDGE

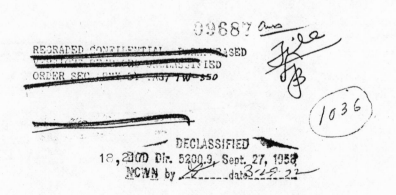

09687

RECRADED CONFIDENTIAL
ORDER SEC

DECLASSIFIED
18,200 Dir. 5200.9 Sept. 27, 1958
NCWN by

(1036)

INCOMING RADIO

RECEIVED : 23 SEPT, 1534 GCT   URGENT

FROM   : LEDO -TORCH-

TO   : AMMISCA

NR   : X 3   FILED : 23 SEPT, 0745 GCT

        EYES ALONE GENERAL STILWELL OR GENERAL HEARN REPEAT EYES
ALONE TRANSFER OF MAJOR RALPH EASY BAIRD QUARTERMASTER CORPS FROM
BASE THREE.COULD SERIOUSLY COMPLICATE OUR PROBLEMS AT THIS TIME (FOR
EYES ALONE OF STILWELL OR HEARN FROM WHEELER) BECAUSE HE IS IN COMMAND
                                              FOR SUPPLY
AT HELL GATE SUB DEPOT WHICH ALSO INVOLVES RESPONSIBILITY/OF TROOPS NOW
MOVING FORWARD AND FOR ROAD PERSONNEL AND MACHINERY ON THE MOVE. THE
FORMER COMMANDER AT HELL GATE (LIEUT COLONEL PRESCOTT) WAS TRANSFERRED
TO GEORGE FOUR BASE HEADQUARTERS TO REPLACE COLONEL ZIKA.MAJOR BAIRD IS
ONLY EXPERIENCED FIELD OFFICER THERE NOW CAPABLE OF TAKING CHARGE. YOUR
RECONSIDERATION OF THIS TRANSFER IS URGENTLY RECOMMENDED. AS YOU KNOW
EYE AM MOST ANXIOUS TO COOPERATE IN OTHER THEATRE PROBLEMS FOR WHICH
PEOPLE ARE BEING TRANSFERRED FROM OUR WORK FROM TIME TO TIME. HOWEVER
IT IS BELIEVED THAT IMPORTANCE OF OUR ACTIVITIES AT HELL GATE JUSTIFY
RETENTION OF OUR KEY PERSONNEL THERE. IT IS RECOMMENDED THAT YOU APPROVE
RETENTION OF BAIRD AT THIS STATION _

                         18,235

EYES ALONE

AMMKUM For DORN FROM
K1482 HEARN.

SEP 24 43 AM

1 Discussed your a 562
with General Stilwell. Your
reference to a portion of the Theater
Staff as "Three great minds"
and the statement "Can run

this Show from Sortcau hooked
and "tell them to leave us alone and do our jobs"
"Miles away", expresses contempt

openly for Gen Stilwells

new Headquarters, borders

on insubordination. Stire
     (cross)

up animosities and affects
adversely a proper attitude.

(1031)

939

This habit of breaking higher authority is prevalent in this theater and the main fault lies with responsible officers. Your redigram was and is read by enlisted personnel at your headquarters and here. It does not have a wholesome effect and impresses them with the lack of military courtesy, military discipline and proper military subordination and procedure which should characterize an army at war. Such sarcastic, derogatory statements will be discontinued.

(1031)

CHUNGKING, CHINA,
24 September 1943.

PERSONNEL DIFFICULTIES

Sample Case - 199 surplus officers were sent to Kunming from Ramgarh for training as radio operators. Only 127 reported for duty at the school. The others are reported to have refused to attend. Of those who reported, 21 left the school without permission. Of the remaining 106, 64 were relived on account of insufficient education or indifference to training. Of the remaining 42, only 8 qualified in their training. 8 out of 199.

Comment.

1. A large surplus of officers was sent to Ramgarh, against our recommendation. We did not need them, but the War Ministry sent them. There were some 450 of these. They have been a source of trouble and worry. We tried to give them training, — two courses, in fact, but there were no places for them, so the experiment of radio training was attempted, with the above result.

2. There are still over 300 left at Ramgarh, their discipline is bad. On one occasion they attacked the officer paymaster who was paying them, and would have maltreated him if General Bergin had not personally rushed him to a car and gotten him out.

3. There is no use in shutting our eyes to conditions such as these. The point is to correct them. In this case an investigation was made and the case was dropped because witnesses would not testify. Authority must be given commanders to take summary action, and when operations begin, the commander of the C.A.I. must have full authority, as the above incident indicates.

4. To be ordered to duty at Kunming, and not report, or to leave without permission after reporting, constitutes desertion. To condone such an offense tends to break down discipline, without which an army becomes a mob.

5. Cases are numerous in which orders are not obeyed, or are evaded in one way or another. Unauthorized absence from training has been the most common delinquency. We have tried to improve conditions at Ramgarh gradually, and they have improved there materially, but time does not allow of our using similar methods in other units.

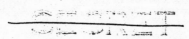

REGRADED CONFIDENTIAL
ORDER SEC ARMY BY TAG/TN-350

941

CHUNGKING, CHINA,
24 September 1943.

PERSONNEL

General Sun, commanding 38th Division.

A good field soldier, courageous and determined. Argumentative, insistent on doing things his way; but much concerned over the well-being of his unit. A capable commander.

General Liao, commanding 22nd Division.

A good field soldier, courageous and determined. He has faithfully complied with all training directives, and as a result his division is now fully as good as the 38th, which had a long start ahead of him. A capable commander.

General Cheng T'ung Kuo, commanding New 1st Army.

This officer may be capable, but he has not yet demonstrated the fact. He appeared to be greatly influenced by General Woon, the deputy Chief of Staff, who has since been relieved. General Cheng has concerned himself principally with demands for the formation of special army units, at the expense of the combat elements of the divisions. He has shown no concern about the basic needs of training, which he does not understand. He is not interested to learn from the bottom up, but expects the finished product to be handed to him to command. This willingness to attempt the command of an intricate organization whose workings he does not understand makes me hesitate to confide authority to him until he has proved himself. As a sample of his attitude, it was agreed that his staff would be kept small, about 30 officers. He now has over 80 officers. As a matter of fact, there is no need whatever for any army staff, as long as the chih hui pu exists. The army echelon will simply transmit orders, and the net result will be merely a delay in execution.

General Hu, commanding 30th Division.

I have had little opportunity to observe this officer. He appears alert, cooperative, and intelligent.

Staff of Chih Hui Pu. In general, very satisfactory. They are very cooperative and are rapidly learning supply procedure. Experience in active operations will make them very valuable.

942

CHUNGKING, CHINA,
24 September 1943.

SAMPLE OF CURRENT REPORTS

"Desertions are common, even among junior officers."

"Even by the present means of forcible recruitment, new recruits cannot make up the losses caused by desertion."

"The unfair and burdensome methods of requisition have caused open resentment and turned the minds of the people against the military."

"It is reliably stated that at the time of the invasion of Chekiang in 1942, Ku Chu T'ung's troops numbered only 25% of their nominal strength, and many of these were coolies engaged in the transport of contraband."

"Two of the main causes for the serious decline in fighting power of the Chinese troops are the lack of proper nourishment, and the fact that pay is far out of line with the rise in prices. This causes undue requisitioning on the people, connivance with smugglers, and other forms of shady business protected by their arms."

True or false, — and I believe them true in the main — such reports are becoming more numerous and are leaking out. There is no way to stop them. The only cure is to take immediate and radical steps to remove their cause.

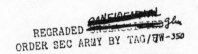

943

BRANCH HEADQUARTERS
UNITED STATES ARMY FORCES
CHINA BURMA INDIA
KUNMING, CHINA

24 September 1943.

His Excellency Governor Lung Yun
Chairman of Yunnan Province
Kunming, China

Sir:

      1. The Service of Supply, U.S. Army Forces in China (Colonel Lewis P. Jordan) has experienced great difficulty and delay in the obtaining of land for necessary building sites for use of U.S. Army personnel. Since 31 July 1943, attempts have been made to procure land in the areas of Hostel Number 2 and Hostel Number 4, and for expansion of hospital facilities in Yang Poo Tau district. All of these projects are essential, and have been delayed for nearly two months by evasive replies, or no replies, from various agencies which deny they have authority to make final arrangements.

      2. Since no results have been achieved by attempting to deal through the usual channels for such matters, I am appealing to you directly for assistance. The following have been unable to give us satisfaction in correspondence during the past two months:

          August 9th   - Colonel Y. T. Yen
                           5th Route Air Force
          August 12th - Mr. Y. Y. Chen
                           Secretary General, Engineering
                                 Commission,
                           National Military Council.
          September 1st- Mr. Y. Y. Chen
          September 2nd- Kunming District Magistrate
                           (who ordered work on hospital
                                    stopped)
          August 20th - General Liu Yao-yang
                           Headquarters Yunnan Provincial
                                      Government
          September 7th- General Liu Yao-yang
          September 13 - Governor Lung Yun

      3. As you can see, it is impossible for the U.S. Army to carry out its proper function of air support and training in China, if its necessary housing, operational, and hospital construction is delayed. This delays the arrival of troops to China from India.

      4. It is hoped that with your assistance these matters can be expedited.

      For LIEUTENANT GENERAL STILWELL:

                                         FRANK DORN,
                                         Colonel, G.S.C.
                                         Deputy Chief of Staff.

(24)

- 1 -

D-R-A-F-T

STATUS OF TRUCKS FOR CEF, SOS

From	Received by SOS	To be furnished later	
YEHTA	*100		
5th Truck Regt.	315	50	Oct. 20
Temp Truck Regt.		90	Oct. 15
Commercial Purchase	56	94	Oct. 30
YB Ry.		200	After air field project is completed.
5th Army		100?	Has failed to do so.
Armies & Divisions		150?	Have failed to do so.
	471	684	

*Of these 60 are being turned over temporarily to Yoke Hq. for liaison teams and miscellaneous needs; 35 turned over to Col. Jordan for air field hauling.

R. M. SANDUSKY,
Col., G.S.C.,
G-4.

- 1 -

CEF, SOS, Western Front, is functioning satisfactorily.

General Tuan, SOS commander for Southern front, assumed office October 1. He has been contacted and promises to start supply operations. Details of supply will be furnished him at once.

R. M. SANDUSKY,
Col., G. S. C.,
G-4.

4 Oct. 1943.

INFORMATION FROM ACTING DIRECTOR YBHEA

Burma Road:

(a) Funds   First 100,000,000 CN. here

50,000,000 CN. due to-day

49,000,000 CN. Restoration not Rec'd.

No fund for paving.

No fund for strengthening bridges.

None contemplated for these though badly needed. (dust will seriously hamper large convoys).

(b) Construction   % Complete

		Earthwork	Culverts & Bridges
Chinese estimates	(K 11-192	100%	95%
Believe they should	(K 192-412	95%	70%
be reduced by 1/5.	(K 412-530	90%	75%
Col. Dawson, now inspecting, will have more accurate data later.	(K 530-574	95%	60%
	(K 574-680	95%	65%
	(K 680-763	To be built with restoration fund.	

Labor Sept. 30   Conscript   22,000

Contract   8,500

Total   30,500

- 3 -

Mitu Road:

    (a) Funds

        Received   50,000,000 CN.

        Promised   70,000,000 CN.

    This 70,000,000 needed badly <u>now</u> as it takes two weeks from Kunming to Mitu for delivery. Failure to receive soon will delay work.

    (b) Construction

    A proposed conscript force of 24,000.

    Done now to Nankien (passable for trucks)

    Scheduled to Kunlang by October 10.

    Scheduled to Wu Cha Chai by November 10.

    Surveys progressing ahead of work.

R. M. SANDUSKY,
Col., G. S. C.,
G-4.

- 4 -

948

RECEIVED IN SECRET CODE

<u>INCOMING RADIO</u>

RECEIVED: 24 SEPTEMBER 0440 GCT

FROM   : AMMDEL

TO   : AMMISCA

NO   : AM 1604 FILED: 23 SEPTEMBER 0550 GCT

    I GET IMPRESSION SOME BRITISH HERE WONDERING (EYES ALONE STILWELL FROM FERRIS) WHAT WILL HAPEN TO ALL US AND CHINESE ARMY INSTALLATIONS IN INDIA, BURMA, THAILAND AND THE REST OF SOUTH EAST ASIA COMMAND WITH THEM IN COMMAND. THEY EVEN GO SO FAR AS TO HINT SOS, REAR ECHELON, JICA, YOU AND CHINESE XXIXXXX WILL BE FOR THEIR USE AS THEY SEE FIT. THIS COMES FROM LOCAL MOSS BACKS AND DOUBT LOUIS WILL TAKE THAT ATTITUDE. BELIEVE WE SHALL HAVE TO BE ON GUARD. THEY MAY EVEN CONSIDER CDS AT THEIR DISPOSAL. NEW SUBJECT COMING HERE RESULT WINGATE REQUEST AT QUADRANT TEN THOUSAND ROUNDS TRACER AMMUNITION FOR CARBINE. DO YOU WANT HALF FOR OUR USE

(1038)

18259

HQ. U.S. ARMY FORCES

CHUNGKING, CHINA
24 SEPTEMBER 1943

A

AGWAR : -767

EYE HAVE ALREADY COMPLIED WITH YOUR INSTRUCTIONS PAREN PERSONAL
TO GENERAL MARSHAL FROM STILWELL REURAD THREE FOUR THREE ZERO SEPT TWENTY
TWO PAREN AND HAVE HAD MORE THAN EQUIVALENT OF TWO WEEKS REST SINCE
RETURNING TO CHUNGKING PD AT PRESENT CMA EYE AM AT CRITICAL POINT OF A
MANEUVER WHICH MAY SMOOTH OUT MANY DIFFICULTIES PD POSSIBILITIES ARE FAR
REACHING IF EYE CAN SIT ON THE EGGS FOR A WHILE LONGER PD WHEN THIS THING
EITHER DEVELOPES OR DIES CMA THE HILLS CAN BE CONSIDERED PD YOUR INTEREST
IS HIGHLY APPRECIATED CMA AND EYE HOPE YOU ARE PRACTICING WHAT YOU PREACH

OFFICIAL:

L.B. Thompson
Maj AGD

ASST. ADJUTANT GENERAL

REC'D IN CODE ROOM _____ DATE _240905_

ACTUAL TIME OF DISPATCH AND METHOD __1000__ JGTB

JWS/ajc

Ref:- 18,217

(1037)

(3)

950

INCOMING RADIO:

RECEIVED: 24 SEPT 1150 Z.   U R G E N T

FROM   : AMMDEL

TO   : AMMISCA (FOR THE EYES OF GEN STILWELL ONLY)

NR   : AM 1626   FILED: 24 SEPT 1026 Z.

EYES ALONE STILWELL FROM FERRIS. CONCERNING GALAHAD
PROJECT AIR MAIL LETTER OPD 320.2 SEC (7 SEPTEMBER 1943)
RECEIVED FROM WAR DEPARTMENT. COPY OF LETTER AND CHARTS OF
PROPOSED ORGANIZATION FORWARDED TO FORWARD ECHELON. TO
ANSWER QUESTIONS IN RADIO 3286 FROM MARSHALL FOR STILWELL
SEPTEMBER 1, FOLLOWING INFORMATION FURNISHED: 1. TRAINING
AREA FOR THIS PROJECT TENTATIVELY SELECTED IN ASSAM 2 MILES
WEST OF MARGHERITA BRIDGE, CONTAINING DENSE JUNGLE, RIVER,
ACCESS TO NAGA HILLS. FINAL RECONNAISSANCE UNDER WAY TO
DETERMINE SUITABILITY. 2. PRELIMINARY STUDY OF T/O, T/E
AND SHIPMENT DIRECTIVES INDICATES A POSSIBLE SHORTAGE IN AIR
DROPPING EQUIPMENT. OTHER TRAINING AND OPERATIONAL EQUIPMENT
GENERALLY APPEAR SATISFACTORY. DEFINITE INFORMATION ON
ADDITIONAL NEEDS WILL BE FURNISHED AFTER DETAILED STUDY. WAR
DEPARTMENT HAD NOT BEEN INFORMED OF THESE FACTS BY REAR ECHELON.

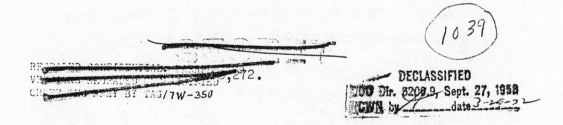

(1039)

DECLASSIFIED
DOD Dir. 5200.9, Sept. 27, 1958

INCOMING RADIO:

RECEIVED: 25 SEPT 1530 Z.

FROM   : RELOT

TO   : AMMISCA (FOR THE EYES OF GEN STILWELL ONLY)

NR   : G 222   FILED: 2 5 SEPT 0650 Z.

EYES OF STILWELL ONLY. EVERYTHING WELL UNDER CONTROL REURAD

OT 11 ONCOCOVMAN (on command) SITUATION HERE. RELATIONS WITH CHINESE HAVE

ALWAYS BEEN MOST CORDIAL BUT OF COURSE EYE AM EMPHASIZING

TRAINING AND THAT WE ARE DEFINITELY GOING BACK INTO BURMA COME

THIS DRY SEASON. YOU KNOW WHY EYE AM DOING THAT AND SHOULD

FEEL CONFIDENT EYE HAVE NO INTENTION TO GO OFF H ALF COCKED

(STILWELL FROM BOATNER) THIRTY EIGHT DIV HERE NOW TOTALS

TEN THOUSAND FOUR HUNDRED, TWO TWO DIV HERE AND ON RAILS

TOTALS FIVE THOUSAND TWO HUNDRED, CORPS TROOPS THREE THOUSAND

THREE HUNDRED. EYE CAN EASILY PLAY ALONG WITH SUN IN COMMAND

ALTHOUGH OTHER UNITS RESENT BEING UNDER HIM. GIFFARD FRANKLY

TOLD ME BRITISH COULD DO NOTHING OFFENSIVE TILL ROADS BUILT

OR REBUILT WHICH WOULD NOT BE TILL JANUARY AT EARLIEST AND

THAT ALL HE COULD DO TO HELP EFFORT HERE WOULD BE ONE WINGATE

COLUMN TOWARD KATHA NOT BEFORE DECEMBER FIFTEENTH. EYE STILL

FEEL ABSOLUTELY CERTAIN ANY CHINESE COMMAND PLACED BETWEEN

YOU AND THESE TWO DIVISIONS WILL PRODUCE ANOTHER LO DASH CHO

DASH YING RPT LO DASH CHO DASH YING HYPH EN TU DASH PI DASH

MING RPT QU DASH LI DASH MING HEADACHE AND CHINESE WILL

INVENT OR MAGNIFY OBSTACLES TO OPERATIONS THIS DRY SEASON

AND WILL CAPITOLIPE ON BRITISH DELAYS AND LACK OF PROMISES.

Eyes alone Gen Stilwell (continued).

BUT COME DECEMBER OR JANUARY YOUR ROAD AND AIRFIELD CONSTRUCTION
UNITS MUST TEB OUCHE FROM SHINGEWIYANG AT WHICH TIME WE MUST HAVE
GONE ON OFFENSIVE IN ORDER CARRY OUT PRESENT MISSION. THIS FORCE
WILL BE REASONABLY READY. UP TO DATE REPORT IMPHAL ROAD
CONSTRUCTION FOLLOWS: TIMAPUR DASH IMPHAL OPEN ALL TRANSPORT WITH
CIRCULATION REDUCED OVERHALF. IMPHAL DASH TAMU OPEN TO CHAMOL
RK 6209 FOR THREE TON TWO WH EELERS AND TO LOKCVAO RIVER RK 7005
FOR FOUR WHEEL DRIVE. NO MAINTENANCE AND NO REPORTS ON ROAD
FORWARD OF SI BONG. IMPHAL DASH TIDDIM ROAD OPEN THREE TON TO
MILE EIGHTY THREE, THREE QUARTER TON FOUR FOUTS TO MILE ONE HUNDRED
THEOCE BY JEEP. NEW SUBJECT: IN MY OPINION SINCE RECENT COMMAND
CHANGE HERE OUR COOPERATION WITH LOCAL SUGAR OBOE SUGAR HAS BEEN
DEFINITELY CORDIAL, FRIENDLY AND EFFECTIVE A ND THEY ARE DOING
BETTER JOB.

1042

18,3 47.

CHUNGKING, CHINA,
26 September 1943.

MEMORANDUM FOR HIS EXCELLENCY GENERALISSIMO CHIANG KAI-SHEK:

1. The Kunming Infantry School has now graduated about 2500 officers and the Artillery School 400. The third class of officers of high rank is now at Ramgarh. If these graduates are used in unit schools promptly, the training can reach most of the men within two months. To supervise this training, one liaison group has been assigned to each group army. These American officers will work with the staff officers of the units, and under the general supervision of the chün hsün pu. Due to distance, delay in arrival of replacements, and lack of proper weapons and facilities, the training will not be all it should be.

2. For various reasons, the first thirty division plan has been so changed that now, counting in the 60th Army and the N22d and the N38th Divisions, it amounts to only 22 divisions. I am assuming that the Yunnan force under the command of Ch'en Ch'eng, will be considered as the first thirty divisions, and training and equipping, will proceed on that basis in the absence of other instructions.

3. A tentative list of divisions in the second group of thirty has been received, and tentative plans have been made for their training. I recommend that Kweilin be selected, on account of the facilities available there, and that officers from the second thirty divisions begin arriving at Kweilin from November 1, as they can be handled. By the time equipment for these units can reach them, all officers should have been through a basic course at the school, and unit schools could be in operation. It is highly advisable to get this work done as early as possible.

4. The formation of new artillery units is necessary. 19 battalions of 75mm howitzers are needed for the first thirty divisions alone, and only 5 have been made available for training. I recommend that drafts from existing infantry units be sent to Kunming for training as artillery to make up this deficiency.

5. The training of tank and mortar units at Ramgarh offers no difficulties and is proceeding smoothly. It is essential that these units remain under American command until the Chinese commanders demonstrate their ability to handle them. I believe they will prove their ability to do so after a reasonable period of training and experience.

- 1 -

(231)

6. The long delay in the furnishing of replacements for the N22d and N38th Divisions, for the N30th Division, and for the Yunnan force, convinces me that the only practicable way of solving the trouble is to break up existing units for this purpose. I renew my recommendation, made over one year ago, that the total number of divisions in the Army be reduced by half so that the remainder can be filled up to strength and have a reasonable supply of weapons. As a result, the Army will be stronger and easier to supply and will partially regain its mobility. If so desired, divisions inactivated can be maintained on a skeleton basis for training and replacement purposes.

7. The commonest causes of rejection on physical examination are trachoma, scabies, and malnutrition. Trachoma requires long treatment, and probably nothing can be done about it. The treatment of scabies is a simple matter; bad cases can be cured in two weeks. Malnutrition is due to inadequate food and an unbalanced diet. The very large number of such cases in the Army prove that commanders do not take the interest they should in the welfare of their men.

8. I urgently recommend that unity of command be established in Yunnan by giving Ch'en Ch'eng command of both the Paoshan and Mengtze fronts, and control of the general reserve. The reasons for this will be obvious to the Generalissimo.

9. If the delays of the past few months continue, the Yunnan force will not be ready for the mission which the Generalissimo has approved.

10. I recommend that General Boatner be named as fu tsung chih hui of the C. A. I., so that in case of my absence, he can act for me.

11. General Woon was relieved as deputy Chief of Staff of the chih hui pu for various irregularities, such as unauthorized correspondence with the War Ministry, unauthorized requests for personnel, the suppression of radios, unwarranted imprisonment of an officer, appointment of several relatives to important positions, and the use of my name on radios unknown to me.

J. W. STILWELL,
Lt. Gen., U.S. Army.

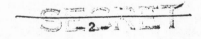

CHUNGKING, CHINA,
26 September 1943.

MEMORANDUM FOR GENERAL HO YING CHIN:

I have just learned that on June 14, General Woon, then deputy Chief of Staff at Ramgarh, sent a radio to the War Ministry without my knowledge recommending an artillery headquarters for the Chih Hui Pu with a table of organization. General Chin Chen has apparently been appointed to head it.

The complications caused by this unauthorized action on General Woon's part are obvious. I do not know, of course, what else he has done, but this assumption of command functions by him makes it extremely difficult for me to carry out the instructions of the Generalissimo.

J. W. STILWELL,
Joint Chief of Staff for the Generalissimo.

MEMORANDUM FOR HIS EXCELLENCY THE GENERALISSIMO:

The Generalissimo has ordered that Chinese officers be assigned to command tank and mortar units in India. He has directed me to get rid of General Boatner, because he is "not on good terms" with the C. A. I., and recommend a new Chief of Staff.

This brings up a matter which should be thoroughly considered before action is taken.

1. When the Generalissimo put me in Command of the C. A. I., he agreed that I could control all matters of organization and training, and could assign American officers to command positions where I considered it necessary. I told him we would stick as closely as possible to Chinese organization, as we have, and that we would use American officers in command positions only when it was essential. I am glad to say that in the divisions, as a result of thorough training, it has been possible to use Chinese officers exclusively. On the staff this has not been possible; American officers have had to be used on account of our dealings with the British, and because the Chinese officers were not familiar with many phases of the work.

2. In the mortar regiment, the personnel is excellent. With Colonel McLaughlin, one of our best officers, as adviser, the Chinese officers can probably command the unit very creditably. In the tank battalions, where the matter of Command is of special importance, I am not satisfied that the Chinese officers have the necessary experience for success. Colonel Brown, the tank instructor, is an officer of long experience; based on his inspection and report, the British have entirely changed their system of tank instruction in India, and have asked to have him detailed with them in charge of this instruction. I refused this request because of our need for him with the Chinese troops. He should command the tank units until the Chinese officers have become experienced enough to take over, as I am sure they will.

3. I do not know who has said that General Boatner is not on good terms with the C. A. I. As far as I have been able to judge, he is on good terms with them. No complaints about him have reached me. I know that he is intensely interested in the Chinese troops and that he would do anything in his power for them. He is a very capable officer, and was chosen for the position on this account and because of his sympathetic attitude towards the Chinese.

4. I wish to request the Generalissimo's careful consideration of the following facts:

The coming operation will be of great importance to the future of China. The part the C. A. I. force will have to play is vital, and we cannot afford to take any chances with the command and operation of that force. It will be supported by a large number of American troops, - medical, engineer, signal, truck transport, aviation, etc. - and its Commander must understand how to handle these units, as well as all the weapons now in the hands of the troops. In case of the temporary absence of the Commander,

- 1 -

the Second-in-Command must be capable of doing this. I do not know of any Chinese officer who has had such experience; if the Generalissimo has someone in mind, a simple practical test could be given him to determine it. The facts seem to be that without further training, there are no Chinese officers available who would have the confidence of both Chinese and American officers and men, and who have the necessary technical experience.

This being so, I strongly recommend —

a. That an American officer, for the reasons stated above, be made Second-in-Command. In my opinion General Boatner is best qualified. He could concurrently be Chief of Staff.

b. That Colonel Brown command the tank units until the Chinese officers have demonstrated their ability.

c. That, as originally agreed, all matters of command, training, and organization be left to the Tsung Chih Hui of the C. A. I.

d. That, when operations begin, the Tsung Chih Hui have full authority to make any necessary changes in personnel, summarily and on the spot, reporting the action to the Generalissimo.

No question should be allowed to enter this matter except the question of efficiency. The Generalissimo is of course vitally concerned that his troops should reach as high a standard as any in the world. Our immediate and vital concern is to open the supply road to China, and I feel that his can be done only if we make efficiency our guide and leave out all other considerations.

JOSEPH W. STILWELL
Joint Chief of Staff for the Generalissimo

958

RECEIVED IN SECRET CODE

<u>INCOMING RADIO</u>

RECEIVED   : 27 SEPT 0715 GCT

FROM   : WAR

TO   : AMMISCA

NR   : 3462   FILED: 26 SEPT, 2138 GCT

PARAPHRASE OF MESSAGE DISPATCHED BY US JOINT CHIEFS OF STAFF

TO BRITISH CHIEFS OF STAFF 24TH SEPTEMBER FOLLOWS (PERSONAL ATTENTION

STILWELL FROM MARSHALL REF YOUR 767 SEPTEMBER 24TH):

PARAPHRASE BEGINS: BECAUSE OF OUR OBJECTIVE OF KEEPING CHINA

IN WAR, POLITICAL IMPLICATIONS WITH CHINA AND PRIOR COMMITMENTS OF THE

PRESIDENT TO CKS RPT CKS THAT 10,000 TONS PER MONTH OVER THE HUMP WILL

BE REACHED THIS FALL, WE DESIRE THAT BEFORE ANY ACTION IS TAKEN TO

LOWER ALLOCATIONS OF TONNAGE FOR AMERICAN AND CHINESE FORCES (CON-

CLUSIVE OF REQUIREMENTS FOR AIR TRANSPORT) THAT MATTER TOGETHER WITH

IMPLICATIONS BE FORWARDED FOR DECISION TO CCS RPT CCS. IN ORDER THAT

THIS LIFT TO CHINA MAY BE ACCOMPLISHED, SOME REDUCTION COULD POSSIBLY

BE MADE IN CIVILIAN AND OTHER NEEDS.

EVIDENTLY A CLARIFICATION OF OUR DECISION IS REQUIRED OF US IN

VIEW OF THE INTERPRETATION OF THE QUEBEC DECISION MADE BY GENERAL

AUCHINLECK INDICATED BY HIS ORDERS TO MOVE CERTAIN BRITISH ENGINEERING

UNITS FROM ULGSAM AIR TRANSPORT AIRDROME CONSTRUCTION TO THE ILPHAL-

TAMU AREA. CCS RPT CCS 27, A MEMO TO THE CCS FROM BRITISH CHIEFS OF

STAFF SET FORTH (IN ONE OF THREE COURSES INTENDED AS A <u>GUIDE</u> FOR THE

SOUTHEAST ASIA SUPREME COMMANDER) THAT MAIN EFFORT COULD ONLY BE AT

EXPENSE OF TONNAGE TO CHINA. WE BELIEVE AUCHLINLECKS INTERPRETATION

WAS BASED ON THIS MEMO.

18,425   SECRET   (1046)

DESIRED BY US CHIEFS OF STAFF THAT YOU INFORM AUCHINLECK AS TO GREAT IMPORTANCE ATTACHED TO MAKING ALL OUT EFFORT TO DEVELOP AND IMPROVE EASTERN INDUUS AND ASSAM LINES OF COMMUNICATION TO EXTENT THAT AT EARLIEST POSSIBLE MOMENT A 10,000 TON MONTHLY LIFT TO CHINA CAN BE ATTAINED.

POSSIBLY MOVEMENT FROM AIRDROME CONSTRUCTION TO IMPHAL TAMU AREA OF BRITISH ENGINEERING MEANS COULD BE SO TIMED AS TO PERMIT TAKING OVER PART OF THE WORK BY US ENGINEER UNITS IN INDIA

NECESSARY MACHINERY FOR THE INTEGRATION WITH OPERATIONS FROM INDIA OF GROUND AND AIR EFFORT FROM CHINA AND FOR DECIDING IN THIS THEATER THOSE MATTERS WHICH AFFECT TONNAGE TO CHINA WITHOUT REFERRING TO CCS WILL BE PROVIDED BY ORGAINZATION OF SOUTHEAST ASIA COMMAND AND POSITION OF GENERAL STILWELL IN THIS COMMAND. HOWEVER PENDING ORGANIZATION OF SOUTHEAST ASIA COMMAND, WE DESIRE THAT FUTURE MATTERS WHICH MAY BRING ABOUT REDUCTION IN AIR LIFT TO CHINA BE FORWARDED TO CCS FOR DECISION. END MESSAGE TO BRITISH CHIEFS OF STAFF

D 2 153.

Arundel   for Ferris.   Eyes alone -

Counting on you to keep us straight with
W. D   I am all tied up here maneuver-
ing and struggling. Slow progress with
good possibilities. Your work is appreciated.
make allowances for Dorn. He has a ticklish job and is working night and day to put
it over -

                              Stilwell -

Secret
Routine

30 Sept

Received 30 0320
Sent   30 0500
         JGT

Dir. 5280.9 Sept. 27, 1958
by ___ date 3___

1045

W-350   834

961

TO ALL GENERAL OFFICERS OF CHINA-BURMA-INDIA COMMAND:

After nosing around the area considerably there are certain points that become obvious. One is that practically everybody is trying to do his job. Some are succeeding better than others, but there are only exceptional cases of dead-beating and laziness. The inefficiency that is only too common is, I believe, almost entirely due to ignorance or inexperience. There are few complaints about the difficulties and inconveniences that are met with; the kicks come mostly from impatience over lack of tools to work with, or over obstructions to getting on with the job, or over medieval methods and mental attitudes. The spirit is good; almost everybody wants to tear into it and do something, and almost everybody craves action. That's all to the good.

What's not so good is as follows:-

1. Action on papers is often slow or perfunctory. All headquarters must perk up and act promptly on all business in and out. Cases of delayed messages must be traced and enough noise made about it to prevent recurrence. The perfunctory disapproval of requests for supplies must stop. If somebody wants something to make his job go, he should get it, if it is at all reasonable, and get it promptly. If he can't have it, he should be told why. No more of this stuff like "this request is not favorably considered". Either give the guy his stuff or tell him why you can't, but don't stop there, either. Take it up with the next higher echelon and see if it can be gotten.

On the other hand, don't ask for the impossible. Everybody knows the limitations on our transportation, and to make a squawk, for instance, for canned beer in China because someone has it somewhere else is not reasonable. And the K. O. who allows such squawks is not playing the game.

2. There is a lot of uncalled for criticism of one agency by another. "The S.O.S. is holding out on us." "Rear Echelon grabs all the good clerks." "I can't get my share of spare parts." "The A.T.C. won't fly." "India gets all the PX stuff." "Ramgarh keeps all the good ordnance officers." etc. etc. I find invariably that the loudest squawkers are the worst offenders. We cannot get the job done unless there is more tolerance for the difficulties that other people are working under. Time after time I have run down complaints and found that they were based on hearsay or misinformation or that they were entirely unfounded. Where they were justified, we are taking action. But in a complex job, like the one we are struggling with, there is necessarily a lot of lost motion, and before criticising someone else, we must make damn sure that there isn't a beam in our own eye.

- 1 -

3. There is, too much loose talking about future plans. Very few people seem able to keep their mouths shut. I recently found a case where the contents of an "eyes alone" radio were common knowledge within twelve hours. This is serious business, and unless it fades out considerably, somebody is going to find himself on a boat bound for the U.S.A.

4. The promotion question is a headache. The quick promotion in the States puts us at a disadvantage here. There are inequalities and injustices. But the Chief of Staff is concerned to hold it within reasonable limits and has called on me to do my part in helping him. The idea is spreading that just because an officer has been in grade for a certain number of months, he is entitled to promotion as a matter of right. This causes constant pressure and dissatisfaction when the action is not taken. I depend on all commanders to help get rid of this idea.

5. There is a great responsibility on all general officers. They must under no circumstances tolerate, much less encourage, criticism of other outfits. This is only common sense; if the team does not work smoothly, every member of it suffers. They must be generous in giving credit to their subordinates, they must be patient with the inexperienced and restrained in their corrective measures. The rank of a general officer makes his disapproval felt in a disproportionate degree. I don't mean that serious cases should be excused, - on the contrary, there has been too much laxity in this respect, and we must tighten up on discipline generally.

6. I am asking you all, as general officers, to help get rid of friction and criticism, to get everybody to be more tolerant of the other fellow and his difficulties, to watch discipline, and to give me any ideas or suggestions for the betterment of the command.

                              JOSEPH W. STILWELL,
                              Lt. General, U.S. Army.
                              Commanding.

- 2 -

963

MEMORANDUM FOR GENERAL PAI CHUNG HSI:

In order to benefit by the experience gained at Kunming, the following changes should be incorporated in the Kweilin set-up:

1. Administrative control must be permanent, and not subject to frequent changes.

2. Demonstration troops must be under the command of the school director.

3. There must be allowances for rations, uniforms, and equipment for the school troops, and for extra pay of assistant instructors, as well as for a good mess for them.

4. The Chinese staff must be carefully selected and kept within reasonable limits. It should not be subject to change without cause.

5. A control board should be set-up, including the American director and his assistant. This board should have power to make necessary changes in the staff personnel.

JOSEPH W. STILWELL,
Lt. Gen., U.S. Army.

reCEIVED IN SECRET CODE

OCT 2 43 PM

INCOMING RADIO

RECEIVED: 28 SEPTEMBER 1245 GCT

DEFERRED

FROM : AMMDEL

DEFERRED

TO : AMMISCA

NO : AM 1653   FILED: 28 SEPT 0902 GCT

EYES ALONE GENERAL STILWELL. FOLLOWING FIFTEEN CODE
NAMES WHICH ARE THE VERY LATEST ARE FURNISHED FOR YOUR INFOR-
MATION (FROM FERRIS) KEYS TO CODE NAMES WILL BE TRANSMITTED
IN A SEPARATE MESSAGE. 1 TRIUMPHANT, 2 CHAMPION, 3 NOTEBOOK,
4 CUTLASS, 5 VALENTINE, 6 SWITHIN, 7 JOURNALIST, 8 PIGSTICK,
9 CUDGEL, 10 BULLFROG, 11 LYNCHPIN, 12 BUCCANEER, 13 CULVERIN,
14 FETTLE AND 15 GALAHAD

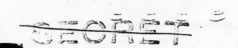

ORDER SEC ARMY BY TAG/TW-350   18482

965

RECEIVED IN SECRET CODE

INCOMING RADIO

RECIEVEB: 29 SEPTEMBER 1305 GCT

FROM : AMMDEL   DEFERRED
                                 DEFERED

TO : AMMISCA

NO : AM 1661   FILED: 29 SEPTEMBER 0537 GCT

EYES ALONE GENERAL STILWELL.   KEYS TO CODE NAMES FOLLOW
(FROM FERRIS) (13) SUMATRA-MALAYA OPERATIONS, (8) AKYAB IN GENERAL
(1) RECONQUEST BURMA, (5) YOKE OPERATIONS, (9) LAND OPERATIONS
                                    WHOLE
ARAKAN COAST NORTH OF AKYAB, (2) WHILE PROGRAM SET OUT IN CON-
CLUSIONS 91ST MEETING COMBINED CHIEFS OF STAFF, (6) XRAY OP-
ERATIONS, (3) AIR TRANSPORT TO CHINA, (12) ANDAMAN ISLAND OPER-
ATIONS, 15 OUR JUNGLE FIGHTERS, (4) OPERATIONS AGAINST NORTH
BURMA, (10) AMPHIBIOUS OPERATIONS AGAINST AKYAB, (7) FOURTH CORPS
OPERATIONS, (14) BUILDING UP INDIA AS A BASE FOR OFFENSIVE
OPERATIONS, (11) RAMREE INLAND OPERATION

ORDER SEC ARMY BY TAG/TW-350

18523

966

CHUNGKING, CHINA,
30 September 1943.

PROGRAM FOR CHINA

China's main needs at the moment, as I see them, are
as follows:

1. A definite policy of reorganization and training,
covered by a general directive, issued by the Generalissimo.

2. A simplifying and speeding up of war ministry
procedure, so that action on decisions can be more prompt.

3. A reduction, by 50%, of existing units, accomplished
by amalgamation.

4. The formation of two field armies, one composed of
the first 30 divisions, the other of the second 30.

5. Elimination of unfit and inefficient officers.

(The two armies in paragraph 4 to be the regular
Chinese Army, all other units to be second line troops,
the best of the second line troops to be used as garrison
units and the others gradually inactivated. They can be
reduced first to brigades, and then by drafts to police
work, gendarmes, anti-smuggling, etc. be eliminated as
troop units.)

China cannot carry the load she is burdened with at
present. It is impossible to properly feed and pay her
large army. The result is that nearly all units are under
strength, full of sickness, immobile, and inefficient. If
the army were a person, a surgical operation would be
performed at once. I propose such an operation for the army,
in the belief that if it is not performed, the patient will
die.

Bad cases require radical treatment. A reduction of
units by 50% would cure many of the ills we are suffering
from. The remaining units would be stronger, and a large
number of men would be released to go back to the farms.
Ten good divisions are certainly better than twenty poor
ones.

How many of China's 300-odd divisions could possibly
be brought to bear against the enemy? Only those where the
enemy chooses to attack, with a few exceptions. Of what
use, then, are the others? There are many divisions that
have not fought at all, or so little as to be a negligible
factor.

- 1 -

234

The designation of two groups of divisions as the regular army of China has many advantages. These troops can be fully equipped and trained. They can be paid and fed and cared for properly. They will then be at least three times as effective as an equal number of the divisions that now exist. They will have a keen sense of loyalty to the Central Government. They can be made mobile and moved to wherever they may be needed. They can quickly become a strong, efficient striking force, backed up by necessary auxiliary units and supplied by a working S.O.S.

The plan can be put into effect as follows:

1. Begin training the remaining divisions in the first 30, and gradually move them to the Yunnan-Kweichow area. If and when the Burma road is opened, the C.A.I. can join the group. Meanwhile training should continue, in anticipation of the receipt of equipment. The first 30, after action in Burma, will be seasoned and experienced, and can then be moved to the Hengyang-Kweilin area, where they will be available for further operations. With such a force in that area, all threats to Chungking and Kunming will be removed.

2. Meanwhile, set up a school in Kweilin and train the officers of the second thirty divisions. After graduates return to their divisions, send U.S. instructor groups to supervise training there. Gradually move the divisions of this group, by exchange with divisions now there, to the Hunan-Kiangsi area, to put them into a position threatening Ichang and Hankow.

3. By the time the first 30 have been equipped and moved to the Hengyang-Kweilin area, the second thirty will be ready for their equipment.

4. Build up the services for the second 30 by cadres taken from the S.O.S. of the first 30.

5. Of the best remaining divisions, designate 30 as garrison units and leave them in key defensive areas -- Sian, Loyang, Lao Ho K'ou, Chekiang, Northern Kiangsi, Shiukwan, etc. These units will not be expected to move; they will be used on the defensive only; and will not need the equipment that the first and second 30 will get.

6. The remaining divisions should be inactivated in one way or another. They can be cut down to brigades at once, by order, and a maximum strength of 4,000 each can be established. Very few of them have more than that, anyway. Some of them can be used to form S.O.S. units for the first and second 30 division groups, and to supply replacements.

968

7. The problem of provincial loyalty will disappear as soon as the first and second 30 are constituted. These two groups will assure the Central Government of obedience to its orders.

8. The problem of surplus officers will have to be solved. Junior officers can be given the chance of demonstrating their ability at the schools. Those who cannot qualify should be released from the army. The number can be cut materially in this way. Senior officers can be sent to the garrison units and carried as extra numbers for the time being. For the surplus ones of very high rank, an advisory body, without authority, but with pay, can be established at Chungking, and they can be used here as a planning board.

The above is a radical procedure. Without it, or something similar, the Chinese Army will go on deteriorating further and further until it falls apart. The eyes of the world are on China; the real state of affairs is becoming known; and the Generalissimo cannot afford to let things drift. Now is the time to take vigorous action. The manifesto of the C.E.C. states that "it is China's responsibility to undertake the major operations on the East Asiatic continent." This will be impossible without a thorough reorganization. With it, China will be able to do her part and refute her critics, and will emerge at the end of the war with the means of assuring her stability.

- 3 -

THE CASE OF GENERAL WOON

General Woon has been deputy chief of staff at Ramgarh.
General Bergin, as acting chief of staff, was in charge.
When I was last in Ramgarh I found that General Woon had had
Lt. Colonel Liu Wen Shih imprisoned because of pique over a
misunderstanding on an administrative matter.

The facts were generally known. Colonel Liu was under
restraint without any real reason, and to fail to take action
on this arbitrary and illegal abuse of authority would have
ruined discipline in the chih hui pu.

In the course of the investigation, I learned that
General Woon had gotten appointments on the staff for four
relatives (Woon H. Yuan, Woon Wei Chun, Woon Yu Ching and
Woon Yu Bui) that one of them was in charge of radio messages,
and that General Woon had been sending and receiving radios
without the knowledge of General Bergin or myself.

Later, in Chungking, I learned that General Woon had
recommended himself and several other officers for the award
of the ch'ing t'ien pai jih decoration, using my name in the
recommendation. This was, of course, without my knowledge
or that of General Bergin.

I also learned that General Woon had asked for the
detail of ten officers from the war college for duty at
Ramgarh. These officers were not needed and neither General
Bergin nor I knew anything about the request.

I have since learned that General Woon, in my name,
recommended the creation of an artillery headquarters at
Ramgarh. This also was done without the knowledge of either
General Bergin or myself.

General Woon on numerous occasions used the seal of the
C. A. I. without authority, and also signed messages and
orders with my name without authority. When asked for certain
messages he could not or would not produce them.

The arbitrary acts of General Woon had so stirred up the
entire staff that to let him continue as deputy chief of staff
would have proven that there was no control over him. He has
caused a great deal of trouble and friction, and even now
I have no way of knowing what further messages he has sent to
the War Ministry over my signature. The only course open to
me, in order to maintain discipline at Ramgarh, was to relieve
him, and I did so, reporting the action at once to the War
Ministry. I recommend, in the interests of good discipline,
that General Woon be tried by court-martial for his misdeeds.

CHUNGKING, CHINA,
30 September 1943.

His Excellency,
General Ho Ying Chin,
Chief of General Staff,
Chungking.

My dear General Ho:

In answer to your letter of September
29, concerning General Woon's action, my views are as
follows:

(a) In my opinion, an artillery headquarters is
not needed at Ramgarh at present. If the personnel
necessary to form and train more artillery units had been
furnished, and we had a large number of organizations in
training, there would be a need for it, but it is a very
simple matter to handle the few units we have, and there
is no apparent prospect of an increase for some time.

(b) Unless it develops that General Woon has
caused further complications in matters still unknown to
me, I am satisfied to consider as settled all the routine
matters of minor importance he has handled.

(c) Any competent staff officer knows that the
duties and responsibilities of a deputy chief of staff do
not extend to the unauthorized use of the seals and the
commanding general's name, and to the suppression of
information and radio messages. The remainder of the
chih hui pu staff understand these things very well, and
there has never been any question about it until General
Woon's arrival.

(d) I shall be glad of the opportunity to see
a copy of General Woon's report in this case.

With my thanks for your prompt answer
and the accompanying documents.

Sincerely yours,

JOSEPH W. STILWELL,
Lt. Gen., U.S. Army.

- 1 -

RECEIVED IN ~~SECRET CODE~~

<u>INCOMING RADIO</u>

RECIEVED: 30 SEPT. 0940 GCT   PRIORITY

FROM   : AQUILA   PRIORITY

TO   : AMMISCA   COGUK

NO   : S 76 T   C 113 TAKS   FILED: 30 SEPT. 0526 GCT

BEEBES RELIEF FROM 14TH AIR FORCE AND APPOINTMENT TO SOUTH
EAST ASIA COMMAND IS NOT IN ACCORDANCE WITH MY RECOMMENDATION.
(STILWELL AND CHENNAULT FOR INFO EYES ALONE FROM STRATEMEYER.)
SEE MY S 40 TB 17 SEPTEMBER IN WHICH I POINTED OUT TO WAR DEP-
ARTMENT THAT BEEBES OPERATIONAL INTELLIGENCE AND BOMBARDMENT
EXPERIENCE NEEDED BY CHENNAULT AND THAT I WOULD DESIGNATE A
QUALIFIED OFFICER (¿ NEC^{RA}SON COMMANDING OFFICER 7TH BOMBARDMENT
GROUP) TO THE SOUTH EAST ASIA COMMAND IF A QUALIFIED OFFICER
COULD NOT BE FURNISHED BY THE WAR DEPARTMENT. IT WAS ALSO
RECOMMENDED THAT BEEBE BE MADE A BRIGADIER GENERAL TO FILL
POSITION OF BOMBARDMENT WING COMMANDER 14TH AIR FORCE. I
EMPHATICALLY BELIEVE THAT THE WAR DEPARTMENT IS STILL NOT
COGNIZANT OF BEEBES VALUE TO CHENNAULT. I URGENTLY RECOMMEND THAT
THE WAR DEPARTMENT BE REQUESTED TO RECONSIDER HIS APPOINTMENT
TO THE SOUTH EAST ASIA COMMAND AND THAT I INTEND TO RELEASE
NECRASON A VERY WELL QUALIFIED OFFICER.

09895

18567

Aquila for Stratemeyer, eyes alone —

Reurad S 76 T. I am sure Arnold has acted on this case — Beebe's replacement, Fisher, is apparently on his way. To me there is little difference in taking Beebe away from the fourteenth A.F. and taking Necrason from the tenth. ~~If you think it is worth while to make a case of this personally with Arnold~~, Davidson needs help as well as Chennault. And presumably Arnold is sending a competent replacement. Unless there are other angles to it, I believe we would get nowhere by objecting further.

Stilwell.

Recd 010340
Sent 010500

JCvB.
J. Rne..

OCT 2 43 PM

RECEIVED
WAR DEPARTMENT
U.S. MILITARY MISSION TO CHINA
CHUNGKING, CHINA

DECLASSIFIED
DOD Dir. 5200.9, Sept. 27, 1958
DOWN by ___ date 3-21-22

(1051)

973

RECEIVED ~~IN SECRET CODE~~

INCOMING RADIO

RECEIVED: 01 ~~SEPTEMBER~~ *Oct* 0850 GCT

FROM   : RELOT   ZZZZ

TO   : AMMISCA

NO   : G 234   FILED: 01 SEPTEMBER 0640 GCT

  FOR THE EYES OF STILWELL ALONE WHEN DO YOU EXPECT TO COME
BACK THRU HERE AND TO DELHI. IF YOU ARE NOT TO BE THERE SUGGEST
YOU GIVE CONSIDERATION TO MY GOING DELHI AS OBSERVER IF COMING
CONFERENCES WILL BE IMPORTANT. IF YOU ARE NOT THERE I FEAR
ASSUMPTIONS AND TACTICAL DECISIONS CONCERNING THIS SECTOR MIGHT
BE MADE THAT ARE FAR FROM LOGICAL AND REALISTIC (STILWELL FROM
BOATNER) I PROMISE TO BE DIPLOMATIC. I HAVE KNOWN WEDEMEYER
FOR 14 YEARS. THINGS HERE ARE GOING ALONG WELL

INCOMING RADIO

RECEIVED: 1 ~~SEPTEMBER~~ *Oct* 0945 GCT

FROM   : AMMDEL

TO   : AMMISCA

NO   : AM 1685   FILED: 1 SEPT. 0615 GCT

EYES ALONE STILWELL FROM FERRIS. WINTERBOTTOM TAKING BRIGADE IN ARAKAN WITH FIFTH DIVISION

HAD SOCIAL TALK WITH ALEX WHO ESTIMATED 5500 TONS WOULD BE TOP FIGURE OVER HUMP FOR SEPTEMBER. SPARE PARTS STILL HIS HEADACHE. RATHER SENSED THAT ALEX FEELING WAS THAT THE MOVE OF ATC HQ TO DELHI WILL NOT SOLVE THEIR TROUBLES.

LOUIS ARRIVES PRESENT PLAN ON SEVENTH AND REPORTS GHQ REMAIN HERE WEEK.

WITH YOUR OKAY WILL GO SEE DORN WITH STRAT AND GET HIS PICTURE FIRST HAND. WE SHALL DO EVERYTHING POSSIBLE TO HELP HIM

18615

AM MDEL. Eyes alone
AD 2157

Boss has no objection

(RvBAD AM 1685 For

Farris From Shaw) to

your taking off with

Strat. Thinks it would

be good for you. Reference

your two last sentences

he says he does not

know the difficulty. Suggest

you get amended here

before you make any

commitment.

100

1111

Know things affecting China
Must first be cleared thru
this office Otherwise
there is a temptation to
play one against the
other- And that does not
make hay. Para. Recently
Davn took exception to one
of your inds. reference
assignment of Censorship Others.
and appealed to the old
Man. He had something in
his favor but with the

10070   (111)

977

Bosses approval / pinned

his ears back

red 0220
Sent TB 0300 10/3

/

(111)

10070

1943. T 691

TIGAR EYE ALONE

Wheeler for Holcombe.
From Hearn.

Several weeks ago I took up
with William the matter
of the transfer of Capt
Lawrence C Lewis Jr.,
Medical Corps, from his
present assignment with
Med. Det 45th Eng. Regt.
to duty with a hospital.
Apparently nothing has
been done.

979

RECEIVED IN SECRET CODE.

INCOMING RADIO:

RECEIVED: 03 OCT 2145 Z.

FROM : AMMDEL

TO : AMMISCA AGWAR AG 2085 (FOR THE EYES OF GENERALS
MARSHALL AND STILWELL)

NR : AM 1705 FILED: 03 OCT 0831 Z.

PRIORITY

RECEIVED

EYES ALONE GENERALS MARSHALL AND STILWELL. CLARIFYING MY 1989 (FROM FERRIS REURAD 3264)

1. AIR TRANSPORT REQUIREMENT IS BROKEN DOWN UNDER 16 HEADINGS AS FOLLOWS: 1. INTERNAL AIR LINES OF INDIA REQUIRE 25 PLANES CONTINUOUSLY FROM JANUARY 1 ONWARDS; 2. PERMANENT REQUIREMENTS OF THE BENGAL COMMAND INCLUDING CHINA SERVICE, MAILS AND TRANSPORT IS 12 PLANES FOR SAME PERIOD; 3. FOR PERMANENT USE IN PARACHUTE TRAINING 25 PLANES SAME PERIOD; 4. FOR SUPPLY DROPPING AT RATE OF 1600 TONS PER MONTH FROM 15 JANUARY TO END OF APRIL TO 2 WEST AFRICAN BRIGADES IN THE KALADAN VALLEY 30 PLANES; 5. 2 LRP GROUPS SUPPLY DROPPING AT RAU *Rate* OF 640 TONS PER MONTH FROM FEBRUARY 1 ONWARDS 20 PLANES; 6. FOR 50 PARACHUTE BRIGADE 50 PLANES IN JANUARY AND 100 FROM JANUARY 15 UNTIL END OF MARCH; 7. MAINTENANCE OF PARACHUTE BRIGADE AND DROPPING 100 TONS FROM MARCH 15 UNTIL 31 MARCH 7 PLANES; 8. FOR FLYING IN AIRBORNE FORCE BETWEEN 16 AND 22 MARCH 175 PLANES FOR ARMY PLUS 30 FOR ROYAL AIR FORCE; 9. MAINTENANCE OF AIRBORNE FORCES FROM 17 MARCH TO 15 APRIL

ORDER SEC ARMY BY TAG/TV 350

- PAGE 2 -

50 PLANES; 10. FOR MAINTENANCE OF MARCHING COLUMN AT RATE OF 600 TONS PER MONTH FROM MARCH 1 TO 15 APRIL 18 PLANES; 11. MAINTENANCE OF THE INDAW FORCE AT RATE OF 2400 TONS PER MONTH FROM APRIL 15 ONWARDS 75 PLANES; 12. MAINTENANCE OF ROYAL AIR FORCE AT INDAW AT RATE OF 600 TONS A MONTH FROM MARCH 17 ONWARDS 25 PLANES; 13. STOCKING AND DEFENSE STORES AT INDAW WHICH WILL REQUIRE DROPPING OF 1600 TONS BETWEEN 15 MARCH AND 15 MAY 25 PLANES; 14. STOCKING OF RAF STORES AT INDAW AMOUNTING TO 600 TONS BETWEEN 15 MARCH AND 15 MAY 12 PLANES; 15. AIRFIELD CONSTRUCTION MATERIALS BETWEEN 15 MARCH TO 30 APRIL AMOUNTING TO EITHER 10630 TONS OR 2830 TONS WILL REQUIRE EITHER 325 PLANES FOR MAXIMUM FIGURE OR 80 PLANES FOR MINIMUM; 16. FOR EVACUATION OF CASUALTIES AND FLYING IN OF REPLACEMENTS FROM MARCH 31 ONWARDS AT RATE OF 50 PERSONNEL A DAY IN AND OUT OF INDAW 5 PLANES HRB TABULATING ABOVE BY MONTHS WILL SHOW REQUIREMENTS AS JANUARY 192 , FEBRUARY 211, MARCH 230 FOR FIRST HALF AND 454 FOR LAST HALF, APRIL 327 OR 572 FOR FIRST HALF AND 334 OR 579 FOR LAST HALF (DEPENDING ON TONNAGE FOR INDAW AIRFIELDS), MAY 304 OR 549 IN FIRST HALF AND 187 IN LAST HALF OF MONTH, JUNE AND SUCCESSIVE MONTHS 187 AIRPLANES.

2. OUR COMMENTS ON THIS PLAN ARE THAT IT DOES NOT REPRESENT A VERY SUBSTANTIAL CONTRIBUTION BY THE BRITISH TOWARDS THE CONQUEST OF NORTH BURMA. THEY PLAN TO DEPLOY A TOTAL FORCE OF 4 DIVISIONS, 2 LRP GROUPS, AND 2 OR 3 PARACHUTE GROUPS WITH STRONG AIR SUPPORT IN NORTH BURMA. CONSIDERING PRESENT STRENGTH AND DISPOSITIONS OF

(1055)

981

JAPS AND OUR STRONG AIR ADVANTAGE A FORCE OF THIS SIZE SHOULD BE ABLE TO CLEAR THE WEST BANK OF THE IRRAWADDY FROM KATHA SOUTH TO THE JUNCTION WITH THE CHINDWIN. GOVEN OUR PRESENT MISSIONS THIS WOULD BE STRATEGIC EQUIVALENT OF CAPTURING MANDALAY.

3. EXCEPT FOR THE EXCESSIVE DEMAND FOR AIR TRANSPORT, BRITISH PLAN IS BELIEVED TO REPRESENT A FEASIBLE OPERATION. HOWEVER, WE DO NOT CONCUR IN NECESSITY FOR A LRP GROUP OPERATING FROM PAVSHAN. THE TONNAGE REQUIREMENT FOR THE INITIAL MOVE COULD BE USED TO GREATER EFFECT BY DELIVERY OF ESSENTIAL SUPPLIES TO CHINESE FORCES ON THE SALWEEN FRONT. WHILE A LRP GROUP OPERATING IN THE LASHIO - GOKTEIK GORGE AREA WOULD HAVE A USEFUL DIVERSIONARY EFFECT, THE RAPID ADVANCE OF SUB T NTIAL FORCES FROM LEDO AGAINST MYITKYINA AND THE OPERATION OF A TASK FORCE WHICH THREATENED THE IMMEDIATE REAR OF THE TENGHUEH - LUNGLING AREA WOULD REPRESENT MUCH MORE SUBSTANTIAL ASSISTANCE TO THE CHINESE ON THE SALWEEN FRONT. SUCH AN OPERATION WOULD REQUIRE AN IMMEDIATE SHIFT IN JAPANESE DISPOSITIONS ON THE SALWEEN WHILE A LRP GROUP THREAT AGAINST GOKTEIK GORGE AREA COULD BE COUNTERED WITH LOCAL RESERVES FROM THE MANDALY AREA.

4. ALL FORCES WITH EXCEPTION OF 18 TRANSPORT SQUADRONS WILL BE AVAILABLE IN INDIA BY ONE JANUARY.

5. THIS PLAN CALLS FOR THE MINIMUM DEMANDS FOR RESOURCES OTHER THAN AIR FROM WITHOUT THE THEATER. AS INDICATED IN MY 1625 OF 1 SEPTEMBER AND 1632 OF 2 SEPTEMBER THE MAIN DEFICIENCY FOR THE YEU OPERATION WAS MOTOR VEHICLES AND FOR THE INDAW - KATHA OPERATIONS IS INFLUENCED A SERIOUS SHORTAGE IN AIR TRANSPORT.

6. BRITISH THOUGHT ON THESE OPERATIONS AS INFLUENCED BY INTANGIBLE FACTORS WHICH ARE MENTIONED HERE SOLELY TO COMPLETE

MILITARY PICTURE AND NOT TO PROVOKE CONTROVERSY. FACTORS ARE FIRST,
BRITISH COMMAND HAS LITTLE CONFIDENCE IN INDIAN DIVISIONS AND KNOWS
THAT BAD SITUATION WILL BECOME WORSE WITH ANOTHER DEFEAT IN BURMA.
THIS RESULTS IN UNWILLINGNESS TO TAKE RISKS, CALCULATED OR OTHERWISE.
SECOND, BRITISH COMMAND HAS NO CONFIDENCE IN ANY CHINESE COMBAT EFFORT,
A MILITARY JUDGMENT STRONGLY REINFORCED BY THEIR COMPLICATED POLITICAL
DIFFERENCES. THIS RESULTS IN UNWILLINGNESS TO ENTER OPERATION
SUCCESS OF WHICH DEPENDS ON CHINESE ACTION, ESPECIALLY WHEN OPERATION
INVOLVES CHINESE AID ON RECAPTURE OF BURMA. THIRD, THEIR APPROACH TO
PLANNING IS THAT OF THE QUARTERMASTER AND NOT THE GENERAL. THEY
BEGIN WITH THEIR LOC AND ASK WHAT OPERATIONS CAN BE SUPPORTED BY A
GIVEN SUPPLY SITUATION. THEY DO NOT SELECT DESIRABLE STRATEGIC
OPERATION AND SET ABOUT TO MOVE HEAVEN AND EARTH TO SUPPORT IT. THIS
IS A HABIT OF MIND OF INDIAN ARMY ARISING FROM SPECIAL CONDITIONS
OUT HERE BUT RESULT IS THAT THEY ARE TOO SENSITIVE TO LIMITATIONS
OF LOC AND TOO INSENSITIVE TO THEIR ABILITY TO IMPROVE IT. THIS
MATTER IS FURTHER COMPLICATED BY FACT THAT CIVIL GOVERNMENT CONTROLS
LOC AND IS NOT GEARED FOR WAR. FOURTH, IDEAS DIE HARD OUT HERE.
THERE IS STRONG OPINION IN SECTIONS OF GEORGE HOW QUEEN THAT BURMA
SHOULD BE BY PASSED. PLAN TO MOVE INTO NORTH BURMA IS LOOKED UPON AS
AN AMERICAN AND NOT A COMBINED PLAN. THIS RESULTS IN AUCHLINLECK
NOT HAVING ENTHUSIASTIC SUPPORT FROM ALL HANDS TO MAKE EFFECTIVE THE
DECISIONS OF COMBINED CHIEFS OF STAFF. SUMMARY: THESE INTANGIBLES
SHOULD NOT BE OVER EMPHASIZED SINCE THEY REPRESENT IMPRESSIONS GAINED
FROM DAY TO DAY STAFF WORK BUT THEY DO REFLECT SOME OF THE ATMOSPHERE
IN WHICH PLANNING GOES FORWARD. PERSONAL RELATIONS ARE UNIFORMLY
EXCELLENT.

1055

7. THIS CABLE DEALS ONLY WITH THE BRITISH SIDE OF THIS PLAN AND DOES NOT CONSIDER AMERICAN - CHINESE PARTICIPATION OR REQUIRE- MENTS. IN GENERAL, OUR REQUIREMENTS ARE MORE OR LESS CONSTANT REGARDLESS OF WHAT PLAN IS ADOPTED BECAUSE WE EXPECT TO USE OUR FIGHTERS AND FIGHTER BOMBERS IN ASSAM, SUPPORT XRAY CORPS, BUILD LEDO ROAD, AND FLY 10000 TONS PER MONTH TO SUPPORT CCHENNAULT AND YUNNAN FORCE.

18,732.

TANKS

Tanks are mobile. They are proof against small-arms fire.
They can move off the roads. They can move over great distance.
They have respectable fire-power. They are vulnerable to 37mm
guns and artillery. They are noisy. They are hard to conceal.
They have limited vision. Their fire when moving is not
accurate. They require considerable maintenance and highly
trained personnel.

They should therefore be used preferably against a serious
objective, — the enemy artillery, his communications, his
reserves, his dumps, etc. When used to support Infantry, they
precede the foot troops to a definite objective and knock out
machine guns and anti-tank weapons by cruising up and down the
position. When the Infantry comes up the tanks withdraw to a
covered rendezvous out of artillery fire, and prepare for their
next move. Each step should be carefully timed and coordinated
with the Infantry. In every attack by tanks, artillery and
other weapons should take the hostile anti-tank weapons under
fire for as long as possible.

The maintenance of tanks is a serious problem. Unless
careful attention is given this matter constantly, there will
be a rapid falling off in tank strength. Mechanical training
is therefore a most important factor in their use.

985

LANDING OPERATIONS

Landing operations are exceedingly difficult and complicated. The most dangerous threat to success is the hostile land-based aviation. The land bases are not vulnerable. The carriers are -- only a limited number of planes can be carried on them, and part of these have to cover the ships, which are also vulnerable to submarine attack.

The landing force has little fire cover until it establishes a beach-head and gets artillery ashore. The landing force cannot move until it gets trucks and munitions ashore, and this is a difficult operation. Thereafter, stocks of all kinds have to be shifted to smaller craft and carried to the beach, often through surf, and usually with no wharfs or unloading facilities. Meanwhile the beach-head is subject to artillery and air bombardment, and Infantry attacks.

Once the landing point is disclosed, the enemy can concentrate against it, and he can do so more quickly than it can be built up. Without air superiority, surprise, careful preparation, good weather, good training, and good equipment, the landing force is at a great disadvantage. It is a race to enlarge the beach-head and get a strong force ashore before the enemy can concentrate enough strength to attack and wipe it out.

Along the shores of Burma, there are long stretches of mud, mangrove swamp, and a network of small streams. Moving of guns, trucks and other heavy equipment is a serious problem. A big concentration of shipping is a good target; yet it must be big to be successful. The Japs have many good airfields within range, and to keep the Jap aviation down, several large carriers are necessary. A landing will require a large number of special type boats, and must be worked out in detail, and executed by good troops. It can be done, but it is an extremely difficult operation, and one that cannot be prepared over-night.

FORMS OF ATTACK

There are various forms of attack, -- frontal, flank, single and double envelopment, penetration, turning movement and combinations of the foregoing.

1. Frontal.

This is the head-on, knock-down form of fighting. There is no maneuver. To succeed, the attacker must have overwhelming strength, especially if the enemy has prepared a position and arranged defensive fires. Casualties are usually very heavy. All the advantages lie with the defense.

2. Flank.

The attack comes in from a flank, so that only a part of the defense can be brought to bear. Effective, if it can be used, but the enemy will rarely be caught and can shift to meet it. It then becomes frontal.

- 1 -

3. Envelopment, single.

If the enemy is engaged lightly along his front (holding attack) and a strong force attacks from his flank, the attack is an envelopment. The holding attack prevents him from readjusting to meet the flank attack, and he is taken at a disadvantage. This is a very common form.

4. Envelopment, double.

Combined with a holding attack, an envelopment is made on either flank. Heavy preponderance of strength is necessary. If successful the results are decisive. Where the two enveloping forces meet, the double envelopment becomes an encirclement.

5. _Turning movement._

Combined with a holding attack, a strong force moves far out around a flank, out of contact with the holding attack, and attacks from the rear or flank. A very effective form of attack. Dangerous if not well executed, because an alert enemy may attack and defeat the holding force before the turning movement can make itself felt. It violates the principle of concentration and therefore incurs risk. It has been successfully used by daring commanders on many occasions.

6. _Penetration._

Against an enemy who is over-extended or in insufficient depth, this form may be successful. The idea is to concentrate against a chosen point, break through it and then attack to the flanks. When successful, it splits the enemy into two parts, which can be handled separately.

7. _Piece-meal._

The worst form of attack. It should be avoided on all occasions. Instead of putting all available means into one strong blow, strength is wasted by successive attacks of small detachments, none of them strong enough to do any good. A common error.

CHOICE OF FLANK FOR ENVELOPMENT

1. Right flank preferable --
cover and ground about the same on
both flanks, but the communications
in rear are more quickly reached
from the right.

2. Left flank preferable --
communications closer on right
flank, but no cover there. On
left flank, cover allows a closer
approach to the rear.

3. Left flank preferable --
ground and cover similar on both
flanks, and communications more
accessible on right, but obstacle
exists there which can be avoided
by going around the left.

990

DEPTH IN ATTACK AND DEFENSE

There must be depth in both attack and defense, to provide successive impulses in the attack, and successive blocks in the defense.

a. In defense, a single line is vulnerable. The enemy can concentrate at any point and break it.

Therefore, the defense is ordinarily set-up in depth, as follows:

An attack on such a position meets continuous resistance. As the attack progresses, casualties make it weaker, and successful resistance at certain points breaks up its cohesion and slows it down.

- 1 -

b. An attack without depth fails at the first successful resistance. Successive impulses are necessary to keep it rolling, and replace casualties.

What chance has this attack of success?

The attack should have been set-up as follows -- then when and if A is stopped, B can be committed, and later, if necessary, C. Enough depth should be provided to make sure of carrying through to the objective.

- 2 -

CHUNGKING, CHINA,
3 October 1943.

DEFENSE

Very few defensive battles have ever been won. The initiative
is necessary to get a decision. It is sometimes necessary to assume
the defensive, but only in order to prepare for the counter-offensive.

The defensive may be active or passive:

(a) In the active defense, the defender holds a position,
but instead of waiting to be attacked, he makes limited objective
attacks in order to dislocate the enemy's dispositions, wear him
down, cause casualties, and gain time.

(b) In the passive defense, the defender waits on the
position to be attacked. He gives the attacker the advantage of
choosing time and place, and making all his preparations unhindered.
If the position is very strong, such action may be justified, but
ordinarily an active defense is much more effective.

(c) In either case, the defender works continuously to
improve his position by clearing fields of fire, digging trenches,
cutting roads, putting in communications, stringing wire, preparing
artillery, machine gun and mortar concentrations, etc. etc. Without
a preponderance of 3 to 1, it is a very serious thing to attack good
troops in prepared positions. They must first be pounded by artillery
and aviation and the attack carefully planned and executed. It is
usually preferable to go around such a position, if possible.

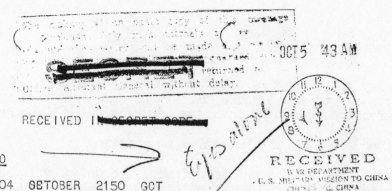

INCOMING RADIO

RECEIVED : 04 OCTOBER 2150 GCT

FROM : WAR

TO : AMMISCA 3495 AMMDEL 3316

NR : 3495   FILED: 02 OCTOBER 0444 GCT

REPLACEMENTS FOR GALAHAD REURAD AMMDEL AG 194 (STILWELL INFORMATION FERRIS FROM MARSHALL). OUR CONCEPTION IS THAT GALAHAD IS PROVIDED FOR 1 MAJOR MISSION OF APPROXIMATELY 3 MONTHS DURATION AND THAT TERMINATION OF THIS OPERATION MAY RESULT IN FOLLOWING CONDITIONS: 35 PERCENT BATTLE CASUALTIES; COMPLETE ANIMAL CASUALTIES; COMPLETE EXHAUSTION OF AERIAL DROPPING EQUIPMENT; LOSS OF 80 PERCENT ORGANIZATIONAL EQUIPMENT; PHYSICAL AND MENTAL FATIGUE OF SURVIVORS NECESSITATING THREE MONTHS HOSPITALIZATION AND REST, WITH PROBABLE WELL DESERVED FURLOUGH IN US FOR SOME PERSONNEL WHO HAVE BEEN IN TROPICS, WITH SOME PARTICIPATING IN COMBAT, FOR AS MUCH AS 2 AND 1 HALF YEARS AND WHO WAIVED EARNED FURLOUGHS TO VOLUNTEER FOR THIS OPERATION. IN LIGHT OF THE ABOVE CONCEPTION, AUGMENTATION OF PRESENT BATTALIONS BY INDIVIDUAL REPLACEMENTS IS NOT REPEAT NOT CONSIDERED FEASIBLE.

REPLACEMENTS NECESSATATED DURING TRAINING PERIOD MAY BE PROVIDED FOR A LIMITED NUMBER BY TRANSFER OF AVAILABLE PERSONNEL WITHIN THE THEATER. PROVISION OF 2 PACK TROOPS WITH 16 OFFICERS AND 160 MEN FURNISHES A 6 PERCENT SURPLUS WITHIN LIMITS OF TENTATIVE T/O. FURTHER ORGANIZATIONS OF THIS TYPE ARE DESIRED FOR

18,754

1056

PAGE TWO

OPERATIONS IN THE DRY SEASON COMMENCING FALL OF 1944, IT IS BELIEVED
NEW UNITS WITH SAME TYPE PERSONNEL AND COMPLETE EQUIPMENT WILL HAVE
TO BE FORMED AND SHIPPED FROM THE US DURING SUMMER OF 1944.
SURVIVING PERSONNEL FROM PRESENT OPERATION, AFTER REST PERIOD, COULD
JOIN NEW UNITS IN KEY POSITIONS. EXACT TYPE AND SIZE OF UNIT AS WELL
AS SPECIAL EQUIPMENT WILL BE DEPEDNENT ON SUCCESS OF PRESENT
ORGANIZATION WHICH IS LARGELY EXPERIMENTAL.

THEREFORE INSTEAD OF SUPPLEMENT PRESENT UNITS FURNISHED YOU
WITH ADDITIONAL HIGH GRADE INDIVIDUAL PERSONNEL IN ACCORDANCE WITH
YOUR REQUEST AND AT THE EXPENSE OF CUIEVAM ORGANIZATIONS IN THE US OR
OTHER THEATERS, IT IS DESIRED THAT YOU CONSIDER THE ORGANIZATIONS
AND OPERATION OF THESE 3 BATTALIONS IN THE NATURE OF A COMBAT
EXPERIMENT. THE SUCCESS OR FAILURE OF THEIR MISSION TOGETHER WITH YOUR
RECOMMENDATIONS FOR FUTURE UNITS OF THIS TYPE WILL DETERMINE WHETHER
OR NOT SUCH SPECIAL BATTALIONS ARE TO BE ORGANIZED FOR FURTHER
EMPLOYMENT IN YOUR THEATER AS WELL AS ESLEWHERE. WITH THIS END VIEW
DETAILED REPORTS ARE REQUESTED DURING EARLY TRAINING AND COMBAT
PERIODS IN ORDER THAT WE MAY CLOSELY ANTICIPATE FUTURE REQUIREMENTS
AND BE PREPARED TO TAKE TIME AND SOUNDEST DECISION IN THE MATTER OF
REPLACEMENTS OR ACTIVATION OF ADDITIONAL UNITS OF THIS TYPE

17785
17787
17866 (eyes alone)
1005 (eyes alone)
18137
17988
18407
10

1C56

18,754

C/S
G-3
T-1

NOTES ON TRAINING

1. Orders for the establishment of the Army Schools were received in late July and early August. With the exception of the 6th Army, all schools were ordered opened before September 1st.

2. XX Group Army (6th Army at present). Nothing had been done to start the schools. No graduates of the ITC had been assembled as instructors. The two divisions of the 6th Army in the Mitu area (the 2nd Reserve and the New 39th) are in bad shape and far under strength; about 5,000 and 7,000 respectively. They do not expect their replacements until late October.

The Chinese head of the Instructional Group has been energetic and cooperative, but has had to face indifference. (Huang Chieh is in Kunming.)

A statement made by the Director of Training of the 6th Army was, "Now that we have the schedule arranged, we can put in the necessary hours. It doesn't matter what we do, so long as we put in the time".

Schools are now in operation and doing well.

3. XI Group (71st Army and 2nd Army). Nothing had been done to start the schools by September 1st. No graduates of the ITC had been assembled as instructors. This situation seems to have been quickly remedied, and the schools are now in operation and doing well. The Chinese head of the Instructional Group has been cooperative and reasonably energetic.

This army seems to be interested, but helpless when it comes to plans or to carrying out plans. All telephones for use in training were immediately installed as inter-office phones in the headquarters. New radios were taken apart, or tinkered with ("examined") and rendered useless. All had to be repaired by the U.S. Signal Officer.

Graduates of the ITC are highly satisfactory as instructors.

General Sung Hsi-lien requested that a medical school with classes of 175 officers be established at Tali. He had failed to send these officers to the ITC as he had been instructed to do. This school will open on October 1st. He also asked that a veterinary school be established at Paoshan. This school will open on October 1st.

4. IX Group Army (52nd Army). Everything had been prepared and was in operation, and the schools got off to an enthusiastic start. Demands for increased American personnel have been beyond our capabilities at this time — 80 officers and 320 enlisted men. Cooperation and enthusiasm have been characteristic of all reports from Colonel Enslow.

General Chao Yao-ming, C. G. of the 52nd Army and a Ramgarh graduate is giving enthusiastic support to the training program. All reports indicate that these schools are doing very well.

- 1 -

996

5. V Group Army (5th Army). Some months previously the 5th Army had established an old-style school with the exception of the weapons courses, in which graduates of the ITC were instructors.

Telephones and radios allotted for training were set-up as head-quarters inter-office phones, and private radio sets for staff officers. This was corrected promptly, but the correction required a threat to report the matter to Chen Cheng. Classes are now in operation — satisfactory but luke warm.

General Chiu Ching-chuan takes a more active part in instruction than is necessary, demonstrating the use of weapons and indulging in long-winded harangues. Outside of these personal idiosyncracies, and a desire to change schedules, he has allowed the school to operate as planned. He causes much time to be wasted.

6. All Armies state that they simply have no graduates of the Kunming school. Since there have been 2,000 graduates, in infantry alone, of which a minimum of 1800 should have had ample time to return to their armies, such statements would seem to indicate a lack of desire on the part of commanders to permit trained junior officers to function as instructors.

7. The supply machinery in the Chinese S.O.S. was not good, but seems to have been corrected quickly. The supply situation in troop units is bad. Each army sent representatives to Kunming or Yunnanyi to draw school equipment and ammunition. The representative of the C.E.F.S.O.S. allowed them to remain waiting in Kunming for two weeks before arranging for the issue of any equipment. Since that time this individual is functioning well, as the result of a conference.

8. In general, the army representatives were indifferent to their responsibilities. Most of them stated that they had no transportation, and were perfectly willing to sit back with no further action. Colonel Tung of the C.E.F.S.O.S. informed me that each army had trucks in Kunming, but that in most cases the representatives of the armies had rented them to civilian agencies for commercial hauling. One representative made no effort to ship equipment for over ten days after he had received it. Another, after having receipted for his equipment, for the 52nd and 54th Armies, stated that he had been given only half of his allotment, and refused to accept the figures on the receipt he had signed himself.

When the equipment arrived at the armies, most of them immediately cached away a good part of the ammunition and varying amounts of equipment. Individuals in authority pocketed small tools indiscriminately, or appropriated items for their own use or storage, with such remarks as — "They can spare these few things." If this had been permitted by the American instructors, probably very little would have remained for training purposes.

9. In spite of the above, all schools are now running satisfactorily, but much time was wasted in getting unit commanders to carry out their orders, both in letter and spirit.

- 2 -

997

10. With the exception of Kuan Lien-chung, who apparently plans an active defense on the Indo-China border, no commanders seem to have any inclination for operations of any kind. Several have stated that they have received word from Chungking to the effect that there will be no operations of any kind this year. The same report has come from the British Military Attache.

11. The motor school at Chuching (Kutsing) graduated its first class, and will start a second larger class utilizing as instructors the graduates of the first class, within the next few days. Shortage of equipment, tools, parts, and American instructors has handicapped the operation of this school, but the Chinese in charge are enthusiastic on the work performed by the American instructors. General Loh, the Commandant, has written me a letter, expressing his appreciation, and recommending promotions for the American officer instructors.

12. The Ordnance Mobile Repair units will be ready to depart for various armies on about October 6th. These units are intended to repair artillery, but are equipped to handle mortars as well.

13. The Field Artillery School at Kan Hai Tze has a new class of 200 artillery officers, and cadres for three battalions in training.

14. The Infantry Training Center at Hei Lin Pu is running out of students. No infantry students reported on September 30th. Repeated requests for students from the 53rd and 8th Armies have not resulted in any arriving.

- 3 -

998

CHUNGKING, CHINA,
5 October 1943.

SAMPLES OF BRITISH OPINION

1. "The Chinese are not only incapable of offense, but would be unable to defend if attacked. This is based on reliable reports I have."

2. "The Ramgarh Chinese are well trained but will not take orders from the Americans. I consider them all right on defense, but slow and unreliable on offense."

3. "A British force attacking from Paoshan is an urgent requirement, and the Chinese will not advance without them."

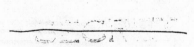

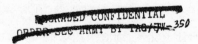

INCOMING RADIO

RECEIVED : 5 OCT 0205 GCT

FROM   : RELOT

TO   : AMMISCA, AMMDEL

NR   : G 240   FILED : 4 OCT 1405 GCT

URGENT

Eyes alone

C/S - G-2 x G-3

FIELD ORDER NUMBER ONE DATED TWENTY ONE SEPTEMBER RECEIVED
OTCOBER SECOND BECAUSE OF TIME INTERVAL NECESSARY FOR COMPLIANCE ORDERS
BEING ISSUED THIS DATE. HOWEVER THE FOLLOWING IS SUBMITTED FOR YOUR
CONSIDERATION: THE THE OCCUPATION OF SHINGBWIYANG AREA WITH QUOTE LINE
OF SECURITY TO THE TANAI RIVER UNQUOTE WILL NOT IN MY OPINION GIVE
SUFFICIENT PROTECTION TO AIR FIELD CONSTRUCTION. THE TANAI IS NO
BARRIER IN DRY WEATHER. (TO STILWELL INFORMATION FERRIS FROM BOATNER.)
EYE BELIEVE THAT ONCE WE START OUT FROM THE FOOTHILLS AROUND SHING-
BWIYANG THAT ADVANCE SHOULD CONTINUE TO AT EAST JAMBU REPEAT JAMBU DASH
BYM FOR IF WE STOP ON THE TANAI RIVER THAT WILL ALERT JAPS AND ALLOW
TIME FOR REINFORCEMENTS *lower* HUKAWNG WITH PERSONNEL AND FORTIFICATIONS.
AT PRESENT THERE IS NO INDICATION OF ANY ENEMY NORTH OF JAMBU BUM OTHER
THAN SMALL MIXED PATROLS AND AERIAL RECONNAISSANCE OCTOBER FIRST REPORTS
ROADS NORTH OF KAMAIXG IN THE HUKAWNG VALLEY FLOODED AND MUDDY SHOWING
LITTLE EVIDENCE OF USE. UNLESS THERE IS SOME REASON KNOWN TO SENTWR SECTOR
HEADQUARTERS AND UNKNOWN TO ME EYE BELIEVE THAT THE STATE OF SUPPLY LINES,
LCIMATIC CONDITIONS AND THE INACTIVITY OF THE ENEMY NORTH OF JAMBU BUM
DICTATES THAT A GENERAL FORWARD MOVEMENT BEYOND SHINGBWIYANG BE DELAYED
UNTIL NOVEMBER FIFTEENTH AND WHEN STARTED BE PUSHED FORWARD CONTINUISLY
TO JAMBU BUM INDICATED IN OUR ALBACORE PLANE. ADDITIONAL TIME WOULD
ALLOW US TOO CONCENTRATE SUFFICIENT FORCE

1 A

18,764

WOULD REQUIRE A LARGER FORCE THAN STIPULATED IN YOUR FIELD ORDER

NUMBER ONE.   EYE STRONGLY RECOMMEND THIS ACTION NEW SUBJECT MY RADIO

NUMBER GEORGE TWO THREE FOUR MISUNDERSTOOD EYE HAVE PLENTY TO DO

HERE AND DO NOT WANT A VACATION

(THIS MESSAGE IS BEING SERVICED, IT WAS GARBLED)

G-3

c/s

G-2

18614 (eyes alone)

2nd copy destroyed

(1062)

OCT 5 43 AM

RECEIVED IN SECRET CODE

INCOMING RADIO

RECEIVED: 05 OCT, 0400 GCT

FROM   : WASSHINGTON

TO   : AMMISCA

NR   : 3513   FILED: 04 OCT, 1743 GCT

MOUNTBATTEN DESIRES TO OFFER GENERAL WHEELER APPOINTMENT
AS PRINCIPAL ADMINSTRATIVE OFFICER, SOUTHEAST ASIA COMMAND. THIS AGREED
TO BY PRIME MINISTER, MINISTER OF DEFENSE AND BRITISH CHIEFS OF STAFF.

(PERSONAL ATTENTION STILWELL FROM MARSHALL) US JOINT CHIEFS
OF STAFF HAVE AGREED.

PROBABLE SCOPE OF WHEELERS NEW DUTIES AND DATE ON WHICH HE
SHOULD ASSUME THESE DUTIES ARE CURRENTLY BEING DETERMINED.

MOUNTBATTEN SHOULD ARRIVE DELHI ABOUT 7 OCTOBER AND HOPES TO
SEE WHEELER UPON HIS ARRIVAL AND OFFER HIM THIS APPOINTMENT. WE ARE
TELLING MOUNTBATTEN THAT WE APPROVE

See 1093

c/s H

DECLASSIFIED
DOD Dir. 5200.9, Sept. 27, 1958
NCWN by ___ data 3-2-5-7

18,767

CEG

1002

1077

AD 2213.

Arundel for Ferris, eyes alone

Boatner's G-240. I agree with Boatner. Tell Auk I much prefer to wait till I see Mountbatten before committing the X force. I recommend November fifteen as tentative date and in view of weather and postponement of other phases of the plan can see nothing to be gained by starting sooner.

Stilwell

Z - Z - Z - Z

FILE

Rec.: 060310
Sent 060320.

(1060)

1003

RECEIVED IN ~~SECRET CODE~~.

<u>INCOMING RADIO:</u>

RECEIVED: 06 OCT 0835 Z.

FROM   : AMMDEL

TO   : AMMISCA   (FOR THE EYES OF GEN STILWELL ONLY)

NR   : AM 1722   FILED: 06 OCT 0456 Z.

     EYES ALONE GENERAL STILWELL. TO GETH THINGS ORGANIZED
FOR GALAHAD A SMALL GROUP OF OFFICERS WILL BE NECESSARY TO ASSIST
BRITISH NOW SO THAT WE WILL WASTE NO TIME WHEN UNITS GET IN
(FROM FERRIS) WE RECOMMEND FOLLOWING; LT COLONELS DANIEL
STILL AND GEORGE GRUNERT. STILL IS NOW ENROUTE TO RAMGARH FROM
KARACHI, EXPERT IN ANIMALS AND PACK TRANSPORT WHO WAS IN GROUP
MERRILL REQUESTED BY NAME IN WASHINGTON. AS PACK UNITS WILL
BE LATE, CONSIDER STILLS ASSIGNMENT AS ABSOLUTE NECESSITY.
AS PLANS AND TRAINING OFFICER TO GET THINGS ORGANIZED AND TO
PERFORM NECESSARY LIAISON WITH LOCAL BRITISH IN ASSAM IS
GRUNERT WHO IS NOW WITH BOATNER. NEED ONE MORE TO HANDLE
SUPPLY AND AM LOOKING AROUND IN OUR OWN SET UP. REQUEST YOUR
AUTHORITY TO ISSUE ORDERS ON INDIVIDUALS MENTIONED FOR WHOM
REPLACEMENTS WILL BE MADE AVAILABLE. WE HAVE SELECTED FIRST
CLASS PEOPLE WHOM WE BELIEVE HAVE POTENTIAL ABILITY FOR FUTURE
USE WITH FORCE.

OK

DECLASSIFIED
DOD Dir. 5200.9, Sept. 27, 195_
NCWN by ___ date ___

ORDER SEC ARMY BY ___   18,841.

RECEIVED IN SECRET CODE

<u>INCOMING RADIO</u>

RECEIVED : 06 OCTOBER 1540 GCT

FROM : AMMDEL   ZZZZ

TO : AMMISCA

NR. : AM 1728   FILED 06 OCTOBER 1100 GCT

EYES ALONE GENERAL STILWELL PRD YOUR ORDERS ON
BOATNERS PROPOSAL WILL BE EXECUTED EXACTLY AS ORDERED BUT EYE
WISH TO RAISE CERTAIN POINTS AS SEEN FROM HERE TO BE SURE YOU
HAVE ENTIRE PICTURE PRD SINCE EYE FEEL SURE AUCHINLECKS APPROVAL
FOR POSTPONEMENT WILL BE GIVEN ALMOST WITH ENTHUSIASM CMA HE IS
NOT BEING APPROACHED UNTIL YOU CONFIRM ACTION DESIRED AFTER CON-
SIDERING THIS MESSAGE PAREN FROM FERRIS REURAD ABLE DOG TWO TWO ONE
THREE PAREN PARA)

BOATNERS GEORGE TWO FOUR ZERO REFERS TO OUR OWN ORDER
BASED ON YOUR INSTRUCTIONS AND COPY SHOULD HAVE REACHED YOUR HEAD-
QUARTERS BY NOW PRD THIS ORDER LIMITS BOATNER TO AN ADVANCE TO
SHINGBWIYANG BETWEEN OCTOBER FIFTEEN RPT ONE FIVE AND NOVEMBER
FIRST RPT ONE AND DIRECTS THAT VIGOROUS AND CONTINUOUS PATROLLING
BE CARRIED OUT PRD FORCE AUTHORIZED CLN ONE RPT ONE INFANTRY
REGIMENT WITH ONE RPT ONE BATTALION ARTILLERY TO SHINGBWIYANG WITH
A RESERVE OF TWO INFANTRY BATTALIONS IN VICINITY TAGAP PRD PARA

MAIN REASONS FOR THIS MOVE ARE CLN ONE PRD TO PERMIT
CLEARING OF AN AIRSTRIP FOR LANDING MACHINERY TO START ROAD BACK

REGRADED CONFIDENTIAL
ORDER SEC ARMY BY TAG/3W-350 18,850

1005

INTO HILLS TOWARDS TAGAP PRD IF ROAD DOES NOT RPT NOT REACH
SHINGBWIYANG BY JANUARY ALL HOPE OF A ROAD LINK THROUGH TO CHINA
NEXT YEAR IS GONE PRD WE NOW HAVE ENOUGH AIRBORNE ROAD MACHINERY
FOR FOUR RPT FOUR ENGINEER COMPANIES WHICH WAS ORDERED FOR THIS
EXPRESS PURPOSE PRD POSTPONEMENT MEANS SERIOUS DELAY ON ROAD WORK
PRD TWO PRD OCCUPATION OF SHINGBWIYANG COMBINED WITH ACTIVE PAT-
ROLLING WILL KEEP JAP NUISANCE PATROLS FROM INTERFERING WITH ROAD
CONSTRUCTION PRD SURVEY PARTIES AND LEADING BULLDOZERS WERE RE-
SPECTIVELY ABOUT FORTY RPT FOUR ZERO AND SIXTY RPT SIX ZERO MILES
NORTH OF SHINGBWIYANG ON SEPTEMBER TWENTY THIRD RPT TWO THREE PRD
THREE PRD BOATNERS FORWARD ELEMENTS ARE WITHIN THIRTY RPT THREE
ZERO MILES OF SHINGBWIYANG NOW PRD ADVANCE FORWARD IN NEAR FUTURE
WILL BE A NECESSITY PRD BOATNER INFORMED HE WOULD HAVE TO MOVE
THERE UNDER ANY CIRCUMSTANCES EARLY IN NOVEMBER TO COVER ROAD WORK
PRD FOUR PRD OUR MOVE SHOULD STIR FOURTH CORPS INTO SOME SEMBLANCE
OF ACTIVITY PRD THEY PLAN ON SOME SIMILAR FORWARD DISPLACEMENT
STARTING IN NOVEMBER CMA AND AS YOU KNOW IDEA OF POSTPONEMENT IS
CONTAGIOUS PRD FIVE PRD IT IS EASIER TO MOVE FORWARD PRIOR TO
TIME JAPS RESUME NORMAL DRY WEATHER ACTIVITIES THAN TO WAIT AND
BE FORCED TO FIGHT THROUGH THE HILLS PRD PARA

DISADVANTAGE OF MOVE AS PRESENTLY ORDERED IS THAT
IT MAY CAUSE UNFAVORABLE JAP REACTIONS PRD JAPS KNOW WHERE ROAD IS
AND THAT FORWARD MOVEMENT IS OUR ONLY POSSIBLE LINE OF ACTION SHORT
OF ABANDONMENT CMA HENCE THEY CAN BE EXPECTED TO REACT ANYWAY PRD
BELIEVE WE ARE BETTER OFF IF WE GET OUT OF THE HILLS AND INTO MORE
FAVORABLE TERRAIN WHERE OUR PROBABLY NUMERICAL SUPERIORITY AND AIR
POWER WOULD COUNT FOR MORE PRD FOR PRESENT PHASE OUR MOVEMENT FOR-

18,850

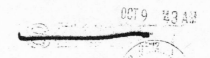

WARD OF SHINGBWIYANG WOULD NOT RPT NOT BE DESIRABLE OR NECESSARY
EXCEPT FOR PATROLS PARA

BOATNER UNDOUBTEDLY HAS IN MIND CONCENTRATION IN FOR-
WARD AREAS OF ENTIRE THIRTY EIGHTH RPT THREE EIGHT DIVISION PRD WE
WOULD NOT CONCUR SINCE CONCENTRATION OF DIVISION NORTH OF SHINGBWI-
YANG MEANS MUCH HEAVIER REQUIREMENTS IN AIR SUPPLY AND IS MORE OF A
GIVE AWAY THAN A SMALLER FORCE RPT FORCE IN SHINGBWIYANG PRD ONE
EFFECT WOULD BE TO REDUCE TROOP CARRIARS AVAILABLE TO SUPPORT DORN
PRD PARA

THERE WILL BE NO RPT NO DIFFICULTIES WITH BRITISH PRD
THEY WILL JUMP AT SUGGESTION TO POSTPONE AND FULL WEIGHT OF FAILURE
TO EXECUTE COMBINED CHIEFS OF STAFF DIRECTIVE WILL IN TIME BE LAID
UPON UNREADINESS OF BOATNER AND LEDO ROAD PRD WE HAVE CONSISTENTLY
SET THE PACE IN EFFORT TO GET ACTION AND THIS MOVE OF BOATNER HAS
BEEN OUR ACE CARD IN INSISTING ON EARLIER ACTIVITY FROM FOURTH
CORPS PRD PARA

IF YOU BELIEVE IT UNDESIRABLE TO CARRY OUT PRESENT PLANS
SUGGEST YOU LET US REVOKE PRESENT ORDERS AND INFORM BRITISH PRD
HOWEVER IF PRESENT ORDERS ARE REVOKED NEW PLANS MUST INDICATE DEFIN-
ITELY AND POSITIVELY WHAT TROOPS CAN BE MOVED FORWARD OF ROADHEAD
PARA

OUR RECOMMENDATION IS THAT PRESENT PLAN STAND PRD IT
IS MORE CONSERVATIVE THAN BOATNERS IN THE IMMEDIATE DEPLOYMENT OF
TROOPS CMA GIVES US A KEY AREA WHICH WE NEED NOW CMA PERMITS ROAD
TO BE BUILT AT MUCH FASTER RATE CMA AND ABOVE ALL GIVES YOU IMPORT-
ANT LEVER TO USE IN DISCUSSIONS WITH MOUNTBATTWN AND COMBINED

18,850

1007

CHIEFS OF STAFF IN FAVOR OF MUCH EARLIER ACTION PRD NO RPT NO
IRRETRIEVABLE COMMITMENT OF XRAY FORCE IS MADE CMA AND DATE IS
SPEEDED UP AT WHICH WE CAN SUPPORT OUR FULL FORCE SOUTH OF SHING-
BWIYANG PRD WE CONCUR WITH BOATNER ON IDEA OF KEEPING MOVING WHEN
THINGS START BUT WE DONT BELIEVE HE CAN DEVELOP SUFFICIENT MOMENTUM
WITH WHAT HE CAN SUPPORT IN NOVEMBER IF WE HANG BACK UNTIL THEN PARA

THIS IS SITUATION AS WE SEE IT AND WE HAVE TRIED TO
BALANCE XRAY AND YOKE FACTORS IN FAIRNESS TO BOTH PRD HONESTLY BE-
LIEVE BOATNERS RADIO PROMPTED NOT RPT NOT BY PLAN ITSELF BUT BY
YOUR LIMITATION ON TROOPS PRD BASED ON YOUR REPLY WE WILL DISCUSS
IMMEDIATELY WITH AUCHINLECK AND ISSUE SUCH INSTRUCTIONS TO BOATNER
AS YOU DESIRE.

1064

GCV   18,850

1008

No. 56

Chungking, China
6 October 1943

MEMORANDUM FOR: His Excellency, The Generalissimo.

    1. We must make the Burma operation a success that will redound to the credit of the Chinese Army, for if it is allowed to fail, I believe the consequences will be extremely serious for China. We must remember that the new South-east Asia Command is British; they are luke-warm about Burma anyway, and failure will allow them to claim that they have proved their point. I believe the entire scene of operations will then shift to Sumatra and Malaya, in which event China may expect to be cut off from all supplies except what comes in by air, for the duration of the war. The effect of this on the Chinese Army is readily apparent.

    2. China is in a position where she must make a determined effort to continue to help herself; otherwise, the risk is serious that all available resources will in future be diverted to operations under British control. Without a road to China, no case can be made for big allotments of supplies, and they will inevitably be diverted to points where they will be used.

    3. The above should receive careful consideration NOW. It will be too late by January 1; in fact it is very late now.

JOSEPH W. STILWELL
Joint Chief of Staff for the Generalissimo

245

+ + +

Letter No. 57   CHUNGKING, CHINA,
                                               7 October 1943.

MEMORANDUM FOR HIS EXCELLENCY THE GENERALISSIMO:

As a matter of information, the following reports are
submitted:

1. Army representatives in Kunming had supplies issued
to them for the training schools. They appeared very
indifferent about their responsibilities and most of them
stated they had no transportation. Colonel Dorn was informed
that every army had trucks in Kunming, but that in most cases
the army representatives had rented them to civilian agencies
for commercial hauling. One representative, after having
receipted for his equipment, stated he had been given only
half his allotment, and refused to accept the figures on the
receipt he had signed himself.

2. The following statements indicate British opinion:

a. "The Chinese are not only incapable of
offense, but would be unable to defend if attacked.
This is based on reliable reports I have."

b. "The Ramgarh Chinese are well trained
but will not take orders from the Americans. I
consider them all right on defense, but slow and
unreliable on offense."

c. "A British force attacking from Paoshan
is an urgent requirement, and the Chinese will not
advance without them."

These remarks were made in India by British officers.

                          JOSEPH W. STILWELL,
                 Joint Chief of Staff for Generalissimo.

14 oct 43

On 13 oct Col Liu
was informed by Col
Lin Hsiung-Kwang
(林祥光) that unsigned
duplicates of these letters
no. 56 and 57 should
be given to General
Stilwell for signature.
Col Liu explained that
duplicates are not signed.
Letter duplicates were returned to Col Lin by Col
Liu - receipt attached.
(OVER)

收回

史迪威將軍十月二日第56号及十月

九日第57号備忘錄两件

将録堂第二組 十一月

These letters forwarded in duplicate to Madame, receipted for by Paul Chen. Madame either kept original or forwarded it to Gmo. The duplicate She sent the Gmo's second section for file. Second section was not aware that an original existed until so informed by Col Lin.

14 oct 43

1013

RECEIVED IN <del>SECRET</del> CODE

INCOMING RADIO

RECEIVED   : 07 OCTOBER 0816 GCT   URGENT

FROM   : AMMDEL   ZZZZ

TO   : AMMISCA

NR.   : AM 1731   FILED 07 OCTOBER 0756 GCT

       STILWELL EYES ALONE FROM FERRIS PRD MET LORD LOUIS
TODAY PRD FIRST IMPRESSION EXCELLENT PRD HE WOULD LIKE TO SEE YOU
KUNMING PRIOR TO CHUNGKING RPT CHUNGKING MEETING TO GET DOPE AND
SCORE PRD UNDERSTAND THAT SOMERVELL GOES TO GISSIMO SOON AND PRIOR
TO LOUIS TO LAY GROUND WORK PRD SOONG BELIEVED TO REMAIN HERE TO
GO CHINA WITH THE ADMIRAL PRD WILL KEEP YOU ADVISED PRD PROBABLY
REQUIRED DOG CHARLIE THREE TYPE PLANE FROM KUNMING YOUR WAY.

 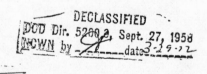

RECEIVED IN ~~SECRET CODE~~

<u>INCOMING RADIO</u>

RECEIVED: 0725 GCT 14 OCTOBER

FROM   : AMMKUN

TO   : AMMISCA

NR   : C 721   FILED: 14 OCTOBER 0521 GCT

BEST REPORT FROM ATC (FOR HEARN FROM DORN) YESTERDAY WE
LOST ONE C-87 WITH 14 PASSENGERS, 2 C-46 PLANES AND ONE CNAC PLANE.
SHOT UP BUT LANDED SAFELY ONE B-24 AND ONE SECOND TROOP CARRIER
DOUGLAS.

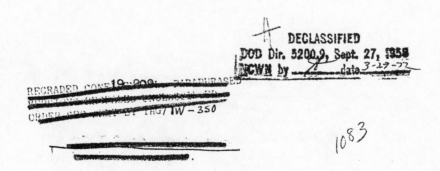

1083

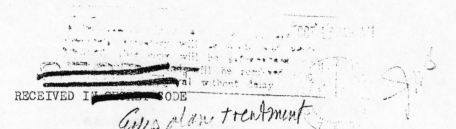

RECEIVED IN SHORT CODE

INCOMING RADIO

Eyes alone treatment

RECEIVED : 14 OCT 2310 GCT

mw —

FROM : AQUILA

PRIORITY

RECEIVED
WAR DEPARTMENT
U. S. MILITARY MISSION TO CHINA
CHUNGKING CHINA

TO : AMMISCA

NR : S 25 OAOX   FILED : 14 OCT 1211 GCT

CONFIRMATION RECEIVED IN MESSAGE FROM HARDIN OF INTER-
CEPTION BY ENEMY FIGHTERS OF TRANSPORTS IN FORT HERTZ AREA AS FOL-
LOWS: (STILWELL FROM STRATEMEYER) EAST BOUND B-24 ATTACKED BY TWO
ZEROS AT HTINGNAN, 2 TROOP CARRIER PLANES DAMAGED BUT RETURNED SAFELY,
1 CNAC AIRCRAFT STILL MISSING REPORTED BY RADIO BEING ATTACKED BY ZERO,
1 B-24 WITH SLUGS FROM FOUR ZERO CALIBER EXPLOSIVE BULLETS ARRIVED
FROM CHINA.   ATC RESCUE SHIP SIGHTED 3 ZEROS SOUTH EAST SUMPRABUM.
UNREPORTED AND OVERDUE ARE 1 C-87 AND 1 C-46.   INFORMATION RECEIVED
FROM KUNMING FOLLOWS: STARTING DAWN 14 OCTOBER , AMERICAN FOURTEENTH
AIR FORCE FIGHTERS WILL GUARD 5588 KILOCYCLES PATROLLING FROM YUNNANYI
NORTHWEST TO RANGE LIMIT.   RESPONSIBLE COMMANDERS HAVE BEEN ADVISED
AND DIRECT VPTAKE NECESSARY ACTION AND TO COORDINATE WITH FOURTEENTH
AIR FORCE TO INCREASE SECURITY OF ATC ROUTE

1084

DR   19233

RECEIVED IN SECRET CODE

INCOMING RADIO

RECEIVED	:	15 OCT 1120 GCT
FROM	:	RELOT
TO	:	AMMISCA
NR	:	G 257

ZZZZ

FILED: 15 OCT 0810 GCT

THIS MORNING SUN LEFT WITH SOMMERVELL PARTY. FOLLOWING IS
PREPARATION FOR HIS PROBABLE SOB STORY. THERE ARE NO SOUND REASONS
TO PREVENT COMPLIANCE WITH YOUR FIELD ORDER NUMBER 1 WHICH WAS RECD
BY HIM ON OCTOBER 5TH. HAS HAD AMPLE TIME FOR PREPARATION ETC.
DAVISON GAVE HIM DETAILED REPORT OF AVAILABLE AIR SUPPORT. WE CAN
AND WILL SUPPLY HIM ADEQUATELY AND ENEMY OPPOSITION CERTAINLY IN-
SIGNIFICANT. SUN HAS PUT OUT HIS USUAL MINOR OBJECTIONS AND ALIBIS
ETC BY MY ORDER GIVES HIM AMPLE LATITUDE AND EYE HAVE MADE IT CLEAR
THAT ALL WE INSIST ON IS THAT LOCALITIES BE OCCUPIED AS ORDERED AND
AS PER SCHEDULE. HE OBVIOUSLY DOES NOT WANT TO ADVANCE NOV 1ST, MAYBE
IS SINCERE IN DESIRING TO MOVE LATER BUT NOT NOW AND MAYBE HIS PRESENT
ATTITUDE IS JUST BLACKMAIL FOR SUPPLIES, SYMPATHY ETC. (STILWELL
FROM BOATNER.) I BELIEVE SUN WILL RELUCTANTLY MOVE AND FIGHT IF WE
CONTINUOUSLY PUSH HIM BUT WILL ALWAYS BE BEHIND SCHEDULE AND SLOW. / IF HOWEVER
HE GETS POSITIVE ORDERS FROM GISSMO BELIEVE WE CAN PUT ON FINE SHOW
AND CAPTURE LDITPYINA. ALL OUR RELATIONS HAVE CONTINUED TO BE MOST
CORDIAL US

JHG

1085

RECEIVED IN SECRET CODE

INCOMING RADIO

RECEIVED: 16 OCTOBER 0600 GCT

FROM   : READDRESSED TO AMUSCA BY AMMDEL FROM WAR

TO   : AMUSCA

NO   : 3606 FILED: 15 OCTOBER 1515 GCT   PRIORITY

INFORMATION ON MATTERS PERTAINING TO YOUR COMMAND CONTAINED IN THE
SECRET REPORT OF THE SENATORIAL COMMITTEE WHICH RECENTLY VISITED ALL
THEATERS IS FORWARDED TO YOU FOR YOUR INFORMATION. (GENERAL STILWELL'S
EYES ALONE FROM MARSHALL). REPORTING ON THEIR ENTIRE TRIP, THEY
WERE PARTICULARLY CONCERNED WINFHYON MORALE CONDITIONS IN DELHI.
AS THE SENATORS PUT IT, THE MAIN DIFFICULTY SEEMS TO BE THAT OUR
OFFICERS AND MEN IN DELHI ARE TOO FAR FROM THE FRONT, OFFICERS ARE
TOO FAR FROM THEIR MEN, AND NO ONE SEEMS TO HAVE ENOUGH TO DO, AND
COMPLAINTS, OFFICERS AND MEN ALIKE, WERE MORE NUMEROUS THAN ANY WHERE
ELSE ON THEIR GLOBAL TOUR. THEY WERE IMPRESSED BY THE MANNER IN
WHICH TROOP OFFICERS IN DELHI WERE FOLLOWING THE BRITISH PATTERN OF
LIVING IN LARGE HOTELS VERY FAR FROM THEIR MEN.

OUR OWN OFFICERS HAVE SEEN THESE CONDITIONS, BUT HAVE BEEN OF THE
OPINION THAT SO LONG AS CLOSE LIAISON WITH BRITISH GHQ WAS NECESSARY,
THAT YOU HAD TO LOCATE YOUR REAR ECHELON HEADQUARTERS AS WELL AS
YOUR SOS AND 10TH AIR FORCE HEADQUARTERS NEARBY.

IN THE MEANTIME SINCE STRATEMEYERS POSITION IN YOUR COMMAND HAS
NOW MADE IT POSSIBLE TO MOVE THE 10TH AIR FORCE HEADQUARTERS FORWARD
TO THE CALCUTTA AREA MUCH OF THE SENATORS REMARKS NO LONGER OBTAIN.
HOWEVER, FURTHER THINNING OUT OF OUR DELHI ESTABLISHMENTS MAY NOW BE
MADE POSSIBLE BY THE ORGANIZATION OF MOUNTBATTENS COMMAND. THIS COMMAND
SHOULD AFFORD MACHINERY FOR LIAISON AND PLANNING WITH THE BRITISH
PREVIOUSLY PERFORMED BY REAR ECHELON HEADQUARTERS AND SOS. WOULD
LIKE TO HAVE YOUR COMMENTS 19315

1092   1087

1018

17 October 1943.

The Honorable T. V. Soong
Chungking
China

My dear Doctor Soong:

In our conference earlier today I spoke to you of the embarrassment of our War Department over the present exchange rate which results in the costs of work performed in China being recorded in our own reports at rates greatly out of proportion to corresponding rates in the United States. The cost of an airport in China, if carried at the official exchange rate, would be up from eight to ten times its cost at home. I am sure that you will understand the problem that this represents to the War Department.

General Stilwell advises me that the monthly expenses of the American Army in China, including airport and road construction, will shortly reach $500,000,000 (Chinese) per month. I would suggest for your consideration that for all American expenditures in China the Chinese Government be credited in the United States with American dollars at the official rate for one-fifth of the expenditures, and that the Chinese Government give General Stilwell a credit of four times this amount to be used to augment the official rate. This five to one ratio would, of course, require periodic adjustment. It would then be possible for our troops in China to be paid in Chinese currency, and our records would reflect costs more nearly comparable to those which would obtain in the United States. Further, it would be my suggestion that this fiscal arrangement be incorporated in a supplemental agreement rather than in a reverse Lend Lease agreement.

I believe that our reverse Lend Lease agreement, inasfar as the War Department is concerned, should provide for the Chinese Government to supply and ration requisite labor for all common projects in China, which would, of course, include those airports and supply routes used jointly by the Chinese and American forces.

I am sure that you understand the importance of an early solution of the exchange agreement. Manifestly, the suggestions contained herein must be considered as informal until I have returned to Washington where they may be discussed with responsible officials of our own government. It would be very helpful, however, if I could return with your own government's views, particularly as to these suggestions, and I am confident that such an exchange will permit a prompt solution soon after my arrival back in Washington.

Please accept once more my appreciation for your delightful luncheon.

Sincerely yours

BREHON SOMERVELL
Lieutenant General
Commanding.

1019

RECEIVED IN SECRET CODE

REDCEIVED: 18 OCTOBER 0450 GCT

FROM   : AMMDEL

TO   : AMMISCA

NO   : AM 1816   FILED: 16 OCTOBER 0605 GCT

STILWELL'S EYES ALONE. TALKING TO WEDEMEYER (FROM FERRIS) INDICATES CLEARLY THAT WINGATE HAS GREEN LIGHT FROM HIGHEST LEVEL ON TRAINING ALL LONG RANGE GROUPS. ALSO HE HAS TASK OF THEIR EMPLOYMENT. PROJECT NUMBER NINE IS AMERICAN AIR SUPPORT FOR ALL LONG RANGE UNITS. MUST SAY THAT MY IMPRESSION IS THAT WINGATE HAS EAR OF WINSTON AND THE PROJECT IS NOW TICKLISH AND POLITICAL. APPARENTLY WINGATE IS IN DISFAVOR AND BAD ~~FCOR~~ ODOR BECAUSE OF HIS ACTIONS. WE ARE CONTINUING WITH OUR TRAINING PLANS

19408

1089

1020

Agwar 813

Renrad 3606. My comments are as follows The British G H Q set-up at Delhi forced us to locate S.O.S. and rear echelon Hqrs. there. (Marshall from Stilwell eyes alone.) We could not have done business efficiently anywhere else. Delhi is of course too far from the front. I don't like that either. The officers live in large hotels because there is no other accommodation for them. I don't know what is meant by officers being too far from their men. Up to now the most of them have been quartered less than two hundred yards from rear echelon hqrs. and tenth air force barracks. Neither do I understand how no one seems to have enough to do. My information indicates the opposite. Not knowing what the complaints are, I cannot answer that. Living conditions are excellent. The messes are very good. There is plenty of amusement for the men. I envy the mental capacity of civilian observers who can do a shirt-tail shoot through a theater the size of the U.S. without knowing anything about its background and can in a few days understand its problems well enough to qualify as experts. When he left Chungking, Senator Russell told me they were just beginning to get an idea of our problems and what we were up against.

PRIORITY

FROM MARSHALL FROM SOMERVELL   EYES ONLY

AGWAR 816

STILWELL AND I RECOMMEND PROMOTION OF COVELL TO MAJOR

GENERAL AND THAT ORDERS BE ISSUED DIRECTING HIM TO

REPORT TO STILWELL AS COMMANDER SOS VICE WHEELER

APPOINTED BY MOUNTBATTEN AS PRINCIPAL ADMINISTRATIVE

OFFICER FOR COMBINED FORCES

Oct 18

HQ U S ARMY FORCES

CHUNGKING, CHINA
19 OCTOBER 1943

AGWAR 8 2 4

    REUBEN CHARLIE HOOD JUNIOR COLONEL ZERO ONE SEVEN EIGHT EIGHT

FOUR AIR CORPS RECOMMENDED FOR PROMOTION TO BRIGADIER GENERAL

PAREN FOR ULIO FROM STILWELL PAREN TO FILL EXISTING POSITION

VACANCY AS CHIEF OF STAFF FOR AIR SERVICE COMMAND THIS THEATRE

WHICH POSITION HE HAS HELD FOR TEN MONTHS

OFFICIAL:

L. B. THOMPSON
MAJOR, A. G. D.
ASST ADJ GENERAL

RECEIVED CODE ROOM _____ EJK _____ DATE 19 0 933 _____

ACTUAL TIME OF DISPATCH AND METHOD _____ 19 0 030· _____

LBT/shc

(See 17339)

(1095)

10312

(1094)

HQ. U. S. ARMY FORCES

CHUNGKING, CHINA
19 OCTOBER 1943

AGWAR 8 23
AQUILA D 591   ROUTINE
AMMDEL AD 2352

NOW RECOMMEND FOLLOWING PROMOTIONS CLN BRIGADIER GENERAL HOWARD

CHARLIE DAVIDSON CMA ZERO DASH THREE FIVE NINE SIX CMA TO MAJOR GENERAL

AND COLONEL AUBREY LOVE MOORE CMA ZERO DASH ONE SEVEN THREE NINE TWO TO

BRIGADIER GENERAL PAREN MARSHALL SIGNED STILWELL INFO STRATEMEYER AND

FERRIS PAREN VACANCIES EXIST FOR DAVIDSON IN TENTH AIR FORCE AS COMMANDING

GENERAL AND FOR MOORE IN STRATEMEYERS HEADQUARTERS WHERE HE OCCUPIES MOST

IMPORTANT POSITION AS ASSISTANT CHIEF OF AIR STAFF OPERATIONS PLANS

INTELLIGENCE AND TRAINING

EYES ALONE
THIS HQ.

OFFICIAL:

L.B. THOMPSON
MAJOR, A.G.D.,
ASST. ADJUTANT GENERAL

Gen. Stilwell approved
this promotions to
me yesterday.
Geo. E. Stratemeyer
Maj. Gen. A.A.U.

(1096)

C/S Larsen

RECEIVED IN CODE ROOM _____ EWR _____ DATE 150933

10311

ACTUAL TIME OF DISPATCH AND METHOD 191030.
AO/3/b (3)

1024

RECEIVED IN SECRET CODE.

<u>INCOMING RADIO:</u>

RECEIVED: 21 OCTOBER 1440 Z.

FROM   : AMMDEL

TO   : AMMISCA (FOR THE EYES OF GEN STILWELL ONLY)

NR   : AM 1850.   FILED: 20 OCTOBER 0938 Z.

FURTHER THOUGHTS ON WINGATE TRAINING AND OPERATIONAL
CONTROL SUBMITTED FOR YOUR CONSIDERATION (FOR EYES ALONE
STILWELL FROM FERRIS) ALL THESE MEN ARE NOW WELL TRAINED AND
SOME COME FROM ACTIVE THEATRE. TROOPS REACTION TO THE
ECCENTRICITIES OF WINGATE MAY BE VIOLENT. MANY WILL ASSUME
INDIANS WITH WHOM THEY TRAIN ON PAR WITH NEGROES WHICH IS
UNWHOLESOME. THIS WILL BE FIRST SUBMISSION KNOWN TO ME OF
UNCLE SUGAR SUBMISSION TO BRITISH TRAINING AND OPERATIONAL
CONTROL. IT SIGNIFIES THIS GAME IS UNKNOWN TO AMERICANS IN
SPITE OF SWP SUCCESSES. REACTIONS OF AMERICAN PUBLIC WILL
BE UNPLEASANT EYE AM SURE AND DEGRADES OUR OWN PROFESSIONAL
SERVICE. IF THESE OPERATIONS SUCCEED, BRITISH WILL ASSUME
FULL CREDIT BUT IF THEY FAIL, THEN IT WILLBE AMERICAN FAULT.

*This was included in
radio summary of 22 oct
to C/S with statement
it ....
.... and had not
been delivered.*

1 9,593.   (1097)

ORDER SEC ARMY BY TAG/SW-350

RECEIVED IN SECRET CODE

INCOMING RADIO

RECEIVED: 22 OCTOBER 0300 GCT

FROM   : AGWAR   PRIORITY

TO   : AMMISCA   AMMDEL

NO   : 3644   3744   FILED: 21 OCTOBER 2044 GCT

PRIORITY

GENERALISSIMO HAS ADVISED THE PRESIDENT THAT OUR COMMITMENTS TO CHENNAULT HAVE NOT BEEN MET. (EYES ONLY TO STILWELL FOR STRATEMEYER FROM ARNOLD)

WE PROMISED HIM THREE SQUADRONS OF MEDIUM BOMBARS AND HE HAS BUT ONE. THE OTHER TWO ARE IN INDIA. USING YOUR BEST JUDGMENT YOU HELD THEM OUT BUT APPARENTLY DID NOT NOTIFY THE GENERALISSIMO OF THIS ACTION. THESE TWO MEDIUM BOMBER SQUAD-RONS ARE NOW DESIRED BY HIM. DISPATCH THESE TWO SQUADRONS TO CHENNAULT WITHOUT DELAY.

TAKE ACTION INDICATED ABOVE AND CABLE UPON COMPLIANCE

action has been initiated

C/S has seen

19618

1026

RECEIVED IN SECRET CODE

INCOMING RADIO

RECEIVED: 22 OCTOBER 0525 GCT

FROM   : AMMDEL
                                        PRIORITY
TO   : AMMISCA   AGWAR

NO   : AM 1855   AG 2383   FILED: 21 OCTOBER 1042 GCT

    EYES ALONE GENERALS MARSHALL AND STILWELL. IN PREPARATION
FOR A MEETING AT GHQ ON OCTOBER 19TH TO DETERMINE THE NOVEMBER
ALLOTMENT ON THE ASSAM LOC THE BRITISH PREPARED JPS PAPER 112
WHICH IS A LENGTHY AND ONE SIDED STUDY OF THREE METHODS BY
WHICH ALL BRITISH REQUIREMENTS MCM THE FOURTH COULD BE MET AT
THE EXPENSE OF THE AIR LIFT TO CHINA. FROM FERRIS. SUMMARY
OF MAIN POINTS OF PAPER FOLLOW: TIME IS RAPIDLY APPROACHING
WHEN AN OVERALL PLAN FOR THE OPERATIONS THIS DRY SEASON MUST BE
DECIDED UPON AND ASSAM LOC TONNAGE ALLOCATED TO THE BEST IN-
TEREST OF THE OVERALL PLAN. REQUIREMENTS TO COMPLETE BRITISH
CONCENTRATION FROM NOVEMBER THROUGH MARCH ARE 154000 PERSONNEL,
12690 VEHICLES, 225 TANKS AND 8500 ANIMALS (THIS INCLUDES RE-
MAINDER THREE DIVISIONS, TRIED TROUPS, TWO LRP GROUPS, RAF,
10,000 RETURNING LAAVES AND 51,000 REPLACEMENTS) REQUIREMENTS
FOR AMERICAN CONCENTRATION ASSAM AND LEDO AREA ARE 73000 PER-
SONNEL, 7500 VEHICLES, 110 TANKS, 526 ANIMALS AND 20,000 NATIVE
LABORERS. TOTAL CAPACITY FOR FIVE MONTHS PERIOD 180,000 PER-
SONNEL, 16500 VEHICLES AND 7500 ᴥᴥᴥᴥᴥᴥᴥ ANIMALS. TANKS MUST
BE MOVED AT THE EXPENCE OF STORES GRAINS. THE RESULTING SHORTAGE
TO BE MET BY A PHASED DIVERSION OR 300 ANIMALS PER TRAIN CAPABEE
OF CARRYING 330 TONS OF SUPPLIES. CONCENTRATION SHOULD BE (1100)

SECRET

POSTPONED AS LONG AS POSSIBLE TO KEEP DOWN MAINTENANCE RE-
QUIREMENTS UNTIL THE TOTAL CAPACITY OF THE LOC BEGINS TO IMPROVE.
IF HUMP TONNAGE IS DRASTICALLY CURTAILED NO FURTHER EXPANSION OF
ATC SHOULD BE NECESSARY IN NEAR FUTURE. MOST FAVORABLE PLAN
(PLAN Z) WOULD ALLOW FOLLOWING TONNAGE TO BE CARRIED TO CHINA:
NOVEMBER THROUGH FEBRUARY 2500-3000 ; MARCH THROUGH MAY 6000-
6500; JUNE 7000. RECOMMENDATIONS ARE THAT: AMERICANS ACCEPT
PLAN Z ; DISCONTINUE FURTHER BUILD UP OF ATC; AMERICAN MOVES
FOR NOVEMBER BE 10,000 PERSONNEL, 1300 VEHICLES AND 750 XXXXXXSS
ANIMALS. END OF SUMMARY. OUR REMARKS. SOME SUCH STUDY SHOULD
BE WORKED OUT JOINTLY BETWEEN AMERICAN AND BRITISH PLANNERS
BEFORE BEING DISCUSSED AT A HIGH LEVEL. THIS WAS ANOTHER CASE
IN WHICH BRITISH SPENT DAYS PREPARING A PAPER AND ASKED US TO
DISCUSS IT ON 24 HOURS NOTICE. THE OVERALL RESULTS WERE
A
 IBORTIVE BUT WE DID ACCEPT THE NOVEMBER TROOP, VEHICLE AND
ANIMAL FIGURE AND A TENTATIVE FIGURE FOR SUPPLIES DURING THE
FIRST TEN DAYS WAS SET AT 3550 TONS FOL AND 1200 TONS SUPPLIES
PER DAY, FOR TOTAL OF 1550 TONS DAILY. EXAMINATION OF BRITISH
FIGURES REVEALS THAT THEY DESIRE TO MOVE UP 61,000 REPLACEMENTS
AND LEAVE PERSONNEL WHICH ALMOST EQUALS OUR TOTAL DEMAND; THE
US DEMAND WOULD ALSO BE ABOUT HALF THAT USED IN BRITISH STUDY
PROVIDED 20,000 LABORERS CAN BE OBTAINED LACALLY WHICH WE AN-
TICIPATE. THIS HEADQUARTERS SEES NO NEED OF TANKS IN THIS
PROPOSED WOODED AREA OF OPERATION AND CONSEQUENTLY ARE AN UN-
NECESSARY BURDEN ON THE LOC. AS STATED IN MY LAST RADIOS
CONSTANT HAMMERING AT HUMP TONNAGE WILL REDUCE ANY AID TO
14TH AIR FORCE AND YOKE FORCE TO AMOUNT MAKING THEIR SUPPLY
FOR OPERATIONS IMPOSSIBLE. SEAC STILL GETTING ORGANIZED AND

(1100)

IT IS UNDERSTOOD TO START FUNCTIONING AS HEADQUARTERS IN
ABOUT ONE MONTH. TIME MARCHES ON. THIS INFORMATION HAS
BEEN FURNISHED IN CASE ANY MENTION OF PAPER SHOULD BE MADE
IN WASHINGTON. WHOLE MATTER IS NOW BEING REEXAMINED AND
WILL BE TAKEN UP AGAIN AFTER RETURN OF SUPREME COMMANDER

gen Hearn has seen

23oct

(1100)

19622

To _____ AMMDEL _____

From _____ RELOT _____

_____ 1037 GCT _____

D-164/23

1145 GCT

WRITERS NR ___ F 354 ___ DATE ___ OCT 23/43 ___ LITERAL COPY

ZZZZ   ZZZZ   ZZZZ

EYES ALONE FOR GENERAL STILWELL

EYES ALONE OF STILWELL PRD SORRY BUT AM NOT CERTAIN EYE UNDERSTAND
URAD ROGER EASY ONE FIVE THREE PRD DO YOU MEAN THAT YOU WANT ME
CANCEL ALL ADVANCE PURSUANT TO YOUR FIELD ORDER NUMBER ONE QUERY
(STILWELL FROM BOATNER PD UNLESS THERE IS SOME REASON UNKNOWN
TO ME EYE RECOMMEND WE GO AHEAD AND TAKE TARO BECAUSE JAPS ARE
DEFINITELY IN THAT CORRADOR AND MUST BE EJECTED TO SAFEGUARD
OUR COMMUNICATIONS PD BELIEVE WE ALSO SHOULD ADVANCE FIVE MILES
SOUTH OF CHINSLOW SAKZY PD THIS MODIFICATION WILL DELAY OCCUPATION
OF SHARAW AND CONSTRUCTION OF AIRFIELD THERE OR IN SHING VICINITY
BUT IT IS NECESSARY TO CARRY OUT MY PRESENT MISSION OF PROTECTING
ROAD PD COMPLETE ARRANGEMENTS MADE FOR FORWARD MOVEMENT TOMORROW
MORNING PD WILL NOT CHANGE ANY ORDERS BUT WILL HAVE PLANS AND
ORDERS ALL SET PENDING CONFIRMATION FROM YOU

1030

RECEIVED IN ~~SECRET CODE~~

<u>INCOMING RADIO</u>

RECEIVED : 24 OCT 0625 GCT

FROM : WAR

TO : AMMDEL 3796, AMMISCA

NR : 3663   FILED : 23 OCT 2129 GCT

APPROVED FOR PROMOTION ON NEXT LIST ARE COLONELS FRANK
DORN ZERO DASH ONE FIVE TWO SEVEN EIGHT FOX ABLE, FRANK DOG MERRIL
ZERO DASH ONE SEVEN SIX THREE EIGHT, AND MALCOM FOX LINDSEY ZERO
DASH SIX NINE ONE FOUR I F (MARSHALL TO STILWELL YOUR NUMBER AMMDEL
TWO TWO ZERO EIGHT OCTOBER ELEVENTH) VERNON EVANS, JOSEPH ABLE CRANSTON
AND THEODORE FOX WESSELS, BRIGADIER GENERALS BEING ASSIGNED CBI RPT
CBI THEATER AND ABOUT SEVEN NOVEMBER ONE NINE FOUR THREE WILL DEPART

AG

C/S

1104

RECEIVED IN ~~SECRET~~

INCOMING RADIO

RECEIVED : 30 OCT 1110 GCT

FROM : AQUILA   (ZZZZ)

TO : AMMISCA

NR : S 65 AOX   FILED : 30 OCT 1015 GCT

AT A CONFERENCE HELD AT CHABUA TWENTY NINE OCTOBER BY
GENERALS DAVIDSON AND OLD, COL HARDIN AIR TRANSPORT COMMAND AND COL
MOORE AS MY REPRESENTATIVE A PLAN WAS PREPARED AND SUBMITTED TO ME
FOR THE PROTECTION OF THE ATC ROUTE WHICH I HAVE APPROVED (STILWELL
FROM STRATEMEYER INFO DAVIDSON AND OLD) ONE PHASE OF THIS PLAN POINTS
OUT THAT IN ORDER TO PROPERLY GUARD OUR TRANSPORTS OVER THE HUMP
IT IS ESSENTIAL THAT WE ESTABLISH OUR AIR WARNING NET TO THE SOUTH
OF SUMPRABUM. SINCE THIS AREA IS AT PRESENT IN ENEMY HANDS PRELIMINARY
TO THE ESTABLISHMENT OF STATIONS TO FURTHER AIR WARNING NET OUR
TROOPS MUST MOVE SOUTH FROM FORT HERTZ. GENERAL BOATNER IS ANXIOUS
TO START QUOTE STRIP TEASE UNQUOTE PLAN AND HAS HIS DETAILED PLAN
READY FOR EXECUTION WITHOUT DELAY. SINCE HIS TROOPS ARE ON THE MOVE
HE IS VERY ANXIOUS TO HAVE A FORCE STARTED FROM FORT HERTZ TO AFFORD
PROTECTION TO HIS LEFT FLANK. WE ARE PREPARED TO SUPPLY THESE TROOPS
BY AIR AFTER THEY ARRIVE IN THE HERTZ AREA AND ARE ALSO PREPARED
TO MAKE AN INITIAL MOVE OF ONE TWO FIVE TRANSPORT LOADS. I URGENTLY
RECOMMEND THAT POSITIVE ACTION BE TAKEN TO SECURE SUFFICIENT FORWARD
AREA FOR THE ESTABLISHMENT OF AIR WARNING STATIONS TO ENABLE TENTH
AIR FORCE TO ACCOMPLISH ITS PRIMARY MISSION OF PROTECTING THE ATC
HUMP ROUTE   20015   CCR

INCOMING RADIO:

RECEIVED: 30 OCTOBER 1615 z.

FROM   : AMMDEL

TO   : AMMISCA AGWAR AG 2542

NR   : AM 1934   FILED: 30 OCTOBER 0730 Z.

MEETING GALAHAD WAS BRINK (FOR EYES ALONE MARSHALL FOR
TIMBERMAN INFO AMMISCA FROM FERRIS) UPON ARRIVAL BOMBAY.
FIFTY REPORTED SICK REQUIRING SOME HOSPITALIZATION. PERSONNEL
FROM SOUTH AND SOUTH WEST PACIFIC PHYSICALLY RUN DOWN.
MALARIA MAY BE EXPECTED FROM THEM. UNCLE SUGAR AND TRINIDAD
UNITS APPEAR IN FINE SHAPE. MORALE OF ALL HIGH.

AT LEAST TWO WEEKS DELAY STARTING TRAINING LIKELY DUE TO
BRITISH FAILURE TO HAVE FACILITIES AT CONCENTRATION AREA TO
RECEIVE THEM. THIS HQ HAD ARRANGEMENTS FOR IMMEDIATE HOUSING
AND TRAINING UPON ARRIVAL IN ASSAM BUT WAS DECLINED BY SEAC
RPT SEAC.

20,043.

Arundel for Ferris. ~~Secret~~ routine

Tank personnel here in urgent need of goggles. Get five hundred pairs from Stratemeyer and arrange for replacement. _New subject._ They tell me here that majority of trucks coming in are six by four instead of six by six. My God, what has happened? Didn't we specify definitely six by six? Answer care of Coughlin at Silty. _New subject._ McLaughlin says there is a project called "Chestnut." This is news to me. Does it mean anything to you? I hate secrets unless I am in on them.

Stilwell —

OUTGOING MESSAGE

INDIA HEADQUARTERS UNITED STATES ARMY FORCES IN
CHINA, BURMA AND INDIA,

TO **AMMDEL**

MESSAGE CENTER NR.
(this space for Msg. Center)

FROM **AMMRAM**   *ROUTINE*

TIME FILED
(this space for Msg. Center.)

MASEP NR **WK 9**   DATE **31 OCT 43**

PHOTO RECORD AT RAMGARH HIGHLY UNSATISFACTORY PAREN FOR COLONEL
WRIGHT SIGNED STILWELL PAREN DONT TELL ME SOME GOOD PHOTOGRAPHERS
ARE COMING PRD MAKE IT YOUR BUSINESS TO STIR UP WHAT WE'VE GOT
PRD EYE SEE NO REASON WHY COX SHOULD BE AN OFFICER PRD EYE HAVE
SPOKEN OF THIS BEFORE BUT NOTHING IS DONE PRD EYE REPEAT THAT
EYE WANT A GOOD PHOTOGRAPHIC RECORD KEPT OF THE TRAINING AT
RAMGARH PRD IF PLAINER WORDS ARE REQUIRED CMA EYE AM PREPARED TO
FURNISH THEM.

RECEIVED
WAR DEPARTMENT
U.S. MILITARY MISSION TO CHINA
CHUNGKING, CHINA

REGISTERED
MESSAGE CENTER
(ORG)
No. 6840
Date 10-31-43
Hour 8:30A

OUTGOING TEL. FILE NO. _____

(1170)

1035

NOV 3 43 ...

RECEIVED
WAR DEPARTMENT
U. S. MILITARY MISSION TO CHINA
CHUNGKING, CHINA

<u>INCOMING RADIO</u>

RECEIVED : 02 NOV 2130 GCT

FROM : AQUILA   *Eyes Alone*

TO : AMMISCA   KONKO DEDAC N 21 AAC

NR : S 4 NAAC   FILED : 02 NOV 0622 GCT

HERE INFORMATION RECEIVED (PAREN TO OLD INFO DAVIDSON
CMA WHEELER AND HARDIN FROM STRATEMEYER PAREN) OF ARMED THIEVERY
OF NATIVE STORES AND HOMES IN CHABUA AREA BY ENLISTED PERSONNEL
AT NIGHT IN GOVT VEHICLES PRD ALSO DRUNKEN BRAWLS AT PLANTERS
CLUB BY OFFICERS WITH NO DISCIPLINARY ACTION PRD REPORT AFTER
INVESTIGATION

c/s #
G-1

See also
(1146)

(1156)

DR   20,172

S̶E̶C̶R̶E̶T̶ (U. S.)
M̶O̶S̶T̶ ̶S̶E̶C̶R̶E̶T̶ (BRITISH)
極̶ ̶秘̶ ̶密̶ (CHINESE)

Chungking, China
November 2, 1943

MEMORANDUM FOR: His Excellency, The Generalissimo.

SUBJECT: Request for approval of special Prisoner of War work in China.

1. There are some 18,000 American Prisoners of War in Japanese hands. Our Armed Services have done nothing for them. Their morale, due to neglect and harsh treatment, is very low. Malnutrition and improper medical care is breaking them down physically. Many have died of the treatment they have received. Many more will die and still others emerge from the war broken in mind and spirit as well as body.

2. In Europe we and the British have established contact with our prisoners and have been able to provide them with news and urgent needs, to use them in the war effort and to assist escapees. As a result the morale of prisoners is unbelievably high, and they see to it they stay fit. Our War Department is extremely anxious that everything possible be done to get in touch with our prisoners and those of our Allies in Japanese hands, and to keep as many of our men out of their hands as possible. We have an organization prepared to undertake this work. To get in touch with prisoners we would like to place a small unit in the vicinity of Shanghai and Yangchow, and another near the Fukien coast opposite Formosa. In due time we hope to extend contact to camps in Japan itself. Each unit should have a portable radio transmitter. As to rescue activities, the work of your troops in bringing our personnel caught behind the enemy lines to safety has been magnificent. Investigation has shown, however, that we could give assistance of considerable value to this work by placing several men in areas of bombing activity, men specially trained and equipped with portable radios.

3. It is understood that the British proposal to help Allied Nationals interned in Hongkong won your enthusiastic approval. In turn it is our earnest hope that you will approve this proposal so that we may do all we can both to prevent our personnel from being captured by the Japanese and also to be of help to our prisoners, for their sake and for ours, before it is too late.

For and in the absence of Lieutenant General STILWELL:

T. G. HEARN
Major General, G. S. C.
Chief of Staff

S̶E̶C̶R̶E̶T̶ (U. S.)
M̶O̶S̶T̶ ̶S̶E̶C̶R̶E̶T̶ (BRITISH)
極̶ ̶秘̶ ̶密̶ (CHINESE)

REGRADED UNCLASSIFIED
ORDER SEC ARMY BY TAG/3W-350

RECEIVED ~~TOP SECRET CODE~~

NOV 4 43.57

RECEIVED
WAR DEPARTMENT
U. S. MILITARY MISSION TO CHINA
CHUNGKING, CHINA

INCOMING RADIO

RECEIVED : 03 NOVEMBER 0434 GCT

FROM ; AMMDEL

TO ; AMMISCA

NR. ; AM 1972   FILED 03 NOVEMBER 0243 GCT

PRIORITY

EYES ALONE GENERAL STILWELL PRD MANEUVERS
RELATIVE TO TRANSPORT PLANES BEAR WATCHING PAREN FROM MERRILL
SIGNED FERRIS PAREN LOOEY SENT SUBSTANTIALLY FOLLOWING TO
BRITISH CHIEFS OF STAFF QUOTE IT IS CLEAR THAT EYE HAVE
NECESSARY AUTHORITY FOR TEMPORARY DIVERSION OF PLANES FROM
FERRY ROUTE PRD THIS IS BASED ON MY PERSONAL RECOLLECTION
SUPPORTED BY MINUTES OF SECOND MEETING BETWEEN PRESIDENT AND
COMBINED CHIEFS OF STAFF ON TWENTY THREE AUGUST UNQUOTE PARA
EIGIT AMNE OF THIS MEETING DOES NOT GIVE THIS IMPRESSION PRD
HOWEVER LOOEY STATES IN SAME MESSAGE THAT PROVISION OF
ADDITIONAL PLANES FROM OUTSIDE INDIA SHOULD BE MADE ASDANY
DIVERSION FROM FERRY ROUTE REDUCES EFFICIENCY OF YOKE FORCES
AND WILL BE DISTASTEFUL TO THE PEANUT RPT PEANUT PRD IN ORDER
TO SEE WHICH WAY WIND IS BLOWING HAVE ASKED FOR A MORE DETAILED
BREAKDOWN OF PROPOSED DIVERSIONS IN EVENT ADDITIONAL PLANES ARE
NOT FORTHCOMING AND STRATEMEYER WILL PREPARE STUDY ON PROBABLE
RESULT TO AIR LIFT.

~~PREPARED CONFIDENTIAL PARAPHRASE~~
~~NOT REQUIRED INCLASSIFIED~~
~~ORDER SEC ARMY BY 517W 364~~ 88,188
GCV

DECLASSIFIED
DOD DIR. 5200.9, Sept. 27, 1958
CWN by ___ date 3-27-72
1161

1038

INCOMING RADIO:

RECEIVED: 3 NOVEMBER 0545 z.

FROM   : AMMDEL

TO   : AMMISCA   (FOR THE EYES OF GEN STILWELL)

NR   : AM 1963   FILED: 3 NOVEMBER 0330 z.

Not in File this HQ

EYES ALONE GENERAL STILWELL. WITH FURTHER REFERENCE TO MY

NUMBER RE 175 DATED OCTOBER 31 A FINAL DECISION ON OPERATIONS TO

START THIS FALL IS EXPECTED IN VERY NEAR FUTURE (FROM MERRILL

SIGNED FERRIS) PRELIMINARY DECISIONS HAVE BEEN REACHED WITH

REGARD TO ARAKAN OPERATIONS, FOURTH CORPS AND TIMINGS. ON

ARAKAN COAST THE LINE INDIN DASH RATHEDAUNG DASH KYAUKTAW WILL

BE TAKEN BY OPERATIONS STARTING ABOUT MIDDLE OF JANUARY. PURPOSE

OF THESE OPERATIONS IS TO OBTAIN A TACTICALLY SOUND POSITION FOR

THE DEFENSE OF CHITTAGONG AREA. HOWEVER THIS IS FIRST OBJECTIVE

ONLY AND FOURTEENTH ARMY INSTRUCTIONS CONTAIN ORDERS TO PLAN ON

EXPLOITING SUCCESS TO EXTENT OF OCCUPYING AKYAB FROM THE LAND SIDE

THESE INSTRUCTIONS ARE SUBSTANTIALLY THE ORDERS THAT SLIM SUGGESTED

HE BE GIVEN. IN FOURTH CORPS SECTOR REGARDLESS OF WHERE THE MAIN

DRIVE WILL HEAD TO THEY MUST START SOUTH DOWN THE KABAW VALLEY

TOWARDS KALEYMO AND KALEWA. WHILE THERE WILL BE SOME MINOR

ACTIVITY IN CONJUNCTION WITH THE BRITISH ROAD CONSTRUCTION AT AN

EARLY DATE NO REAL ACTIVITY WILL START UNTIL ABOUT THE MIDDLE OF

FEBRUARY WHEN THE LRP GROUPS GO OUT. THEY WILL BE FOLLOWED AFTER

A WEEK TO TEN DAYS BY THE MAIN GROUND FORCES. ABOUT TWO WEEKS AFTER

THE MAIN BODY OF FOURTH CORPS MOVES OUT AIRBORNE OPERATIONS WILL

START. BRITISH STATEMENT THAT NET RESULT OF THE AIRBORNE OPERATIONS

(162)

PAGE 2.

WILL APPROXIMATE A START IN DECEMBER HAS SOME TRUTH IN IT IF THEY
ACTUALLY DO THE JOB PLANNED. THERE IS STILL NO DECISION AS TO
OBJECTIVE OF FOURTH CORPS. WEDEMEYER AND EYE ARE HOLDING OUT FOR
MANDALAY AREA AND THINK LOOEY IS WITH US BUT THE OPPOSITION IS VERY
STRONG. REGARDLESS OF WHERE THE OBJECTIVE IS LOOEY STILL BELIEVES
FIRMLY IT IS A BRITISH OBLIGATION TO TAKE ON AS MANY JAPS AS
POSSIBLE BEFORE THE YUNNAN FORCE DOES ANYTHING IN A BIG WAY. LOOEY
REQUESTS THAT YOU CONSIDER THIS AND DISCUSS IN HIS NAME WITH
PEANUT IF YOU THINK ADVISABLE WITH A VIEW TO GETTING THE REACTION
TO SOME DATE BETWEEN FIFTEEN FEBRUARY AND MARCH FIFTEEN AS MOST
SUITABLE FOR YOKE TO JUMP. LOOEY HAS REPORTED TO BRITISH CHIEFS OF
STAFF THAT REGARDING THE INSTRUCTIONS SENT TO YOU AND AUCHINLECK TO
GET TOGETHER ON MINIMUM HUMP TONNAGES THAT AN AGREED RECOMMENDATION
BY YOU TWO CANNOT BE DECIDED UNTIL FINAL DECISIONS REGARDING
OPERATIONS ARE REACHED. ATTITUDE APPEARS TO BE THAT YOU MUST HAVE
TEN THOUSAND TONS OVER THE HUMP FROM NOW ON FOR AS LONG A PERIOD
AS POSSIBLE AND THAT IF ANY REDUCTION TAKES PLACE IT MUST COME AS
LATE IN THE GAME AS POSSIBLE.

20,189.

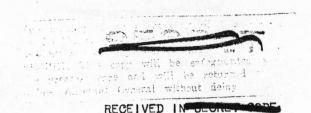

RECEIVED
WAR DEPARTMENT
U.S. MILITARY MISSION TO CHINA
CHUNGKING, CHINA

RECEIVED IN ~~SECRET CODE~~

INCOMING RADIO

RECEIVED : 03 NOV 1209 GCT

FROM : AMMDEL

TO : AMMISCA VIA SILTY

NR : S114   FILED: 01 NOV 1148 GCT

PRIORITY

GOGGLES FIVE ZERO ZERO RPT FIVE HUNDRED WILL BE SHIPPED
THIS WEEK BY AIR FROM KARACHI PRD COUGHLIN FOR STILWELL FROM FERRIS
PRD

MAJORITY OF TWO AND HALF TON TRUCKS NOW BEING RECEIVED ARE
SIX BY FOURS PRD MERRILL INFORMS ME THAT WHILE IN WASHINGTON YOU
STRUGGLED WITH WAR DEPARTMENT ON THIS SUBJECT AND YOU HAD TO ACCEPT
SIX BY FOURS WHICH ARE TRUCKS NOW ON HAND PRD WE HAVE CONSISTENTLY
HELD OUT FOR SIX BY SIX IN REQUESTS TO WAR DEPARTMENT AND CHECK BEING
MADE TO INSURE THIS POINT AND AGAIN INSISTING WAR DEPARTMENT FURNISH
THEM TO US PRD WE HAVE NOTICE OF FEW SIX BY SIX NOW AFLOAT AND ON WAY
HERE PRD

CHESTNUT

CODE CORD QUESTIONED IN PARA THREE OF URAD IS AN OUTLINE
ALTERNATE PLAN FOR OPERATIONS AGAINST NORTHERN BURMA CALLING FOR USE
OF TWO UNCLE SUGAR DIVISIONS FROM IMPHAL AGAINST MANDALAY AREA PRD
YOU SAW THIS AND DIRECTED FURTHER PLANNING ALONG LINES INDICATED

ZAR

RECEIVED IN SECRET CODE

NOV 5 43 PM

INCOMING RADIO

RECEIVED ; 03 NOVEMBER 1317 GCT

FROM ; AMMDEL

TO ; AMMISCA

NR. ; AM 1967   FILED 03 NOVEMBER 1046 GCT

PRIORITY

RECEIVED
WAR DEPARTMENT
MISSION TO CHINA
KING, CHINA

EYES ALONE GENERAL STILWELL PRD SEAC HAS
RECEIVED A DIRECTIVE WHICH IS SIMILAR TO THE ONE YOU HAVE
RECEIVED CONCERNING PROPOSALS FOR FUTURE OPERATIONS PRD
SEAC IS COVERING OPERATIONS GENERALLY ALONG THE LINES OF
ANNEX ONE TO COMBINED CHIEFS OF STAFF PAPER THREE ONE NINE
SLANT TWO REVISED COPY OF WHICH YOU HAVE PRD BELIEVE YOUR
REPLY TO WAR DEPARTMENT SHOULD BE CONSIDERED FROM POINT OF
VIEW THAT IT WILL PROBABLY BE PASSED TO BRITISH THROUGH
COMBINED CHIEFS OF STAFF AND THAT YOU SHOULD CAREFULLY
CONSIDER UNFAVORABLE REACTIONS HERE IF YOU COVER ANYTHING
PERTAINING TO SEAC OTHER THAN PLANS ALREADY AGREED ON AND
YOUR METHOD OF CARRYING OUT OUR PART PAREN FROM MERRILL
SIGNED FERRIS PAREN BELIEVE EXTREME CAUTION NECESSARY TO
END THAT WE DO NOT IN ANY WAY APPEAR TO BE ATTEMPTING TO
INFLUENCE SEAC THROUGH BACK DOOR APPROACHES AND THAT AT ALL
COST YOU PERSONALLY MUST NOT EVEN REMOTELY BECOME INVOLVED
IN ANYTHING THAT CAN LATER BE USED AGAINST YOU PRD AT CON-
FERENCE LOOEY STATED HE WAS THE BOSS AND THAT ANYONE WHO
STARTED A BACK DOOR CAMPAIGN WOULD GET THE AXE PRD IT IS

REGRADED CONFIDENTIAL
ORDER SEC ARMY BY TAG/TW-3 20,210

(1172)

ALREADY ABOUT TO FALL ON MORRIS WHO TRIED TO PULL A FAST ONE
AND GOT CAUGHT PRD ON THE OTHER HAND FOR OPERATIONS IN THE
THEATER WHICH FALL OUTSIDE OF SEAC EYE FEEL YOU SHOULD GO TO
TOWN PARTICULARLY ON ANYTHING PERTAINING TO TWILIGHT PROJECT
AND ALSO ON POSSIBLE OPERATIONS FROM CHINA TOWARD CANTON AND
HONGKONG PRD SEAC IS EXCHANGING VIEWS WITH SOUTHWEST PACIFIC
AND MAIN THING CBI THEATER WILL BE CONCERNED IN WILL BE THOSE
EYE HAVE MENTIONED ABOVE PRD REALIZE SITUATION ON THIS THAT
WE DO NOT CONTROL THESE MATTERS BUT FACT REMAINS THAT UNLESS
YOU SUGGEST SOMETHING SOMEONE ELSE WILL. CONCRETELY EYE FEEL
THAT UNLESS YOU MENTION ABOVE POINTS THAT BRITISH WILL PROPOSE
SOME EXTENSION TO PRESENT SEAC TO PERMIT THEM TO WORK IN CLOSER
COOPERATION WITH MACARTHUR PRD THIS EXTENSION WILL BE JUSTIFIED
BY DEFINITE PROPOSALS TO ASSIST HIM BY WORKING UP THE CHINA
COAST WHICH WILL NECESSITATE THEIR WORKING IN CLOSE COLLABOR-
ATION WITH CHINESE GROUND FORCES ETCETERA ETCETERA.

No. 72

CHUNGKING, CHINA,
8 November 1943.

MEMORANDUM:

TO   : Her Excellency, Madame Chiang Kai Shek.

    If Ch'en Ch'eng's sickness prevents his continuing
in command, the selection of a replacement becomes of
great importance. A man of great determination is needed,
and I believe that Hsueh Yueh is the best choice. There
are rumors that Wei Li Huang will be appointed. The
Generalissimo knows him much better than I do, and can
judge whether he is suitable, but his record in Shansi
makes me doubt his ability.

    A possible solution, looking to the future, would
be to appoint Hsueh Yueh to command the Y-force, (which
will become the first group of thirty divisions) and
shift Ch'en Ch'eng to the command of the second thirty
divisions, which are now starting to train. This will
allow time for Ch'en Ch'eng to recover and meanwhile he
can supervise the organization and training of the
second thirty. I strongly recommend this course unless
the Generalissimo has already made up his mind about it.

                                        JOSEPH W. STILWELL,
                                        Lt. Gen., U.S. Army.

Chapter XIII
THE END OF 1943

Situation in China

In early November 1943 the complexion of affairs in China had assumed a somewhat healthier hue. The annual election of officials had tended to stabilize the government and to continue the political dominance of the Kuomintang Party. Chiang Kai-shek and the principal officials, who were elected, had been well received by the Chinese and were satisfactory to the Allied nations. A general belief prevailed that the Japanese would be ultimately defeated, and as a result of that defeat Chinese business executives expected China to profit politically and economically, as well as from the subsequent collaboration in which they expected to participate. The general opinion existed that the Central Government would now make more potent commitments to the war effort.

The Americans could expect that the continued support of their war effort would be limited by the Chinese capabilities and their natural inclination to avoid unnecessary sacrifices. If the campaign in Burma should fail, or if the Burma Road should remain closed, there would unquestionably arise in China a feeling of deep disappointment and increasing discouragement, resulting in an inevitable drop in public morale.

The Japanese activities in China at the time pointed either to diversionary attacks to disrupt any Chinese plans, reconnaissances in force, or raids for seizing newly harvested crops. The more dependable of the 324 Chinese divisions were generally disposed in central China to counter any possible attack directed against Chungking. The Yoke Force had 15 divisions on the Yunnan-Burma border, six on the Indo-China border, and three in the vicinity of Kunming. Chinese units in general were understrength, which reduced their combat effectiveness, and much of their equipment was unserviceable. In the Y-Force, reports indicated that the divisions had only about 50% of the arms and weapons prescribed in the Tables of Equipment, and at least half of these were unserviceable because they lacked critical parts. Similar conditions obtained in the other 300 divisions.

A steady improvement in the Chinese attitude towards the methods of American training had been shown by the higher authorities in their readiness to accept and to approve the establishment of new training centers and American-supervised training within Chinese units. Definite improvement was being made in the combat efficiency of organizations which had received American instruction.

With the possible exception of Yoke and X-Ray Forces, there was little expectancy of an offensive spirit until equipment, training, and improved rations were forthcoming. The Japanese would probably continue their training maneuvers, food foraging expeditions, and other diversionary moves in order to disrupt the American-Chinese training schedules, and to divert the Fourteenth Air Force from its prescribed missions into support of Chinese ground troops, or to relieve local pressure.

Tactical Situation in North Burma

On 6 November the situation in Assam was:

CBI had received a directive from SEAC for the Chinese to advance to the general line of Taro-Taipha Ga-Sharaw. The valley troops had reached the following positions: The 1st Battalion,

Chinese 112th Regiment had reached Ningam Sakan, advancing southeast. The 2nd Battalion of the same regiment had reached Sharaw Ga and was fighting in the vicinity of Ningbyen with one company of the 2nd Battalion at Yupbang Ga where fighting was also in progress. The 3rd Battalion, 112th Regiment had reached a point six miles northwest of Taro. The 1st Battalion, Chinese 114th Regiment was moving from Tagap to Shingbwiyang.

The latest construction target for the Ledo Road was a one-way all-weather road to Shingbwiyang by 1 January 1944. Metalling had now reached Mile 53, with approximately 54 miles to go to reach Shingbwiyang. SEAC now recognized the need for Hump tonnage to support the Fourteenth Air Force and Y-Force, and was working to adjust the Assam LOC to meet CBI's full requirements.

By the middle of November 1943 the elaborate plans for an all-out amphibious attack on Burma were still being studied preparatory to the Cairo Conference, and again the difficulties of this extremely intricate command arose. As Deputy Supreme Commander to Lord Louis Mountbatten, Stilwell had been advised by the War Department that all American troops in China, Burma and India were under his command; that he was to employ these forces, including any Chinese troops which the Generalissimo might allot to him, to insure that SEAC made an effective and united effort. Should any American troops come under British direction for combat, the individual and unit training as well as administration and supply would remain the responsibility of CBI. However, the training of such units was to be closely coordinated with that of the British so that battalion or even smaller units could operate with the British or vice versa. American units of all types should retain their identity.

The Cairo Conference, Late November-Early December 1943

The specific operations in 1944 approved at the Cairo Conference were largely an endorsement of the Quebec decisions:

"Operations for the capture of Upper Burma in order to improve the air route and establish overland communications with China . . . . Continuance of operations during the autumn of 1944 within the limits of the forces available to extend the position held in Upper Burma . . . . Should the means be available, additional ground offensive operations."

In regard to air operations, the Cairo Conference made specific plans for the execution of long range bombing from bases in India and forward staging airfields in the Chengtu, China area. This project had already been approved at the Quebec Conference. The Cairo Conference reported that the VLR* planes would be available early in 1944, and operations could start earlier than was thought at Quebec if *four* fields in India and *five* in China could be constructed in time. American units and equipment would need to arrive by 15 January, and certain resources would have to be diverted from Ledo. All this would probably delay road construction progress six weeks to two months.

In their estimate of the enemy situation the U. S. Joint Chiefs of Staff (JCS) stated:

"It may be expected that Japan will initiate local offensive actions to forestall operations by the United Nations in Burma and to prevent the establishment of air bases by the United Nations in China."

On Chinese capabilities, the JCS said:

"We believe that, with the possible exception of the American trained Chinese divisions, no large number of troops can be expected to undertake more than limited objective offensive operations at the present time."

Events proved these estimates to be substantially correct.

As a result of the Cairo Conference the current plans, which had been drawn up and studied in the fall for the capture of Burma, were considerably curtailed. The heavy demands for equipment

---

* Very Long Range, i.e., B-29's. *Editorial note.*

and personnel in the European and Mediterranean Theaters had so drained the stock piles of the United Nations that tentative commitments to SEAC had of necessity to be denied. Consequently, upon returning from the Cairo Conference the planners were faced with the painful necessity of revising the Burma plans on a greatly reduced scale.

What the scheme amounted to now was a limited operation in north Burma, the establishment of a bridgehead over the Chindwin by the British troops in the Imphal area, and a drive on Akyab down the Arakan coast. This greatly simplified plan meant that diversions of aircraft from the Hump run could be considerably reduced, but as far as Allied progress in Burma was concerned, it held little promise.

When the plan was presented to the Generalissimo, Chinese reluctance to undertaking any offensive in Burma without a major contribution by other powers was again apparent. In a meeting between Stilwell and Chiang Kai-shek about 21 December [sic. Almost certainly, 16 December 1943], the Generalissimo said he would go ahead with training and with the concentration of troops with a view to attacking in the spring provided the time was ripe and the conditions suitable. Chiang Kai-shek said the decision would be made by himself and Admiral Mountbatten. The Generalissimo agreed, however, to attack at any time a full-scale amphibious operation was ordered. Within a few days, Washington urged the Generalissimo to accept Mountbatten's present plans, indicating to him that the real solution to Chinese difficulties lay in improved communications.

The Generalissimo replied that as he did not participate in the conference which decided to use all available resources to defeat Germany first, he had consequently been given no opportunity to express his views. The fact that the China Theater had been relegated to the background had he claimed given rise to serious misgivings. He still felt that the landing of a strong force in south Burma was necessary to success in the North Burma campaign. He had committed all the Chinese troops in India to this operation, but under no circumstances could he commit any more without being assured that a strong force would land in south Burma. The Generalissimo expressed the opinion that an unfavorable turn of events at this point might adversely affect the entire Pacific campaign.

The viewpoints of the three nations involved varied widely. The Chinese wanted the land route opened, and had already expressed willingness to consider a reduction in Hump tonnage if necessary to achieve this goal. The Americans were definitely committed to north Burma operations, and their plans all pointed east toward China. British wishes, on the other hand, lay to the south. Consequently a meeting of the international minds and agreement to commit "on hand" resources to a united, limited operation posed certain obstacles that had not yet been cleared.

The Cairo Conference disapproved the SEAC amphibious plans against the Andaman Islands, and later withdrew for use in the Mediterranean operations the amphibious equipment earmarked for SEAC. This unhappy situation left SEAC and CBI in a position where it was much more difficult to get the Generalissimo to agree to the commitment of his Yunnan force to assist in opening a land route to China.

The abandonment of plans for an offensive in Burma would probably have forced another year of inactivity; at least any worthwhile and forceful combined operation against the Japanese would have been impossible. Therefore, the year might have ended on a rather discouraging note but for the fact that the North Burma campaign was actually launched.

<u>INCOMING RADIO</u>

RECEIVED: 2 JULY 43 0915 GCT

FROM   : WASHINGTON DC

TO   : AMMISCA FOR DELIVERY TO GISSIMO

NR.   : 2917 THIRTIETH   FILED: JUNE 30 2128 GCT

        PERSONAL AND SECRET TO THE GENERALISSIMO FROM THE

PRESIDENT. SGD ROOSEVELT.

        I HAVE CONCLUDED A SERIES OF VERY SATISFACTORY TALKS

WITH MME CHIANG KAI-SHEK WHICH SHE WILL TELL YOU ABOUT.

        I HAVE TOLD HER OF MY ANXIETY TO MEET YOU SOMETIME

THIS FALL. I THINK IT IS VERY IMPORTANT THAT WE GET TOGETHER.

IF YOU AGREE WITH THIS I SUGGEST SOME PLACE MIDWAY BETWEEN OUR

TWO CAPITOLS. I WOULD APPRECIATE VERY MUCH HEARING FROM YOU

RELATIVE TO THIS PROPOSAL.

*THIS MESSAGE MUST BE PARAPHRASED BEFORE DELIVERY TO ADDRESSEE

(623)

14508

Urgent.

~~SECRET~~

630

Eng: RH

Filed: 090502z

Disp:

Agwar for the eyes of Gen. Marshall alone —

Following message just received for transmission to the President quote — — — — — — — ~~unquote~~ Signed Chiang Kai Shek unquote —

Stilwell —

URGENT

10 July 43

43 AM

~~SECRET~~

RECEIVED
WAR DEPARTMENT
~~ARMY MISSION TO CHINA~~
CHUNGKING, CHINA

~~SECRET~~ ~~CONFIDENTIAL~~ PARAPHRASED
~~REGRADED CONFIDENTIAL~~ PARAPHRASED
~~REGRADED UNCLASSIFIED~~
TAG? CW-350

DECLASSIFIED
DOD Dir. 5200.9, Sept. 27, 1958
NCWN by _____ date 3-27-72

7835

(636)

PRESIDENT ROOSEVELT WASHINGTON D. C.

YOUR TELEGRAM OF FOURTH JULY HAS BEEN RECEIVED. AND I AM IN
FULL ACCORD WITH YOUR SUGGESTIONS. MADAME CHIANG HAS INFORMED
ME IN DETAIL OF HER CONVERSATIONS WITH YOU. I AM DELIGHTED
WITH THE RESULTS AND THAT WE SEE EYE TO EYE ON MANY QUESTIONS.
I ANTICIPATE WITH PLEASURE OUR MEETING IN THE NEAR FUTURE.
FOR MANY YEARS I HAVE BEEN WISHING THAT WE COULD DISCUSS
TOGETHER IN PERSON VARIOUS PROBLEMS OF MUTUAL INTEREST. I
VENTURE TO SUGGEST THAT ANY TIME AFTER SEPTEMBER WOULD BE
MOST CONVENIENT AND SUITABLE TO YOU WOULD BE POSSIBLE FOR
ME. SHOULD NECESSITY ARISE, HOWEVER, FOR OUR MEETING BEFORE
THEN, I SHOULD APPRECIATE YOUR LETTING ME KNOW AT LEAST A
FORTNIGHT IN ADVANCE OF MY DEPARTURE.

                    CHIANG KAI-SHEK

    CHUNGKING, SZECHUAN

    JULY 9, 1934

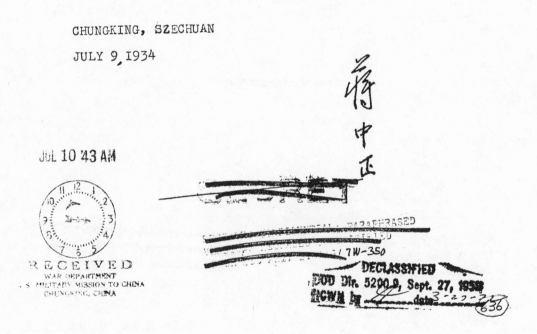

INDIA HEADQUARTERS UNITED STATES ARMY FORCES IN
CHINA, BURMA AND INDIA.

TO   GEN STILWELL

6695
MESSAGE CENTER NR.
(this space for Msg. Center)

FROM   T V SOONG

TIME FILED
(this space for Msg. Center.)

WRITERS

NR 2405   DATE 10 AUG 43   COPY

THAT SUCH SHORTAGE MEN TO FILL THREE DIVISIONS GREATLY SUR-PRISES ME. (THIS PARAPHRASE OF MESSAGE RECEIVED FROM T V SOONG LONDON RELAYED BY WAR DEPT TO AMMDEL FOR STILWELL REF STILWELLS AMMRAM CK 11 AUGUST 6). AT ONCE I SHALL INSIST THAT NECESSARY PERSONNEL BE SENT; IF NECESSARY SHALL SUGGEST SOME EXISTING DIVISION AT KUNMING BE BROKEN UP AND SENT TO INDIA. PLEASE LET ME KNOW IF (IN ONE WEEK) YOU DONT HAVE SATISFACTION OR HEAR FROM ME.

SHOULD THERE BE OTHER MATTERS IN WHICH I CAN ASSIST I WISH YOU WOULD LET ME KNOW PROMPTLY.

Aug. 17

INCOMING TEL. FILE NO.

Agwar   for Chief of Staff.

727

In dealing with the Chinese on the scale we are now approaching, more rank is needed for the officers who deal directly with them. I recommend that our allotment of general officers be increased by ten ~~ten~~ and that the following colonels be promoted at once to the grade of brigadier general: —

✓ George W. Sliney, F.A., O-3545.
✓ Malcolm F. Lindsey, Inf. O-6914.
✓ Richard M. Sandusky, Inf. O-8291.
✓ John E. McCammon, Inf. O-11140.
✓ Frank Dorn, F.A.   O-15278
✓ Frank D. Merrill, Cav. O-17638.

All of the above officers have demonstrated their ability and their fitness for promotion

Stilwell

Recd code Room 9/6 0655 elk
Sent via JGTB 0730

OCT 11 43 AM

Agwar for the eyes of Gen. Marshall alone   729.

KUO MIN TANG

Plenary session of kuo min tang under way. All
sorts of rumors. Concensus of opinion is that G-mo will
emerge with further centralization of power. One nasty
rumor is that liquidation of communists will be discussed. One estimate overheard was that they could be
cleaned up in three months, while Russia is fully
occupied. If any such crazy policy prevails, the consequences are unpredictable, but you can see where it
would put us with respect to Russia to be backing
this gang under such circumstances. I repeat that
above is only rumor as yet, but I want you to be
prepared for possible eventualities. There is no single
indication that any matter connected with the prosecution of the war will be discussed.

                                        Stilwell.

SEP 8 '43 AM

Received   Sent
080130   080230

RECEIVED
WAR DEPARTMENT
U. S. MILITARY MISSION TO CHINA
CHUNGKING, CHINA

REGRADED CONFIDENTIAL
ORDER SEC ARMY BY TAG PER W-350

UNCLASSIFIED
REGRADED
ORDER SEC ARMY
BY TAG PER
7230 85

788

WERTZ.

1054

RECEIVED IN SECRET CODE

INCOMING RADIO

RECEIVED: 2115 GCT 09 SEPT

FROM   : AMMKUN

TO   : AMMISCA

NR   : C 476   FILED: 09 SEPT 0429 GCT

OF

MARKED ON ALL CHINESE MILITARY MAPS IS AREA/NORTH

EAST BURMA TO INCLUDE SADON, VICINITY OF MYITKYINA AND EAST EDGE OF HUKAWNG

VALLEY AS A HSIEN OR COUNTY OF YUNNAN. CHINESE IN EXTREME NORTH ARE SEMI

INDEPENDENT BUBSIDIZED TROOPS:/ FURTHER SOUTH ARE ARMY AND GUERRALAR AND

UNITS OF ELEVENTH GROUP ARMY. BULK OF THIRTY SIX DIVISION NOW IN HPIMAW

DASH LUSHIU DASH NORTH OF MAMIEN PASS AREA (FOR HEARN AND BOATNER FROM

DORN) THIS FOR YOUR INFO AND QOTECY NOT TO BE PASSED ON TO BRITISH.

CHINESE HAVE NO INTENTION OF EVER MOVING OUT. FOR US EYE BELIEVE BETTER

ACCEPT SITUATION

TO ACCEPG SIMUDTEYN AS THEY WILL WITHOUT DOUBT CLAIM ALL OF NORTH BURMA

OCCUPIED BY THEIR TROOPS AND INTEND TO MAKE THEIR BORDER CONTINGENT WITH

ASSAM.

**** DO YOU WISH THIS MSG SERVICED ****

C/S _____

G-2 _____

G-3 _____

REGRADED CONFIDENTIAL
ORDER SEC ARMY BY TAG /7W-350

17,606

/7W-350   795

HQ. U.S. ARMY FORCE

CHUNGKING, CHINA
SEPTEMBER 11, 1943.

AGWAR 737

EYES ALONE

VARIOUS CHINESE SOURCES RATED CHARLIE DASH TWO PAREN MARSHALL FROM STILWELL PAREN REPORT THAT TAI LI IS NOW IN DISGRACE PRD TAI HEADS SECRET POLICE CHARGED WITH SURVEILLANCE OF FOREIGNERS CMA TRAITORS AND SMUGGLING WHILE KUOMINTANG SECRET POLICE SEEK TO SUPPRESS DANGEROUS THOUGHTS PARA TAI IS SAID TO HAVE FALLEN FROM GRACE BECAUSE IN RETALIATION FOR HIS MUSCLING IN ON KUNG RACKETS AND ROUGH HANDLING OF KUNG PROTEGES THE KUNGS AND MME CHIANG EXPOSED TO THE GMO FINANCIAL MISDEEDS OF THE GESTAPO CMA BECAUSE MISSIMO NEEDLED THE GMO ON TAIS EVIL REPUTATION IN THE UNITED STATES AND BECAUSE TAIS ENEMIES WHO ARE LEGION FORTHWITH JOINED IN THE ATTACK PRD WHATEVER THE GMOS DECISION ABOUT TAI HE CANNOT DISPENSE WITH SECRET POLICE PRD EVEN IF TAI GOES THE SYSTEM WILL REMAIN

OFFICIAL:

ASST. ADJUTANT GENERAL

REC'D IN CODE ROOM _____ DATE & TIME 9/11 __1425

ACTUAL TIME OF DISPATCH & METHOD __JGTB____ 1600

JMS,JR/flr/G-2.

SEP 12 4?AM

(3)

REGRADED
ORDER SEC ARMY BY TAG PER
723653

REGRADED CONFIDENTIAL
ORDER SEC ARMY BY TAG/?W-35

(793)

1056

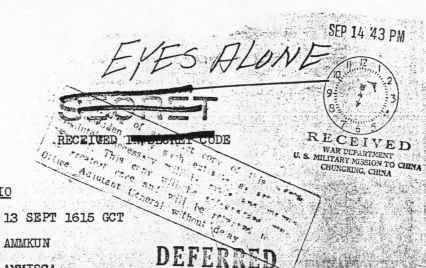

EYES ALONE

~~SECRET~~

RECEIVED IN SECRET CODE

DEFERRED

INCOMING RADIO

RECEIVED : 13 SEPT 1615 GCT

FROM   : AMMKUN

TO   : AMMISCA

NR   : C 497   FILED: 13 SEPT 0754 GCT

SOME INSTRUCTIONS REQUESTED REGARDING EVACUATION
PLAN FOR US ARMY PERSONNEL FROM YUNNAN IN CASE JAP ADVANCE FROM
WEST OR SOUTH (FOR GENERAL STILWELL FROM DORN) HOPE WE WILL
NOT NEED THIS, BUT BELIEVE WE SHOULD PREPARE. QUESTIONS:
DO WE TRY TO FLY TO INDIA, MOVE NORTH INTO SZECHUAN OR
MARCH OUT THROUGH NORTH BURMA?

G-3
c/s

17752

139

Agwar for eyes of Gen. Marshall alone

Plenary session of Kuo min tang ends to-day. Net result probably establishment complete dictatorship. Action on communist question uncertain. Their liquidation has been discussed. Allied successes in Europe have had bad effect here. Chinese tend more and more to loaf on the job. CKS announced that war would be over perhaps in six months and probably in one year. In this session there was no attention given to prosecution of the war. Main points of interest were consolidation of power by the gang, and chances of getting foreign capital for reconstruction after the war. We will ~~have to have~~ need pressure to get action.

Stilwell

rec'd msg cih 0410
sent JGTB 0530

REGRADED ~~CONFIDENTIAL~~
ORDER SEC ARMY BY TAG/ZW-350

09393   798

1058

INCOMING RADIC:

RECEIVED: 15 SEPT 1500 Z.

FROM   :   WASHINGTON.

TO   :   AMMISCA   (FOR THE EYES OF GENERAL STILWELL ONLY)

NR   :   3372   FILED: 15 SEPT 0120 Z.

        I APPRECIATED YOUR GRACIOUS LETTER OF JUNE 30 AND HAVE HAD

THE MATTERS YOU OUTLINED CAREFULLY EXAMINED. (FOR GENERAL STILWELL

TO DELIVER THE FOLLOWING MESSAGE FROM THE PRESIDENT TO MADAME CHIANG

KAI DASH SHEK SIGNED ROOSEVELT) WE ARE TAKING THE NECESSARY STEPS

TO ASSIGN TWO ADDITIONAL FIGHTER SQUADRONS FOR THE FOURTEENTH AIR FORCE

AS SOON AS ADEQUATE PROTECTION FOR THE ASSAM AREA CAN BE PROVIDED WHICH

SHOULD BE BY THE LATTER PART OF SEPTEMBER. WE ARE ALSO PROVIDING

ADEQUATE REPLACEMENTS FOR THE FIGHTERS AND MEDIUM BOMBERS NOW A PART

OF THE FOURTEENTH AIR FORCE, ALTHOUGH OUR SCHEDULE WAS INTERRUPTED

WHEN A SHIP CARRYING PLANES WAS SUNK. I REGRET THAT PETER DASH

FIFTY ONES CANNOT BE DELIVERED AT THIS TIME BUT FEEL THAT THE FIGHTER

ROLE CAN BE FULFILLED BY THE PRESENT PETER DASH FORTIES AVAILABLE,

REINFORCED BY THE PETER DASH THIRTY EIGHTS. WE ALSO PLAN TO TRANSFER

ADDITIONAL MEDIUM BOMBERS NOW IN INDIA TO CHINA AS SOON AS THEY CAN BE

SUPPLIED AND MAINTAINED THERE. THIS, OF COURSE, IS IN ADDITION TO THE

FIGHTERS AND BOMBERS WHICH HAVE BEEN ALLOCATED TO THE CHINESE AIR

FORCE, EIGHTY NINE FIGHTERS OF WHICH HAVE ALREADY BEEN SHIPPED. IT

IS EXTEMELY UNFORTUNATE THAT OUR AIR DELIVERIES TO CHINA HAVE BEEN

HAMPERED BY THE WEATHER, FLOODS AND FAILURE TO COMPLETE AIRDROMES AS RAPIDLY AS HAD BEEN PLANNED. THE MATTER HAS ALSO BEEN COMPLICATED BY THE NECESSITY FOR THE ADJUSTMENT OF MECHANICAL DEFECTS USUAL IN NEW PLANES AND WHICH HAVE BEEN NECESSARY IN THE CARE OF THE CHARLIE DASH FORTY SIX TRANSPORTS. I BELIEVE THAT WE HAVE GONE A LONG WAY TOWARDS MEETING THE DIFFICULTIES AND WE WILL DRIVE AHEAD TO REACH OUR GOAL OF TEN THOUSAND TONS PER MONTH AS SOON AS IT IS WITHIN OUR POWER TO DO SO.

IT IS HOPED THAT THE ESTABLISHMENT OF THE SOUTHEAST ASIA COMMAND WILL VITALIZE THE UNITED EFFORT AGAINST JAPAN AND THE RAPID DEVELOPMENT OF THE AIR ROUTE THROUGH BURMA TO CHINA. GENERAL STRATEMEYER, WHO HAS BEEN RECENTLY SENT TO INDIA, IS AN OFFICER OF THE ABILITY AND WIDE EXPERIENCE AND WILL, I AM SURE, CONTRIBUTE MATERIALLY TO THE SOLUTION OF OPERATIONS AND MAINTENANCE OUT OF INDIA INTO CHINA.

AS YOU KNOW, MRS. ROOSEVELT IS STILL IN THE SOUTHWEST PACIFIC BUT IF SHE WERE HERE SHE WOULD JOIN ME IN VERY WARM REGARDS TO YOU AND THE GENERALISSIMO.

SEP 16 43 AM

RECEIVED

17,815.

(807)

CHUNGKING, CHINA,
16 September 1943.

MEMORANDUM FOR HER EXCELLENCY MADAME CHIANG:

The following message has just been received from President Roosevelt.

"Your gracious letter of June 30 was appreciated, and I have had the matters you outlined examined carefully. The necessary steps are being taken to assign two additional fighter squadrons to the 14th Air Force as soon as proper protection can be assured for the Assam area. This should be accomplished by the last of September. Adequate replacements are also being provided for the medium bombers and fighters now a part of the 14th Air Force, although the schedule was interrupted by the sinking of a ship carrying planes. I am sorry that we cannot deliver P-51's at this time, but I feel that the fighter role can be fulfilled by the P-40's available at present, with P-38's to reinforce them. We also plan on the transfer to China of additional medium bombers now in India, as soon as they can be supplied and maintained in China. This is in addition, of course, to the bombers and fighters which have been allocated to the Chinese Air Force, of which eighty-nine fighters have already been shipped. It is extremely unfortunate that the weather and floods and the failure to complete airdromes on schedule have hampered our air deliveries to China. This matter has also been complicated by the necessity for adjusting certain mechanical defects usual in all new types of planes, a necessity which has arisen in the case of the C-46 transports. I believe we have made good progress in overcoming our difficulties, and we will continue to drive towards our goal of ten thousand tons a month.

I hope that the united effort against Japan and the rapid development of the China-India air route will be vitalized by the establishment of the Southeast Asia Command. General Stratemeyer, who has recently arrived in India, is an officer of wide experience and ability, and I am sure that he will contribute materially to the solution of questions of maintenance and of operations between India and China.

Mrs. Roosevelt, as you know, is still in the southwest Pacific. If she were here, I know she would join me in warm regards to you and the Generalissimo. Signed Roosevelt."

JOSEPH W. STILWELL,
Lt. General, U.S. Army.

OFFICE OF THE COMMANDING GENERAL

UNITED STATES ARMED FORCES

CHINA BURMA INDIA

Amitieu for Dorn — EYES ALONE.

K 1467

Battle for Kweilin continuing. It looks now as if we would win and take over the entire plant there, the military academy to move elsewhere. Tell Arms he can make tentative plans on this basis and I will inform ~~him~~ when decision is definite. We will shoot for November first as opening day. To justify the fuss we are making, everything must click when we start. Are you getting necessary material ~~and personnel~~ lined up?

Stilwell.

Cherry
Okell
by C.S.

recd
0322

Sent
0430

R 2 1 43 PM

(1026)

OFFICE OF THE COMMANDING GENERAL

UNITED STATES ARMED FORCES

CHINA BURMA INDIA

Silty   for Coughlin — EYES ALONE.

DN 299

I understand you have a shipment of stuff including drugs, motion picture apparatus, etc., consigned to the madame and now held at Cha-bua. For good and sufficient reasons, this stuff should be shipped promptly. Disregard priorities and customs formalities and get it started. The issue is important. Mark it plainly for delivery at Chungking, and let me know weight and also date you ship.

Stilwell

rec'd   0 3 0 7

Sent   0430

See   18205

and answer this.

RECEIVED IN SECRET CODE

INCOMING RADIO--

RECEIVED: 23 SEPTEMBER 0750 GCT

FROM : SILTY

TO : AMMISCA

NO : AA 99 FILED: 23 SEPTEMBER 0510 GCT

PRIORITY

PRIORITY

CONFIRMING URAD DN 299 SEPTEMBER 21 GENERAL STILWELL EYES ALONE
FROM COUGHLIN WE SHIPPED 10 PACKAGES WEIGHING 1013 POUNDS IN A TOMMY
CHARLIE PLACE 402 DEPARTING FOR KUNMING SEPTEMBER 23 CONSIGNED CHUNGKING
FOR MISS KUNG SECRETARY TO MADAME. PREVIOUS SHIPMENT COMPRISED 20
PACKAGES WEIGHING 3921 POUNDS IN AMMISCA PLANE 49 DEPARTED KUNMING
SEPTEMBER 3. TOTAL RECEIVED FOR FORWARDING WAS 30 PACKAGES WHICH
FROM CHABUA NOW ARE CLEARED

C/S

17438
09239

23 Sept.

SEP 25 23 1~

PRIORITY

RECEIVED
WAR DEPARTMENT
U. S. MILITARY MISSION TO CHINA
CHUNGKING, CHINA

INCOMING RADIO

RECEIVED : 24 SEPT, 1858 GCT

FROM : AMMKUN

TO : AMMISCA

NR : C 576   FILED: 24 SEPT, 0817 GCT

PARCELS IN URAD K 1471, FOR GENERAL STILWELL FROM

DORN, WILL BE SENT ON NEXT PLANE.   YOUR MESSAGE CAME TOO LATE FOR

TODAY.   OTHER SHIPMENT TURNED OVER TO KISSIMOS HEADQUARTERS AS

PER PREVIOUS INSTRUCTIONS AND PRESUMEABLY SENT BY TRUCK.   CHINESE

HERE INFORM US THAT TWO SHOPS HAVE BEEN OPENED IN CHUNKING FOR

DISPOSAL OF THIS STUFF

C/S

25 Spt

1041.

09621

18,292

INCOMING RADIO:

RECEIVED: 29 SEPT 0835 Z.

FROM   : AMMDEL

TO   : AMMISCA (FOR THE EYES OF GENERAL STILWELL ONLY)

NR   : AM 1658   FILED: 29 SEPT 0334 z.

AM SENSING QUITE A BUILD UP (EYES ALONE STILWELL FROM FERRIS) OF A BRITISH STAFF TO ACCOMPANY CHINESE INTO BURMA FROM YUNNAN. WILSON BRAND ALREADY IN KUNMING WHICH IS BEGINNING. MORE WILL BE ADDED. THIS IS SPONSORED BY CIVIL GOVERNMENT WITH EYE TO THE FUTURE.

18,507.

(1049)

MEMORANDUM - CK-1581:

In to see me was Brigadier Wilson-Brand (Eyes alone Dorn from Hearn). He is coming to Kunming on Wednesday. He is discussing with Chinese a responsibility Boundary. I told him a demarcation of areas of responsibilities for coordination purposes prior to D-day seemed desirable but as to where the boundary should be or was not in position to know. Para. He enquired about Jang to Tali and Paoshan, and with whom of our personnel should he take up the matter. I told him that in Kunming areas you were Gen. Stilwell's representative. No decisions were given him, & no authority to go any where was granted him.

Recd - 100430
Sent -

1068

RECEIVED IN SECRET CODE

INCOMING RADIO

RECEIVED: 15 OCTOBER 1723 GCT

FROM   : AMMKUN

TO   : AMMISCA

NO   : C 730   FILED: 15 OCTOBER 0849 GCT

RITY

PRIORITY

CHINESE REQUEST FOR AIR SUPPORT WEST OF SALWEEN MOST REASONABLE IN SCOPE (FOR GENERAL STILWELL EYES ALONE FROM DORN) THIS MORNING I PROPOSED DIVISION OF SECOND ARMY MOVE FROM CHENKANG TO VICINITY OF PINGKA AND THEN ATTACK MANGSHIH AND LUNGLING WITH IDEA OF FORCING JAPS TO WITHDRAW PRESSURE FROM 36 DIVISION AND 28 DIVISION BATTALIONS. AFTER CONFERENCE WITH CHIN CHENG, THE PLAN IS APPROVED AND WILL BE PUT INTO EFFECT AT ONCE. THIS NOT MAJOR OPERATION BUT HIT AND RUN TACTICS TO STRIKE MAIN COMMUNICATION LINES OF JAPS. BIG SURPRISE THAT PLAN WAS APPROVED. SECOND RESERVE DIVISION ORDERED TO TSAOKEN REPEAT TSAOCHIEN

Gen Stilwell has replied

1086

1306

HQ U S ARMY FORCES

CHUNGKING, CHINA
16 OCTOBER 1943

AGWAR

IT IS TRUE THAT THERE WAS MISCONDUCT IN SOME CHINESE UNITS LAST YEAR PD
FOR STRONG REURAD THREE SIX ZERO ZERO OCT FOURTEEN FROM STILWELL PD IT IS
ALSO TRUE THAT BURMESE KILLED MANY OF OUR WOUNDED PD AT PRESENT EYE BELIEVE
OUR RELATIONS WITH BURMESE ARE ON GOOD BASIS CMA AND EYE DO NOT EXPECT ANY
SERIOUS TROUBLE BETWEEN THEM AND CHINESE PD THE BRITISH HAVE AN AXE TO GRIND
IN HARPING ON PROBABLE TROUBLE BETWEEN CHINESE AND BURMESE PD THEY ARE
TRYING TO CREATE IMPRESSION THAT BURMESE WILL RECEIVE THE BRITISH BACK AGAIN
WITH OPEN ARMS WHICH IS VERY QUESTIONABLE PD AMERICAN RELATIONS WITH ALL
TRIBES WITH WHOM WE ARE IN CONTACT ARE EXCELLENT CMA AND CHINESE ARE AWARE
OF NECESSITY OF MAINTAINING THEM

OFFICIAL:

L. B. THOMPSON
MAJOR, A. G. D.
ASST ADJ GENERAL

RECEIVED CODE ROOM _____ DATE _____ _____

ACTUAL TIME OF DISPATCH AND METHOD _____

JWS/shc

(See 19260)

Eyes alone
this HQ

REGRADED CONFIDENTIAL
ORDER SEC ARMY BY TAG/SW-350

10210

1

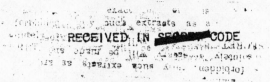 

RECEIVED IN SECRET CODE

RECEIVED
WAR DEPARTMENT
U. S. MILITARY MISSION TO CHINA
CHUNGKING. CHINA

INCOMING RADIO

RECEIVED: 2225 GCT 17 OCT

FROM : AMMKUN

TO : AMMISCA

NR : C 748   FILED: 17 OCT 0452 GCT

3
CONVOY OF/TRUCKS CONTAINING 17 OFFICERS, 2 ENLISTED MEN AND
2 CHINESE (FOR GENERAL STILWELL FROM DORN) ATTACKED BY BANDITS ABOUT
10 MILES EAST OF ILIANG RPT ILIANG. THIS WAS NEW GROUP OF INSTRUCTORS
TO 9TH GROUP ARMY. DURING 20 MINUTE FIGHT 5 RPT FIVE OFFICERS WERE
WOUNDED, 1 SERIOUSLY, BANDITS LOST TWO CONFIRMED, SEVERAL PROBABLES
AND NUMBER OF NEAR MISSES. WM REPORTING MATTER COMPLETELY TO CHINESE
AND DEMANDING DRASTIC ACTION. (GISSIMO MIGHT BE INTERESTED IN UNITED
FRONT
FROST THIS REPRESENTS ON YUNNAN.) WOUNDED ARE COLONEL HUTCHINSON, MAJOR
PENN OYER, MAJOR WOODWARD, CAPT VON SCHAILM AND LIEUT ABBOTT.

19,389

SL

Agwar   For Gen. Marshall, eyes alone

820

During last few days we have been having a battle over my relief, which was demanded by CKS when Somervell saw him. Reasons given were that I am arrogant and a threat to the cordial relations between the U.S. and China. The unnamed persons behind this campaign had poisoned the mind of CKS to the point where the demand was categorical and apparently irrevocable. None of the crimes imputed to me had been brought to my notice. Last night I conferred with certain supporters and saw CKS. I simply stated my position, aims and motives and assured him of full co-operation, whereupon he reversed himself and accepted me on the same terms as before. The ground had been prepared for this, and I am told that my relations with him are now on a much more solid basis and that future attacks of this nature are far less likely. Somervell has full information on this matter, The game was won only in the last minute of play.

Stilwell

0939   18th

Sent TB 1030 GCT

10290

1074

1071

HQ. U. S. ARMY FORCES

CHUNGKING, CHINA,
21 October 1943.

RECEIVED

AGWAR *828*

FOR MARSHALLS EYES ALONE FOR THE PRESIDENT FROM STILWELL

COLON MADAME CHIANG KAI SHEK HAS REQUESTED THE FOLLOWING

MESSAGE BE DELIVERED TO THE PRESIDENT OF THE UNITED STATES PD

MESSAGE BEGINS COLON EYE WISH TO THANK YOU FOR YOUR KIND

TELEGRAM PD ADMIRAL MOUNTBATTEN CMA GENERAL SOMERVELL AND

GENERAL STILWELL HAVE HELD SEVERAL CONFERENCES WITH THE

GENERALISSIMO AND HIS STAFF PD EYE AM GLAD TO INFORM YOU THAT

SO FAR AS EYE KNOW EVERYTHING PORTENDS TO THE FULLEST

COOPERATION AND THAT THE GENERALISSIMO IS VERY FAVORABLY

IMPRESSED WITH BOTH ADMIRAL MOUNTBATTEN AND GENERAL SOMERVELL

PARA YOU WILL ALSO BE GLAD TO KNOW THAT YOUR HOPES OF WHAT

GENERAL STRATEMEYER CAN ACCOMPLISH SEEM TO BE TAKING PLACE PD

WITH WARM GREETINGS TO YOU AND MRS ROOSEVELT IN WHICH THE

GENERALISSIMO JOINS PD SGD MAYLING SOONG CHIANG PD MESSAGE

ENDS PD THERE IS NO MORE

OFFICIAL:

L. B. THOMPSON,
Major, A. G. D.
Asst. Adjutant General

RECEIVED IN CODE ROOM _____ DATE 10/21 0245

ACTUAL TIME OF DISPATCH AND METHOD TB 0320

10337   (1101)

1072

RECEIVED IN ~~SECRET~~

INCOMING RADIO

RECEIVED   :   23 OCTOBER 1435 GCT

FROM   :   AMMKUN

TO   :   AMMISCA AMMDEL D814

NR.   :   C 803   FILED 23 OCTOBER 0821 GCT

LOCAL CHINESE ARE GETTING CONCERNED ABOUT BANDIT INCIDENT
(FOR GENERAL STILWELL AND HEARN FROM DORN) EYE WILL LET THEM STAY
CONCERNED AND AM INFORMING THEM ALL IT IS OUT OFMY HANDS AS US
GOVERNMENT IS TAKING ACTION OFFICIALLY.

c/s W.S.D.
Gen Hearn Hazards

JJG   19,877

RECEIVED IN ~~SECRET CODE~~

INCOMING RADIO

RECEIVED: 23 OCTOBER 1620 GCT

FROM   : 6QGUK

TO   : AMMISCA   AQUILA

NO   : M 70 E   A 145 OE   FILED: 23 OCT 1148 GCT

    TO WAR DEPARTMENT QUERY THIS IN REGARD, ON USE OF CHENGTU FOR LONG RANGE BOMBERS THE FOLLOWING ANSWERE ARE SUBMITTED. FOR STRATMEYER INFO STILWELL SIGNED CHENNAULT. 1: CHENGTU AREA CAN BE DEFENDED WITH THE MODERNIZED CHINESE FIGHTER UNITS PLUS ONE ADDITIONAL MODERN US FIGHTER GROUPS WHICH IS ADEQUATE BUT THIS DOES NOT MEAN P-40 SERIES. 2: 5 FIELDS WITH SIX TO EIGHT THOUSAND FOOT RUNWAYS CAN BE CONSTRUCTED IN CHENGTU AREA (1 SUITABLE FIELD NOW EXISTS LESS QUARTER), IF CHINESE GOVERNMENT GIVES COMPLETE COOPERATION, AND MEETS NO FINANCIAL DIFFICULTIES, 4 ADDITIONAL CAN BE COMPLETED IN SIX MONTHS FROM XXX TIME CONSTRUCTION IS STARTED. 3: NECESSARY QUARTERS CAN BE CONSTRUCTED FOR DESIRED NUMBER PERSONNEL. 4: SURFACE TRANSPORTATION IS NOT AVAILABLE FOR TRANSPORT OF NINE THOUSAND TONS OF EQUIPMENT BETWEEN KUMMING AND CHENGTU, AND CONDITIONS OF ROAD IS SUCH THAT IF TRUCKS WERE AVAILABLE THE TRIP WOULD REQUIRE A MINIMUM OF THREE WEEKS ONE WAY. UNABLE TO OBTAIN AMOUNT OF CHINESE ANTI DASH AIRCRAFT AND HAVE REQUESTED AMMISCA TO FURNISH THAT INFORMATION. XXX THREE FIVE SIX TONS (ONE) WOULD BE REQUIRED PER MONTH TO MAINTAIN TWO FIGHTER GROUPS FOR NORMAL OPERATIONS IN THE CHENGTU AREA. IT WILL BE NECESSARY TO FLY ALL EQUIPMENT FROM INDIA TO CHENGTU FOR OPERATIONS OF LR BOMBERS. 14TH AIRFORCE WITH PROPOSED STRENGTH AS OF EARLY 1944 TO CONTINUE WITH PRESENT ASSIGNED MISSION

19705

INCOMING RADIO

RECEIVED: 24 OCTOBER 0334 GCT

FROM : AGWAR   PRIORITY

TO   : ANMISCA AMMDEL

NO   : 3669   3803   FILED: 23 OCT. 1030 GCT

TEXT QUOTED IN YOUR 830 FROM CHUNGKING 20 OCTOBER IS
ACCEPTABLE TO US RPT US CHIEFS OF STAFF. (STILWELL EYES
ALONE FOR SOMERVELL FROM MARSHALL END) FOR YOUR INFORMATION,
QUADRANT DECISION (CORRIGENDUM TO CCS 308/3 DATED 6 SEPTEMBER
END) EXCLUDED INDO CHINA FROM SOUTHEAST ASIA THEATER BUT
INCLUDED THAILAND. GENERALISSIMOS BELIEF THAT INDO CHINA WAS
INCLUDED UNDER MOUNTBATTENS COMMAND AND HIS CONSEQUENT ACCEPTANCE
OF THE DELINEATION OF A BOUNDARY IN INDO CHINA AS WELL AS IN
THAILAND BETWEEN THE TWO THEATERS TO US IS QUITE SATISFACTORY

REGRADED
ORDER SEC ARMY
BY TAG PER
7230 P

REGRADED CONFIDENTIAL
ORDER SEC ARMY BY TAG/TW-350

1103

19710

1075

INCOMING RADIO

RECEIVED: 24 OCTOBER 1440 GCT

FROM   : AMMKUN

TO   : AMMISCA, AMMDEL D835,

NR   : C817   TIME FILED: 24 OCTOBER 0623 GCT

        GOVERNOR LUNG IS VERY CONCERNED AND DEEPLY REGRETS
BANDIT ATTACK PRN FOR GENERAL STILWELL FROM DORN PRN BUT HAS DONE
NOTHING CONCRETE SO FAR PRD HE HAS SUSPENDED TWO MAGISTRATES BUT
PLACED SAME TWO IN CHARGE OF HIS INVESTIGATION PRD CHUNGKING EM-
BASSY HAS TAKEN LUKEWARM ATTITUDE AND IS TRYING TO BURY ENTIRE
MATTER WITHOUT ACTION ACCORDING TO KUNMING CONSUL PRD WAR MINISTRY
AND OTHER CHINESE CONCERNED ARE WORRIED AS TO WHAT WE MAY DO CMA
WHICH INFORMALLY EYE HAVE TOLD GO BETWEENS WILL PROBABLY BE PLENTY
IF APPROPRIATE ACTION IS NOT TAKEN PRD CAN OUR EMBASSY BE PUSHED
INTO ACTION PRD ENTIRE ATTITUDE OF CHINESE INDICATES THEY FEEL
THEY MUST MAKE AMENDS CMA BUT WILL DO NOTHING UNLESS WE PUSH THIS
AFFAIR

Eyes Alone

C/S *Gen Hearn*

Col Drysdale has seen
Suspend for C/S upon
his return

CONFIDENTIAL PARAPHRASE, 737
VERSIONS REGRADED UNCLASSIFIED
ORDER SEC. ARMY BY TAG/2W-250

(1113)

RECEIVED IN ~~SECRET CODE~~

INCOMING RADIO

RECEIVED   : 25 OCTOBER 1414 GCT

FROM   : AMMDEL

TO   : AMMISCA

NR.   : AM 1886   FILED 25 OCTOBER 1132 GCT

            REFERENCE REVERSE LEND-LEASE (FOR HEARNS
EYES ALONE FROM STILWELL) WE MUST WAIT FOR DECISION AT
WASHINGTON ON PROPOSALS INITIATED BY PLAY PRD GIST OF THIS
IS THAT CHINESE PUT UP FOUR DOLLARS AND WE PUT UP ONE PRD
CLAY PROMISED TO NOTIFY US PROMPTLY PRD NEW SUBJECT PRD
WILL TELL NIXON TO DO SOMETHING FOR ARMS CMA BUT I ALSO
EXPECT ARMS TO DO SOMETHING FOR HIMSELF PRD NEW SUBJECT
PRD YOU ARE TO LEAVE FOR KUNMING ON FIRST AVAILABLE PLANE
AND SPEND TWO WEEKS THERE PRD I WILL BE THERE IN FEW DAYS
TO CHECK UP.

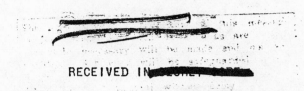

RECEIVED IN ~~SECRET~~

INCOMING RADIO

RECEIVED: 25 OCTOBER 1520 GCT

FROM   : AMMKUN

TO   : AMMISCA

NR   : C821   TIME FILED: 25 OCTOBER 0903 GCT

    EYE REQUEST BANDIT AND SHOOTING INCIDENT BE BROUGHT TO
ATTENTION PERSONNALLY OF TARE VICTOR SOONG PAREN FOR HEARN FROM
DORN PRN GOVERNOR HAS DONE NOTHING CONCRETE SO FAR AND TWO ADDI-
TIONAL BANDIT AFFAIRS HAVE OCCURRED NEAR CHENGKUNG AFTER REPEAT
AFTER THE IMPORTANT ONE PRD NO ONE WAS HURT IN THE LATER SCRAPES
PRD SOONG CAN BRING PRESSURE ON LUNG YUN BETTER THAN MOST

LF _____ 19,784

The Ambassador has already taken this incident up with T. V. Soong, who has informed the Ambassador that he has informed the Generalissimo about the affair. The Ambassador has demanded appropriate action and believe this procedure will strengthen the hand of the Central Government vs the Provincial Government. I believe this procedure will get better results than making local demands on Lung Yun.

W.S.D.
4.1.

Oct 26 1943 EYES H: ONE   SPECIAL CODE
AGuar - 840..   PRIORITY

Following message for Mrs Roosevelt

from Madame Chiang-Kai-Shell.
(For Ulio from Hearn).
Message begins: The Generalissimo
and I are distressed to learn from
the papers of the President's
indisposition. Will you kindly convey
to him our sincerest wishes for
his speedy recovery. Signed
Mayling Soong Chiang. Message
ends.

RECEIVED : 260745
SENT : 260330.

106627.

(1119)

Civil Affairs Officers with Yunnan Force

At the recent meeting held with the Generalissimo he raised the question of how the civil affairs of the Burma territory reconquered by the Yunnan Force was to be carried out. I accepted the responsibility for arranging this and said I would send Air Marshal Joubert out to Chungking when he arrived.

It is essential that this question should be examined at once and that proposals should be got ready for me to approve before Air Marshal Joubert arrives on about the 10th November.

Certain principles seem clear (a) that the Civil Affairs Officers must be British Military Officers with a specialised knowledge of the task; (b) that they should be provided with their own portable wireless sets and crews to enable them to maintain communication between each other and S.E.A.C; (c) that the question of enforcing order by means of Chinese troops requires investigation; (d) the degree of control to be exercised by the Chinese Military Commanders on the spot will require defining.

I should like this to be taken in the presence of General Stilwell to obtain his views before he leaves New Delhi.

Supreme Commander
27th October, 1943.

[254]

RECEIVED IN ~~SECRET CODE~~

INCOMING RADIO

RECEIVED   :   27 OCT 2320 GCT

FROM   :   WAR

TO   :   AMMISCA, AMMDEL 3888

NR   :   3697   FILED : 27 OCT 2208 GCT

URGENT

STUDIES AND REPORTS CONCERNING DEVELOPMENTS SINCE QUADRANT ARE
BEING PREPARED FOR CONSIDERATION AT THE NEXT UNITED STATES DASH BRITISH
STAFF CONFERENCE. TO ASSIST WITH THIS PREPARATION THE JOINT CHIEFS OF
STAFF HAVE DIRECTED (FOR STILWELL FROM MARSHALL) THAT YOU SUBMIT A
SUMMARY OF THE PRESENT SITUATION IN CHINA AND A REPORT ON PLANS FOR
FUTURE OPERATIONS. AS SOON AS POSSIBLE AND NOT RPT NOT LATER THAN
NOVEMBER SIXTH THIS SUMMARY AND REPORT ARE REQUIRED

Eyes alone

C/S H

G-3 *Has Seen*

Headline in WHSH
6 Nov
F/c 4 Nov

JRH

19,873

1120   28 Oct

RECEIVED ~~IN SECRET CODE~~

INCOMING RADIO:

RECEIVED: 28 OCTOBER 0745 Z.

FROM   : WASHINGTON.

TO   : ALMISCA   (FOR THE EYES OF GENERAL STILWELL ONLY)

NR   : 3701   FILED: 28 OCTOBER 0119 Z.

PRIORITY

PERSONAL AND SECRET TO THE GENERALISSIMO FROM THE PRESIDENT. I HAVE BEEN VERY PLEASED TO HEAR FROM YOU OF YOUR SATISFACTION WITH YOUR MEETING WITH MOUNTBATTEN AND SOMERVELL. THE CONFERENCE AT MOSCOW HAS MADE SPLENDID PROGRESS UP TO THE MOMENT AND I AM VERY HOPEFUL THAT THE RESULTS WILL BE BENEFITING ALL AROUND. I AM PRESSING FOR THE FULL BLOWN PARTNERSHIP OF CHINA GREAT BRITAIN RUSSIA AND THE UNITED STATES. I AM NOT YET SURE WHETHER STALIN CAN MEET ME BUT UNDER ANY CIRCUMSTANCES I AM ANXIOUS TO MEET YOU WITH CHURCHILL AT A REASONABLY EARLY DATE SOMEWHERE BETWEEN THE TWENTIETH AND THE TWENTY FIFTH OF NOVEMBER. I THINK ALEXANDRIA WOULD BE A GOOD MEETING PLACE . THERE ARE GOOD ACCOMODATIONS THERE. I WILL BRING A SMALL STAFF WITH ME INCLUDING OUR HIGHEST RANKING ARMY NAVY AND AIR OFFICERS. I SHOULD THINK THE CONFERENCE WOULD LAST ABOUT THREE DAYS. I KNOW YOU WILL NOT WANT TO BE AWAY FROM CHINA LONG BUT IT IS FAR BETTER FOR ME TO GET AWAY NOW THAN LATER. I AM LOOKING FORWARD TO SEEING YOU BECAUSE I AM SURE THERE ARE MANY THINGS THAT CAN ONLY BE SATISFACTORILY SETTLED IF WE CAN MEET FACE TO FACE . PLEASE KEEP THIS VERY CONFIDENTIAL.

Seen by:
General Hearn
Lt Col Cahill
Maj. Thompson
Lt. McCall

Capt King

No. 63

CHUNGKING, CHINA,
28 October 1943.

MEMORANDUM:

TO   : His Excellency, The Generalissimo.

The following message has been received from President Roosevelt for transmission to your Excellency:

"PERSONAL AND SECRET TO THE GENERALISSIMO FROM THE PRESIDENT.

I HAVE BEEN VERY PLEASED TO HEAR FROM YOU OF YOUR SATISFACTION WITH YOUR MEETING WITH MOUNTBATTEN AND SOMERVELL. THE CONFERENCE AT MOSCOW HAS MADE SPLENDID PROGRESS UP TO THE MOMENT AND I AM VERY HOPEFUL THAT THE RESULTS WILL BE BENEFITING ALL AROUND. I AM PRESSING FOR THE FULL BLOWN PARTNERSHIP OF CHINA GREAT BRITAIN RUSSIA AND THE UNITED STATES. I AM NOT YET SURE WHETHER STALIN CAN MEET ME BUT UNDER ANY CIRCUMSTANCES I AM ANXIOUS TO MEET YOU WITH CHURCHILL AT A REASONABLY EARLY DATE SOMEWHERE BETWEEN THE TWENTIETH AND THE TWENTY FIFTH OF NOVEMBER. I THINK ALEXANDRIA WOULD BE A GOOD MEETING PLACE. THERE ARE GOOD ACCOMODATIONS THERE. I WILL BRING A SMALL STAFF WITH ME INCLUDING OUR HIGHEST RANKING ARMY NAVY AND AIR OFFICERS. I SHOULD THINK THE CONFERENCE WOULD LAST ABOUT THREE DAYS. I KNOW YOU WILL NOT WANT TO BE AWAY FROM CHINA LONG BUT IT IS FAR BETTER FOR ME TO GET AWAY NOW THAN LATER. I AM LOOKING FORWARD TO SEEING YOU BECAUSE I AM SURE THERE ARE MANY THINGS THAT CAN ONLY BE SATISFACTORILY SETTLED IF WE CAN MEET FACE TO FACE. PLEASE KEEP THIS VERY CONFIDENTIAL."

For and in the absence of Lt. General STILWELL:

T. G. HEARN

Major General, GSC

RECEIVED IN ~~SECRET~~

INCOMING RADIO

RECEIVED   : 28 OCTOBER 0855 GCT   PRIORITY

FROM   : WAR

TO   : AMMISCA

NR.   : 3702   FILED 28 OCTOBER 0119 GCT

FROM THE PRESIDENT TO THE GENERALISSIMO PERSONAL
                       YOU CAN
AND SECRET. I GREATLY HOPE XEGOGTN AUTHORIZE YOUR AMBASSADOR

TO SIGN THE MOSCOW PACT IT IS AT THE LEAST AN EXCELLENT START.

GCV   19,911

~~SECRET~~

1085

No. 64   CHUNGKING, CHINA,
                                               29 October 1943.

MEMORANDUM:

TO   : His Excellency, the Generalissimo.

        The following message has been received from President
Roosevelt for transmission to your Excellency:

            "FROM THE PRESIDENT TO THE GENERALISSIMO PERSONAL
                            YOU CAN
AND SECRET. I GREATLY HOPE XEGOCTM* AUTHORIZE YOUR

AMBASSADOR TO SIGN THE MOSCOW PACT IT IS AT LEAST AN

EXCELLENT START."

            * Received garbled.

        For and in the absence of Lt. General STILWELL:

                                    T. G. HEARN
                                    Major General, GSC.
                                    Chief of Staff

SOUTH EAST ASIA COMMAND HEADQUARTERS,
NEW DELHI,
INDIA.

29th October, 1943.

Since writing my letter of the 25th October I have
received your Excellency's very charming telegram for which I wish
to offer my heartfelt thanks.   I am so glad that you too have the
feeling that my visit was the beginning of a personal friendship.

I have been discussing with General Stilwell how we can
best ensure that the arrangements which have been made direct
between Your Excellency and Prime Minister Churchill about General
Carton de Wiart can best be given effect to.

To begin with I understand that you have accepted
General Carton de Wiart as the personal representative of our
Prime Minister with you.   In addition you will remember that the
Prime Minister said that General de Wiart would be a member of my
staff.

In the former capacity he would ~~he would~~ presumably have
direct access to yourself, but in the latter capacity I feel that it
is essential that he should be subordinate to General Stilwell who
is the Deputy Supreme Commander in the South East Asia Command.
General Stilwell has kindly offered office accommodation at his
Headquarters to General de Wiart and his staff officer Colonel
Dobson.

When General Stilwell is present he will see Your
Excellency personally on any matters connected with the South East
Asia Command, but in his absence he will depute General de Wiart
to see you in any matters that concern this command.   I understand
that it is quite impossible to obtain any living accommodation in
Chungking, on account of the great housing shortage, unless Your
Excellency gives the necessary orders yourself, and I am therefore
hoping that you will be kind enough to place a small house at the
disposal of General de Wiart and Colonel Dobson.

I am giving this letter to General Stilwell to deliver
in order that he may be able to discuss in person the arrangements
proposed in this letter.

We are now all hard at work on plans for the coming
campaign and General Stilwell will be able to tell you that I have
left no stone unturned to increase the Assam Lines of Communication
to a point at which they will carry enough for the campaign and for
the supply into China.   This has proved a very difficult matter,
and the solution is not yet certain.   General Stilwell will be able

(253)

Mr. Gauss.

(over)

1087

to explain some of the difficulties we are really encountering.

Please convey my kindest regards to Madame Ch'iang Kai Shek, I should like to assure you both I have the happiest memories of Huang Shan.

RECEIVED ~~IN SECRET CODE~~

INCOMING RADIO

RECEIVED : 30. OCT 0155 GCT

FROM : WAR

TO : AMMISCA

NR : 3720   FILED: 29 OCT 2120 GCT

MANY THANKS FOR KIND WIRE. (FROM MRS ROOSEVELT TO MADAME CHIANG KAI SHEK, PERSONAL AND SECRET) PRESIDENT GREATLY IMPROVED

Eyes alone

C/S Hasleen

β 30 oct

TA   ~~10,931~~
            20,000

                                    1/32   DECLASSIFIED
                                    DOD Dir. 5200.9, Sept. 27, 1958
                                    NYCWN by   date 3-21-72

No. 65

CHUNGKING, CHINA,
30 October 1943.

MEMORANDUM:

TO   : Her Excellency, Madame Chiang Kai Shek.

The following is a message from Mrs. Roosevelt to Her Excellency:

"PERSONAL FROM MRS ROOSEVELT TO MADAME CHIANG KAI SHEK. PRESIDENT GREATLY IMPROVED. MANY THANKS FOR KIND WIRE. MESSAGE ENDS."

For and in the absence of Lieutenant General STILWELL:

T. G. HEARN,
Major General, G.S.C.
Chief of Staff.

- 1 -

HEADQUARTERS   RPW/bc
U. S. ARMY FORCES IN C. B. I.

31 October 1943
Chungking, China

ALMDEL   - AD 2451.

BIOLOGIC AND GAS WARFARE POSSIBILITIES PAREN EYES ONLY

FERRIS FROM HEARN REFERENCE AGWARS TWO THREE TWO EIGHT MARCH

TWO ZERO REPEATED TO YOU ON TWENTY TWO MARCH PAREN FOR YOUR

INFORMATION COLN CHINESE REPORT OCTOBER FOUR THAT EACH FAMILY

IN TENGCHUNG CMA CHINESE DASH BURMA BORDER CMA REQUESTED BY

JAPS TO FURNISH THREE LIVE MICE PD GEORGE TWO CHINESE REPORTS

OCTOBER TWENTY SECOND. JAPS PUT IN TWO GAS FACTORIES SOUTH OF

ROGER ROGER STATION HANKU NEAR TIENTSIN CMA THIS IN AREA OF

SALT PRODUCTION CMA MAY BE ~~INTRUDING~~ *INTENDING* TO MAKE CHLORINE STOP

BURMA FRONTIER MEDICOS ALERTED AGAINST PLAGUE CMA WE TAKE NO

OTHER ACTION EXCEPT CONTINUING SURVEILLANCE PD JACOBS CMA

SIMMONS AND MARQUAND HAVE BEEN NOTIFIED

Th. Surg........

G-2...........

OFFICIAL

L. B. THOMPSON,
MAJOR, A. G. D.
ASST. ADJUTANT GENERAL

REGRADED CONFIDENTIAL. PARAPHRASED
VERSIONS REGRADED UNCLASSIFIED
ORDER SEC ARMY BY TAG

DECLASSIFIED
DOD Dir. 5260.9, Sept. 27, 1958
NCWN by ___ date 3-27-72

REC'D IN CODE ROOM.............DATE. 310440.

ACTUAL TIME OF DISPATCH AND METHOD..... 310700.   10545

1091

RPW/bc

31 October 1943
Chungking, China

AGWAR — 8 41.

INDICATIONS OF POSSIBLE BIOLOGIC WARFARE PAREN EYES ONLY

JACOBS FROM STILWELL REURAD TWO THREE TWO EIGHT MARCH TWENTY

CMA REQUEST REPEAT TO SIMMONS AND MARQUAND OF SURGEON GENERALS OFFICE

PAREN ON FOUR OCTOBER CHINESE REPORT THAT JAPS REQUESTED EACH

FAMILY IN TENGCHUNG CMA BURMA DASH YUNNAN BORDER CMA FURNISH

THREE LIVING MICE RPT MIKE ITEM CHARLIE EASY STOP SURGEONS

ALERTED FOR PLAGUE CMA OTHERWISE WE TAKE NO ACTION BUT CONTINUE

OBSERVATION

Th. Surg........
G-2........
C/S........

OFFICIAL

L. B. THOMPSON,
MAJOR, A. G. D.
ASST. ADJUTANT GENERAL

REC'D IN CODE ROOM.............................DATE. 3.10.41

ACTUAL TIME OF DISPATCH AND METHOD........ 3.18.7.0.0.

(1138)

10546

1092

31 October 1943
Chungking, China

AGWAR — *842.*

POSSIBLE PREPARATIONS FOR GAS WARFARE PAREN EYES ONLY OF
JACOBS REURAD TWO THREE TWENTY EIGHT OF MARCH TWO ZERO FROM
STILWELL CMA PLEASE REPEAT TO MARQUAND AND SIMMONS OFFICE OF
SURGEON GENERAL PAREN TWENTY TWO OCTOBER CHINESE GEORGE DASH
TWO REPORTS JAPS ESTABLISH TWO GAS FACTORIES SOUTH OF HANKU
RAILROAD STATION NEAR TIENTSIN STOP THIS IS SALT PRODUCING
AREA CMA FACTORIES COULD MAKE CHLORINE STOP WE WILL TAKE NO
ACTION BUT CONTINUE OBSERVING

Th. Surg........

G-2........

C/S........

OFFICIAL

L. B. THOMPSON,
MAJOR, A. G. D.
ASST. ADJUTANT GENERAL

REC'D IN CODE ROOM............DATE....31044Z.

ACTUAL TIME OF DISPATCH AND METHOD.....31.0.700.

(136)

10547

<u>INCOMING RADIO</u>

RECEIVED   : 31 OCTOBER 0720 GCT

FROM   : WAR   **PRIORITY**

TO   : AMMISCA

NR.   : 3734   FILED 31 OCTOBER 0458 GCT

        EYE HAVE NOT RPT NOT HEARD DEFINITELY FROM
MARSHAL STALIN BUT THERE IS STILL A CHANCE OF CHURCHILL AND
ME MEETING HIM NEAR PERSIAN GULF PD VERY CONFIDENTIALLY CMA
I HOPE YOU WILL MAKE ARRANGEMENTS TO MEET WITH CHURCHILL AND
ME IN GENERAL NEIGHBORHOOD OF CAIRO ABOUT NOVEMBER TWENTY
SIXTH PD FROM THE PRESIDENT TO GENERALISSIMO CHIANG KAI DASH
SHEK PD ROOSEVELT PD I AM DELIGHTED THAT SUCH EXCELLENT
PROGRESS IS MADE FOR FOUR POWER PROPOSAL PD WE HAVE CRACKED
THE ICE CMA AND I THINK THAT YOU AND I HAVE SUCESSFULLY
ESTABLISHED THE PRINCIPLE PD BEST REGARDS.

Seen by:
General Hearn
Lt Col Cahill
Maj. Thompson
Kelly
Nietsch
GCV   20,067

1094

No. 67

CHUNGKING, CHINA,
1 November 1943.

MEMORANDUM:

TO   : His Excellency, The Generalissimo.

The following message has been received from President
Roosevelt for transmission to your Excellency:

"EYE HAVE NOT RPT NOT HEARD DEFINITELY FROM MARSHAL
STALIN BUT THERE IS STILL A CHANCE OF CHURCHILL AND ME
MEETING HIM NEAR PERSIAN GULF PD VERY CONFIDENTIALLY CMA
I HOPE YOU WILL MAKE ARRANGEMENTS TO MEET WITH CHURCHILL
AND ME IN GENERAL NEIGHBORHOOD OF CAIRO ABOUT NOVEMBER TWENTY
SIXTH PD FROM THE PRESIDENT TO GENERALISSIMO CHIANG KAI DASH
SHEK PD ROOSEVELT PD I AM DELIGHTED THAT SUCH EXCELLENT PROGRESS
IS MADE FOR FOUR POWER PROPOSAL PD WE HAVE CRACKED THE ICE CMA
AND I THINK THAT YOU AND I HAVE SUCCESSFULLY ESTABLISHED THE
PRINCIPLE PD BEST REGARDS."

For and in the absence of Lt. General STILWELL:

                              T.G. HEARN
                         Major General, GSC.
                            Chief of Staff

No. 69   CHUNGKING, CHINA,
                                              2 November 1943.

MEMORANDUM:

    TO   : His Excellency, The Generalissimo.

        Admiral Mountbatten has advised that a Carton De
    Wiart, Colonel Dobson, Major Gale and Sergeant Brown
    are in Delhi awaiting the availability of housing
    accomodations in Chungking before proceeding onward.
    Since the first mentioned individual is carrying a
    letter from the Prime Minister to the Generalissimo,
    Admiral Mountbatten is anxious for this party of four
    to proceed at the earliest practicable date. It is
    requested that when the necessary housing arrangements
    have been decided upon, this Headquarters be notified
    in order that forward movement of the personnel concerned
    may be effected.

        For and in the absence of Lieutenant General
    STILWELL:

                                    T. G. HEARN,
                                 Major General, G.S.C.
                                    Chief of Staff.

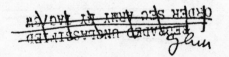

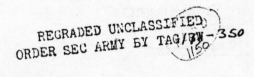

TO: RELOT (EYES OF GENERAL STILWELL ALONE)

FROM: AMMDEL

WRITERS NR: RE-175/31ST/0915 (LOCAL)

PRIORITY

LITERAL

EYES ALONE GENERAL STILWELL PRD AT CONFERENCE THIS MORNING SUBJECT
OF OPERATIONAL COMMAND OF CHINESE FORCES WAS DISCUSSED PRD LOUIS
STATED PEANUT AGREED TO HIS COMMANDING ALL CHINESE TROOPS ENGAGED
IN BURMA FUNCTION ASSISTED BY YOU PRD THEREFORE HIS REACTION TO
COMMAND PROBLEM IS TO PLACE BOATNER UNDER EITHER GIFFARD OR SLIM
PRD IN FORMER CASE BOATNER WOULD RECEIVE DIRECT INSTRUCTION
FROM GROUND FORCE COMMANDER PRD IN LATTER CASE HE WOULD BE EQUIVALENT
TO A RPT ABLE CORPS COMMANDER OF FOURTEENTH ARMY AND TAKE ORDERS FROM
SLIM PRD CONCERNING YOURSELF LOUIS STATED THAT WHILE HE KNEW YOU
WOULD HELP HIM OUT ON BOTH SIDES WITH THE CHINESE PROBLEM HE WOULD
APPRECIATE YOUR TAKING PERSONAL CHARGE OF THE YUNNAN SITUATION PRD
ASKED THAT ABOVE BE SENT YOU FOR REMARKS PAREN (FROM MERRIL SIGNED
FERRIS) PAREN STILL OBSCURE ARE MAJOR DECISIONS AS MUCH DEPENDS ON
LONDON PRD TWO DEFINITE DECISIONS ONLY HAVE BEEN REACHED PRD ARAKAN
GROUND SHOW DEFINITELY ON FOR FIRST WEEK JANUARY PRD GIFFARD WANTED
RPT WANTED THIS TO BE A RPT ABLE LIMITED AFFAIR BUT LOUIS WANTS THE
PLANS TO INCLUDE AKYAB RPT AKYAB PRD AMPHIBIOUS PARTY DEFINITELY ON
FOR FIRST WEEK FEBRUARY BUT LOCATION OF PARTY NOT RPT NOT YET SETTLED
PRD ALL OUTFITS LIKE GALAHAD WILL BE IN FIELD FIRST WEEK FEBRUARY AND
ALTHOUGH NO RPT NO DECISIONS REACHED THERE IS GENERAL AGREEMENT
THAT YOUR PROPOSALS FOR JUNGLE OUTFIT ARE SOUND AND FIT INTO OVERALL
(GUNS/PLAN)
PLAN PRD BOATNERS GLNU* WILL PROBABLY HAVE TO BE AT NEXT PHASE LINE
BY FIFTEEN FEBRUARY CMA FOURTH CORPS WIQL BE HEAVILY ENGAGED ABOUT █

(113)

SAME TIME PRO TO GIVE YUNNAN FORCE MAXIMUM CHANCE LOUIS THINKS IT

SHOULD NOT RPT NOT JUMP UNTIL JAPS THOROUGHLY ENGAGED ON ALL

OTHER FRONTS PRO THEREFORE AS A RPT ABLE GENERAL BASIS FOR

PLANNING HE SUGGESTS JUMP OFF ACROSS RIVER FOR YOKE BE TENTATIVELY

SET BETWEEN FEBRUARY FIFTEEN AND TWENTY EIGHT PRO PRIOR TO THAT

PERIOD HE THINKS HE WILL BE ENGAGING AS MANY JAPS AS POSSIBLE AND GIVE

YOKE MAXIMUM CLEAR FIELD PRO LOUIS WANTS MANDALAY BUT HAVING

DIFFICULTIES WITH LONDON THIS POINT

*AS DECODED

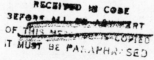

(1193)

TO: RELOT (EYES OF GENERAL STILWELL ALONE)

FROM: AQUILA

WRITERS NR: 0-497-F/31ST/1031(LOCAL)

Z Z Z Z

LITERAL

FOR THE EYES OF GENERAL STILWELL ALONE COLON A CONFERENCE WAS HELD
TWO NINE OCTOBER AT CHABUA BY GENERAL OLD GENERAL DAVIDSON
COLONEL HARPING OF ABLE TARE CHARLIE AND A REPRESENTATIVE OF MY
OFFICE AT WHICH A PLAN WAS PREPARED AND SUBMITTED TO ME PAREN
STILWELL FROM STRATEMEYER) PAREN I RPT ITEM HAVE APPROVED THEIR
PLAN HOWEVER THEY POINT OUT THAT TO ENABLE THEM TO EFFECTIVELY
GUARD OUR TRANSPORTS ON OVER THE HUMP RUN IT IS ESSENTIAL THAT
OUR AIR WARNING NET BE EXTENDED SOUTH FROM SUMPRABUM FRD THE NET
CANNOT BE EFFECTIVE UNLESS IT IS ESTABLISHED IN TERRITORY HELD
BY OUR FORCES WHICH WOULD NECESSITATE A MOVEMENT SOUTH FROM FORT
HERTZ PRD GENERAL BOATNER IS ANXIOUS TO EXECUTE QUOTE STRIPTEASE
UNQUOTE PLAN AND WOULD BE ABLE TO PLACE IT IN OPERATION WITHOUT
DELAY PRD HE IS ALSO ANXIOUS TO PLACE THIS FORCE IN POSITION FOR
PROTECTION OF HIS LEFT FLANK PRD AIRCRAFT ARE AVAILABLE FOR INITIAL
MOVEMENT OF TROOPS REFERRED TO ABOVE AND WE ARE PREPARED TO SUPPLY
THEM PRD IN ORDER TO ENABLE THE ONE ZERO AIR FORCE TO CARRY OUT
ITS PRIMARY MISSION OF PROTECTION OF THE ABLE TARE CHARLIE HUMP
ROUTE I RPT ITEM URGENTLY RECOMMEND THAT POSITIVE ACTION BE
TAKEN TO SECURE FORWARD AREA FOR THE ESTABLISHMENT OF DEPENDABLE
AIR WARNING NET

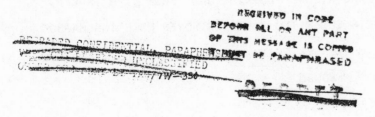

NOV 1   43 PM

DECLASSIFIED
DOD Dir. 5200.9, Sept. 27, 1958
NCWN by _____ date _____

INCOMING RADIO

RECEIVED: 01 NOV 0505 GCT

FROM   : DRONE

TO   : AMMISCA, COGUK D 643

NR   : D 643   FILED: 01 NOVEMBER 0020 GCT

Treat Eyes alone

PARTIAL COVERAGE DUE TO CLOUDS AT SASEKO.   MINIMUM
41750
TOTAL FOUR ONE SEVEN FIVE ZERO TONS MERCHANT SHIPPING, FIFTEEN NAVAL
(STILWELL FOR MILES AND BROWN INFO OLMAN FROM COHOB) INNER HARBOR
MINIMUM TOTAL THREE SEVEN ONE FIVE ZERO TONS MERCHANTS AND THIRTEEN
NAVAL, ONE - FIVE FIFTY FOOT MERCHANT, ONE - THREE SIXTY CARGO, ONE -
TWO NINETY CARGO, ONE - TWO FIFTY TANKER, ONE - THREE FORTY CARGO, ONE
- THREE FIFTY CARGO, ONE - ONE SEVEN FIVE CARGO, ONE PROBABLE ONE SIXTY
TANKER, ONE - ONE SIXTY MERCHANT, ONE PROBABLE ONE SIXTY CARGO, FOU
- ONE TWO IVE COLLIERS, FOUR - ONE FORTY VESSELS, ONE - ONE FIFTY VESSEL,
TWO - ONE TWENTY BY TWO FORTY BARGES WITH CRANES, NWH - TWO TEN SEAL
PROPELLING BARGES, MANY VESSELS LESS THAN ONE HUNDRED FEET, ONE - TWO
EIGHTY DESTROYER, ONE - TWO SEVENTY DESTROYER BEGINNING, ONE PROBABLE
THREE FORTY NAVAL, ONE PROBABLE TWO SIXTY DESTROYER, ONE - THREE HUNDRED
FOOT SUB, EIGHT PROBABLE ONE HUNDRED FOOT NAVAL.   SHIPPING SASEBO HARBOR
MINIMUM FOUR SIX HUNDRED TONS MERCHANTS AND TWO NAVAL, ONE DASH THREE
                                                      FIVE
THREE FIVE CARGO ENTERING HARBOR, ONE PROBABLE ONE THREE VIVE TANKER,
ONE - ONE SIXTY VESSEL, ONE - THREE TWO FIVE DESTROYER ENTERING HARBOR,
ONE PROBABLE ONE ZERO FIVE CUTTER ENTERING HARBOR.   NAVAL DOCKYARD

20096

(1144)

MOQUO COVERED. PARTIAL COVERAGE NAGASAKU DUE TO CLOUDS, MINIMUM TOTAL
ONE ONE TWO FIVE ZERO TONS MERCHANTS AND ONE NAVAL, ONE – FOUR TWO FIVE
MERCHANT, ONE – TWO TEN MERCHANT, ONE – ONE TWENTY MERCHANT, ONE POSSIBLE
THREE HUNDRED FOOT PROBABLE DAMAGED VESSEL, TWO – ONE HUNDRED FOOT
VESSELS, ONE CARRIER RYUJA RPT RYUJV

G2 8 _____

air off _____

G3 _____

3rd copy Burn DB

See 1143   1144

B

20095

1101

No. 71

CHUNGKING, CHINA,
2 November 1943.

MEMORANDUM:

TO   : Her Excellency, Madame Chiang Kai Shek

    Your letter of November 2nd and inclosure thereto
were received this afternoon. The message has been
dispatched in a special code to avoid paraphrasing.
All necessary measures are being taken to insure secrecy.

                    Sincerely,

                    T. G. HEARN,
                    Major General, G.S.C.
                    Chief of Staff.

- 1 -

From the Generalissimo to His Excellency President Roosevelt:

     I am in receipt of your telegrams transmitted to me
by General Hearn on October 28 and 29 and November 1.
I am delighted to accept the suggestions contained in your
last telegram and am looking forward to meeting you and
Mr. Churchill.   Everything will be kept strictly secret here.
The signing of the four nation declaration is a splendid
success which is entirely due to your firm stand for justice
and solidarity.   This declaration constitutes one of the
greatest contributions to the peace and security of the
post-war world.   Please accept my warm and sincere thanks
for your deep concern for our common cause and kindly
convey to Mr. Hull my appreciation of the excellent results
he has achieved at the Conference.   Best regards.

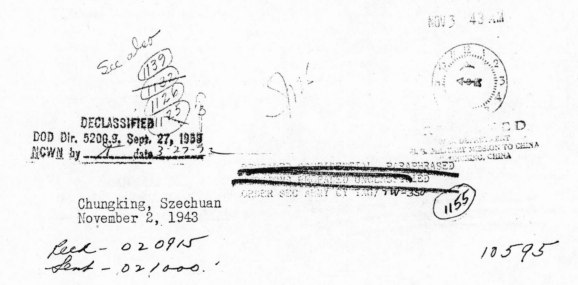

DECLASSIFIED
DOD Dir. 5200.9, Sept. 27, 1958
NCWN by _____ date 3-27-73

Chungking, Szechuan
November 2, 1943

Recd - 020915
Sent - 021000.

10595

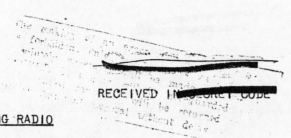

RECEIVED IN SECRET CODE

INCOMING RADIO

RECEIVED : 03 NOV 1945 GCT

FROM : AMMKUN

TO : AMMISCA

NR : C 890   FILED : 03 NOV 0955 GCT

   WITH REFERENCE TO WILLIAM DOG RADIO ON SCIENTIFIC WAR-
FARE FORWARDED BY YOU NOVEMBER FIRST PAREN DICKEY FROM CLEVELAND
SIGNED DORN PAREN IN WUG PERIODIC REPORT FOR PERIOD ENDING OCT-
OBER TWENTY SIX WAS DISCUSSED POSSIBLE USE OF RATS BY JAPS TO
SPREAD BUBONIC PLAGUE

Eyes Alone
DCB

G-2

State Surgeon

AGWAR 851
ABDEL A02481

CHUNGKING, CHINA,
4 NOVEMBER 1943.

THIS MESSAGE IS IN TWO PARTS COLON THE FIRST CMA SUMMARY OF SITUATION IN CHINA
(HEARN) EYES ALONE (SIGNED STILWELL)
AND THE SECOND CMA PLANS FOR FUTURE OPERATIONS PAREN STILWELL FOR MARSHALL REURAD THREE
EYES ALONE
SIX NINE SEVEN OCTOBER TWO SEVEN INFORMATION FERRIS REURAD ABLE MIKE ONE NINE ONE FIVE
OCTOBER TWO EIGHT PAREN PART ONE REPEAT PART ONE DASH ANNUAL ELECTION OF OFFICIALS HAS
TENDED TO STABALIZE PRESENT GOVERNMENT AND CONTINUE THE KUOMINGTANG AS DOMINANT
POLITICAL PARTY PD CHIANG KAI DASH SHEK AND THE PRINCIPAL OFFICIALS ELECTED ARE WELL
RECEIVED BY CHINESE AND ARE SATISFACTORY TO ALLIED NATIONS PD THERE IS NOW GENERAL
BELIEF IN THE ULTIMATE DEFEAT OF JAPAN PD GOVERNMENT OFFICIALS AND BUSINESS EXECUTIVES
EXPECT THAT CHINA WILL PROFIT POLITICALLY AND ECONOMICALLY AS RESULT OF THAT DEFEAT CMA
AND SUBSEQUENT COLLABORATIONS IN WHICH THEY WILL PARTICIPATE PD CENTRAL GOVERNMENT
AUTHORITIES ARE MORE WILLING TO MAKE CMA AND THE CHINESE PEOPLE WILL ACQUIESCE MORE
FREELY IN CMA CHINESE COMMITMENTS TO THE WAR EFFORT PD CARE MUST BE TAKEN AS IN THE
PAST TO DEFEAT NATURAL TENDENCY INHERENT IN CHINESE OFFICIALDOM TO RECEIVE THE UTMOST
OF PROFIT FROM MINIMUM OF COOPERATION AND SACRIFICE PD WE CAN EXPECT CONTINUED SUPPORT
OF OUR WAR EFFORT LIMITED ONLY BY CHINESE CAPABILITIES AND DESIRE TO AVOID NECESSARY
SACRIFICES PD HOWEVER SHOULD THE BURMA CAMPAIGN FAIL OR THE BURMA ROAD REMAIN CLOSED
CMA THERE WILL BE FEELING OF GREAT PART TWO DISAPPOINTMENT AND INCREASED DISCOURAGEMENT CMA
WITH LOWERING OF MORALE PD PARA LATEST ESTIMATES OF ECONOMIC SITUATION INDICATE SOME
IMPROVEMENT PD CROP PROSPECTS ARE GOOD AND PRICES ARE FAIRLY STABLE AT LEAST
TEMPORARILY ALTHOUGH CURRENCY CIRCULATION CONTINUES TO INCREASE ABOUT SEVEN PERCENT
PER MONTH PD OPTIMISM OVER UNITED NATIONS FINAL VICTORY IS BEGINNING TO HAVE
FAVORABLE EFFECT IN REDUCING HOARDING PARA JAPANESE FORCES AFFECTING CHINESE FORCES
COLON ABLE DASH BURMA DASH FOUR DIVISIONS CMA THAILAND DASH UNKNOWN CMA FRENCH
INDOCHINA DASH ONE DIVISION CMA SOUTH CHINA DASH ONE AND ONE THIRD DIVISIONS AND ONE
INDEPENDENT MIXED BRIGADE CMA CENTRAL CHINA DASH TWELVE DIVISIONS AND THREE
INDEPENDENT MIXED BRIGADES CMA NORTH CHINA DASH TEN DIVISIONS AND TEN INDEPENDENT
MIXED BRIGADES CMA KNOWN TOTAL COLON TWENTY EIGHT AND ONE THIRD DIVISIONS AND

(1173)

FOURTEENTH INDEPENDENT MIXED BRIGADES PD BAKER DASH THERE ARE NUMEROUS UNVERIFIED REPORTS OF REINFORCEMENTS IN BURMA CMA THAILAND CMA AND INDO CHINA PD CHINESE REPORT TOTAL OF ONE HUNDRED AND FIFTY THOUSAND TROOPS OF WHICH BURMA HAS ONE HUNDRED AND TWENTY THOUSAND PD CHARLIE DASH JAPANESE HAVE SEIZED AND ARE HOLDING LINE OF SALWEEN RIVER WITH FIFTY SIXTH DIVISION PLUS ONE HUNDRED AND FOURTEENTH REGIMENT OF EIGHTEENTH DIVISION PD DOG DASH NO INDICATION OF PROJECTED JAP ATTACK IN NORTH OR CENTRAL CHINA PD AN ATTACK FROM KWANGCHOWAN TOWARDS NANNING OR TO SEIZE

PART 2.

THE COASTAL ROAD TO FRENCH INDOCHINA REMAINS A CAPABILITY PD NO INDICATION OF AN ATTACK IN FORCE TOWARD KUNMING FROM FRENCH INDOCHINA CMA THAILAND CMA OR BURMA PD DIVERSIONARY ATTACKS TO DISRUPT ANY CHINESE PLANS FOR AN ATTACK CMA TO RECONNOITER IN FORCE CMA OR TO SEIZE NEWLY HARVESTED CROPS APPEAR TO BE THE OBJECT OF PRESENT JAPANESE ACTIVITIES PARA CHINESE FORCES COLON ABLE DASH MAJORITY OF LIST OF THREE HUNDRED AND TWENTY FOUR CHINESE DIVISIONS ARE GENERALLY DISPOSED IN CENTRAL CHINA TO COUNTER POSSIBLE ATTACK DIRECTED AGAINST CHUNGKING PD BAKER DASH YOKE FORCE NOW COMPRISING TWO FOUR DIVISIONS HAS ONE FIVE DIVISIONS ON THE YUNNAN DASH BURMA BORDER SMCLN SIX ON THE INDOCHINA BORDER SMCLN AND THREE IN THE VICINITY OF KUNMING PD PRESENT OPERATIONS IN WESTERN YUNNAN WILL DEPLETE CMA IF NOT ANNIHILATE CMA ONE DIVISION OF THIS FORCE CMA INTERRUPT TRAINING AND ADVERSELY AFFECT BUT NOT PREVENT PREPARATIONS FOR THE USE OF THIS FORCE AS A PART IN THE BURMA CAMPAIGN PD CHARLIE DASH CHINESE UNITS IN GENERAL ARE UNDERSTRENGTH SMCLN SICKNESS AND MALNUTRITION FURTHER REDUCE THEIR COMBAT EFFICIENCY PD ACCORDING TO THE STANDARDS OF MODERN WAR CMA EQUIPMENT IS INSUFFICIENT CMA OBSOLESCENT OR UNSERVICEABLE PD IN YOKE FORCE CMA REPORTS INDICATE THAT DIVISIONS HAVE BUT FIFTY PERCENT OF THE SMALL ARMS WEAPONS PRESCRIBED IN TABLES OF EQUIPMENT AND THAT OF THAT FIFTY PERCENT AN AVERAGE OF FIFTY PERCENT WILL NOT FIRE BECAUSE OF LACK OF PARTS PD THESE CONDITIONS IN OTHER THREE HUNDRED

1106

PART 4

DIVISIONS MUST BE WORSE PD THE EVILS OF MALNUTRITION ARE WIDE SPREAD

IF NOT APPALLING PD ONE EYE WITNESS ESTIMATE IS THAT ONLY TEN PERCENT

OF THE ENTIRE STRENGTH OF CHINESE ARMIES ARE REALLY PHYSICALLY CAPABLE

OF HARD CAMPAIGNING PD PHYSICAL EXAMINATION OF THOSE PRESENTED FOR

SHIPMENT OVER THE HUMP LEAD TO THE CONCLUSION THAT THE TRUTH LIES

SOME WHERE BETWEEN TEN PERCENT AND FIFTY PERCENT AND PROBABLY NEARER

TO TEN THAN FIFTY PERCENT PD DOG DASH STEADY IMPROVEMENT IN THE

ATTITUDE TOWARD AMERICAN METHODS OF TRAINING IS SHOWN BY THE HIGHER

AUTHORITIES IN THEIR READINESS TO ACCEPT THE ESTABLISHMENT OF NEW

TRAINING CENTERS AND AMERICAN SUPERVISED TRAINING WITHIN CHINESE

UNITS PD TRAINING PLANS FOR THE SECOND THIRTY DIVISIONS HAVE BEEN

ACCEPTED PD DEFINITE IMPROVEMENT IS BEING SHOWN IN THE COMBAT

EFFICIENCY OF UNITS WHICH HAVE RECEIVED AMERICAN INSTRUCTION PD

ALL EFFORTS MUST BE DIRECTED TO INTENSIVE TRAINING TO ASSURE DEGREE

OF COMBAT EFFECTIVENESS IN FUTURE CONTEMPLATED OPERATIONS PD EASY

DASH OFFENSIVE SPIRIT CMA WITH POSSIBLE EXCEPTION OF YOKE PAREN AND

XRAY PAREN FORCES CMA HAS LITTLE OR NO EXPECTANCY UNTIL EQUIPMENT

CMA TRAINING AND IMPROVED RATIONS ARE FORTHCOMING PD FOX DASH TRAINING

- 3 -

MANEUVERS CMA FOOD DASH FORAGING EXPEDITIONS AND OTHER DIVERSIONARY MOVES BY THE
JAPANESE MAY BE EXPECTED TO INTERRUPT TRAINING CMA DISRUPT LOCAL DEFENSES AND
CAUSE DIVERSION OF THE UNITED STATES AIR FORCE FROM THEIR PRESCRIBED MISSION IN
ORDER TO SUPPORT OR RELIEVE PRESSURE ON CHINESE GROUND TROOPS PARA AIR FORCES
COLON ABLE DASH CHINESE AIR FORCE DASH MISSION TO DEFEND CHUNGKING AND CHENGTU
CAN BE PERFORMED DURING WINTER [PART 5] MONTHS WITH PRESENT OBSOLESCENT EQUIPMENT AUGMENTED
BY PETER DASH FORTIES NOW ARRIVING PD OUR RECORDS SHOW NO OFFENSIVE MISSIONS AND
ONLY ONE DEFENSIVE MISSION CMA WHERE CONTACT WITH ENEMY WAS MADE CMA PERFORMED SINCE
JUNE PD WE CAN EXPECT LITTLE OFFENSIVE HELP FROM CHINESE AIR FORCE PD BAKER DASH
CHINESE DASH AMERICAN WING DASH FIRST TWO FIGHTER SQUADRONS AND MEDIUM BOMB SQDN
NOW ENROUTE CHINA FOR EMPLOYMENT BY CHENNAULT PD WE EXPECT FAIR COMBAT EFFICIENCY
FROM THESE UNITS THOUGH THEY HAVE NOT YET PROVED THEMSELVES PD BY APRIL ONE NINE
FOUR FOUR THIS WING SHOULD CONSIST OF TWO FIGHTER GROUPS PAREN TWELVE PLANE SQDNS
PAREN AND ONE MEDIUM GROUP PAREN TEN PLANE SQDNS PAREN PD CHARLIE DASH FOURTEENTH
AIR FORCE CONSISTING OF TWO FIGHTER GROUPS CMA ONE HEAVY GROUP CMA ONE MEDIUM GROUP
PAREN TWO SQDNS STILL ENROUTE CHINA PAREN PLUS ONE RECONNAISSANCE SQDN CAN BE EXPECTED
TO CARRY OUT MISSIONS OF PROTECTING FERRYING ROUTE CMA GIVING AIR SUPPORT TO YOKE
FORCES AND CONDUCT LIMITED OFFENSIVE ACTIONS FROM EASTERN AIRDROMES KWEILIN AREA PD
CAPACITY OF HEAVY GROUP TO CONDUCT STRATEGIC OFFENSIVE OPERATION AGAINST JAPANESE
OBJECTIVES NOW LIMITED BY PROVISION THIS GROUP FERRY OWN SUPPLIES FROM INDIA PD
DOG DASH LONG RANGE BOMBERS COLON DASH TWILIGHT PLAN NOT YET APPROVED PD BELIEVE
MODIFIED TWILIGHT USING CHENGTU AS STAGING AREA INITIALLY HAS GOOD CHANCE OF
ACCOMPLISHING STRATEGIC BOMBING ON JAPAN PROPER BY JUNE ONE NINE FOUR FOUR PD NO
AERIAL KNOCK OUT BLOW CAN HOWEVER BE EXPECTED FROM CHENGTU BASES PARA [PART VI] ASSUMING NO
INCREASE IN MINIMUM TONNAGE OF FOUR THOUSAND SEVEN HUNDRED OVER HUMP FOR FOURTEENTH
AIR FORCE CMA FIRST THIRTY CHINESE DIVISIONS CAN BE EQUIPPED FOR FULL REPEAT FULL
COMBAT BY ONE JANUARY ONE NINE FOUR FIVE AS REPORTED IN REAR ECHELON LETTER DATED
ELEVEN OCTOBER ONE NINE FOUR THREE PD OUR ESTIMATE OF DATE ON WHICH MINIMUM NEEDS
OF YOKE FOR THREE MONTHS COMBAT WILL BE MET REMAINS JANUARY ONE NINE FOUR FOUR PD IF

FOURTEENTH AIR FORCE MINIMUM REQUIREMENTS AS STATED BY CHENNAULT ARE INCREASED TO
FIVE EIGHT ZERO ZERO TONS AND MAINTENANCE OF GROUND TROOPS REDUCED TO FIVE ZERO TONS
PER DIVISIONS PLUS AMMUNITION CMA APPROXIMATELY SAME SCHEDULE CAN BE MET PD IF FINAL
YOKE FORCE CONTAINS ONLY ONE EIGHT DIVISIONS CMA IT IS PLANNED THAT AT LEAST ONE TWO
DIVISIONS OF CHARLIE FORCE BE EQUIPPED BY END ONE NINE FOUR FOUR PD FOREGOING
ASSUMES NO PARTICIPATION IN TWILIGHT PLAN BY PRESENT ABLE TARE CHARLIE PLANES PD
LABOR AND FINANCIAL SITUATION ON AIRFIELD CONSTRUCTION IS BECOMING MORE DIFFICULT PD
WHEN CONDITIONS PERMIT IT IS PLANNED TO FLY IN SOME ENGINEER AIR BORNE MACHINERY PD
IF REVERSE LEND LEASE PLAN IS NOT CONSUMATED IN MANNER TO MEET THESE DIFFICULTIES CMA
IT MAY BE NECESSARY IN NEAR FUTURE TO CONTRIBUTE UNITED STATES FUNDS TO ACCELERATE
CONSTRUCTION PD HIGHWAY TRANSPORTATION EAST OF KUNMING REMAINS CRITICAL AND STUDIES
ARE IN PROGRESS TO MAKE BEST USE OF AVAILABLE FACILITIES CMA WHICH MAY REQUIRE
ADDITIONAL AMERICAN PERSONNEL PRIOR TO OPENING BURMA ROAD PD PARA PART TWO REPEAT
PART 7:
TWO PARA ONE MAJOR EFFORT IS BEING MADE TO EQUIP AND TRAIN UNITS OF YOKE FORCE FOR
PARTICIPATION IN THE BURMA OFFENSIVE AND THE PROTECTION OF YUNNAN PROVINCE PD PLAN
BEING DEVELOPED UNDER OVERALL PLAN SEA *South East Asia* THEATER FOR RECAPTURE BURMA PARA TWO
REORGANIZE CMA EQUIP AND TRAIN THE SECOND THIRTY DIVISIONS FOR THREE POSSIBLE LINES
OF ACTION COLON ABLE DASH DEFENSE OF AN AREA AND ADVANCE AIRFIELDS NOW IN POSSESSION
OF CHINESE IN EASTERN OR CENTRAL CHINA FOR FUTURE OFFENSIVE OPERATIONS AGAINST JAPAN
PROPER SMCLN BAKER DASH TO ASSIST IN THE CAPTURE OF A SEAPORT IN EASTERN CHINA CMA
NAMELY CANTON CMA HONGKONG OR HAIPHONG IN INDO CHINA SMCLN CHARLIE DASH FOR OFFENSIVE
ACTION DESIGNED TO DRIVE THE JAPANESE FROM THE YANGTZE RIVER VALLEY PD THE PLANS IN
ABLE CMA BAKER AND CHARLIE ABOVE WILL BE WORKED OUT IN DETAIL IN CONJUNCTION WITH
CHINESE STAFF CMA WHEN CHINESE CAN BE ASSURED OF THE EQUIPPING OF THE SECOND THIRTY
DIVISIONS PARA THREE DEVELOPMENT AND IMPROVEMENT OF THE CHINESE AIR FORCE TO THE
EXTENT OF SUPPORTING CHINESE GROUND TROOPS AND ENGAGE IN TACTICAL AND STRATEGICAL

5.

AIR OPERATIONS AGAINST THE JAPANESE IN CHINA PD DIRECTIVE FOR DEFENSE OF PRESCRIBED

AREAS AND PLANS THEREFOR ARE MADE PD PLANS FOR OFFENSIVE ACTION WILL BE WORKED OUT IN

DETAIL UNDER GENERAL CHENNAULTS DIRECTION WHEN CHINESE AIR FORCE IS AUGMENTED

SUFFICIENTLY

OFFICIAL:

   L. B. THOMPSON,
    Major, A. G. D.
  Asst. Adjutant General.

RECEIVED IN CODE ROOM _____ DATE _____

ACTUAL TIME AND METHOD OF DISPATCH _____

(3)

HQ U.S. ARMY FORCES

CHUNGKING, CHINA
NOVEMBER 5, 1943

AGWAR 8^{52}

     BASE USED WAS SUICHWAN RPT SUICHWAN ONE ONE FOUR DEGREES THIRTY

MINUTES DASH TWENTY SIX DEGREES TWO FIVE MINUTES PAREN MARSHALL FROM

STILWELL PAREN REURAD AMMISCA NUMBER THREE SEVEN FOUR SIX NOVEMBER THREE

PRD OBSERVATION BY ONE FOUR AIR FORCE FOX THREE ON AERIAL RECONNAISSANCE

CMA OCTOBER THREE ONE PRD ACK ACK ENCOUNTERED WAS ZERO CMA DUE TO HIGH

ALTITUDE OF PLANE IT IS BELIEVED JAPS MAY NOT KNOW OBSERVATION WAS MADE

OFFICIAL:

L. B. THOMPSON
Major, A. G. D.
Asst. Adjutant General

REC'D IN CODE ROOM _____ DATE & TIME _ _0_5_0_4_1_5_._ _ _ _

ACTUAL TIME OF DISPATCH AND METHOD _ _ _ _0_5_0_5_0_0_ _J_G_T_B

JKD/ctr/G-2.

(3)

NOV 5 '43 PM

Handle Eyes alone this HQ

RECEIVED
WAR DEPARTMENT
U. S. MILITARY MISSION TO CHINA
CHUNGKING, CHINA

10651

SECRET

ORDER SEC ARMY BY TAG/7W-350

1111

HQ. U. S. ARMY FORCES

CHUNGKING, CHINA
5 NOVEMBER 1943

COGUK *A 5711*

COMING FROM FRENCH SOURCES PAREN CHENNAULT SIGNED STILWELL PAREN
ONE THREE ZERO ZERO ZERO RPT THREE THOUSAND TON FREIGHTER LOADED WITH
PHOSPHATE WAS SUNK BY MAGNETIC MINE X RPT MINE IN NARROW CHANNEL AT
HAIPHONG ON TWENTY SECOND OCTOBER REPORTED TO HAVE BLOCKED CHANNEL

OFFICIAL:

L.B. THOMPSON
MAJOR, A.G.D.,
ASST. ADJUTANT GENERAL

RECEIVED IN CODE ROOM _____ DATE *11/5   0820*

ACTUAL TIME OF DISPATCH AND METHOD _____ *0835*

AO/JR/b

(3)

1112

Agwar   for Arnold, eyes alone from Stilwell

Targets in KYUSHIU now accessible from SUICHWAN. Chennault wants to start hitting them. Not knowing how such action would fit other possible plans, I am holding him off until I get word from you. Understood your policy was to wait until a really serious effort could be made and then go to town. Our attack now would be weak and sporadic. ~~It~~ ~~Suitable~~ Numerous targets closer home are available and better suited to our resources. Can you give us a policy on this matter?

                                    Stilwell –

56/3

1180

INCOMING RADIO:

RECEIVED: 5 NOVEMBER 0300 Z.

FROM   : WASHN.

TO   : AMMISCA   (PERSONAL FOR GEN STILWELL)

NR   : 3759   FILED: 4 NOVEMBER 2135 Z.

PRIORITY

RECEIVED
WAR DEPARTMENT
U. S. MILITARY MISSION TO CHINA
CHUNGKING, CHINA

PLEASE CONVEY TO STRATEMEYER AND TO CHENNAULT MY APPRECIATION
OF THE AGGRESSIVENESS, INITIATIVE AND ENERGY WHICH PROMPTS
RECONNAISSANCE FLIGHTS OVER JAPAN AND EFFORTS TO BOMB THE JAPANESE
AT HOME. (PERSONAL FOR STILWELL FROM ARNOLD) IT IS THAT SPIRIT
THAT ASSURES THE INEVITABLE DEFEAT OF THE JAPS.

YOU KNOW I HAVE PLANS AFOOT AND OPERATIONS UNDERWAY TOWARD
THE EARLY INITIATION OF SUSTAINED HEAVY BOMBARDMENT ON JAPAN. ALL
WILL BE FRUITLESS IF WE SHOW OUR HAND TOO EARLY.

IT IS THEREFORE MY DESIRE THAT A POLICY BE ESTABLISHED AND
ADHERED TO THAT THERE SHALL BE NO RPT NO FLYING OVER JAPAN
INCLUDING KYUSHU UNTIL FURTHER WORD FROM ME. ALSO DECISIONS ON
OPERATIONS, RECONNAISSANCE OR BOMBING, SHOULD BE INFLUENCED BY
PROBABLE AFFECT UPON THE JAP WILL AND ABILITY TO SEIZE OUR
ADVANCED BASES. AS TIME PROGRESSES AND CIRCUMSTANCES CHANGE LESS AND
LESS OF THIS DISTASTEFUL CONDITION SHOULD BE REQUIRED.

AT PRESENT THE INCREASING LOSSES BY OUR TRANSPORTS TO JAP
FIGHTERS OVER THE HUMP IS OF GRAVE CONCERN TO ME. OPERATIONS TO
PROTECT THAT LIFE LINE SHOULD HAVE MUCH HIGHER PRIORITY THAN
OPERATIONS DIRECTED TARD THE JAP HOMELAND.

A 510

Coquí — fr Chennault, Eyes alone

Answer from Arnold ref. your
proposition to me. Arnold appreci-
ates aggressive spirit indicated, but
directs that there be no flying over that
area or any part of it until he gives
the word. He considers it of extreme importance not to show our hand. He
is concerned over loss of transports, and
indicates that this matter rather than the
other should receive our first consideration. Let me know you have this message
and understand it.   Stilwell.

Recd 050500   1053
Sent 050515

1115

RECEOVED I~~N SECRET CODE~~

INCOMING RADIO:

RECEIVED: 5 NOVEMBER 0700 Z.

FROM   : COGUK   OPERATIONAL PRIORITY ~~CEIVED~~

TO   : AMMISCA   CGAAF W 23 NE

NR   : M 18 NE   FILED: 4 NOVEMBER 1202 Z.

PHOTO INTERPRETATION FIRST (EYES ALONE ARNOLD AND STILWELL
FROM CHENNAULT) ON PHOTO COVER OFF SASEBO HARBOR AND INNER HARBOR
OCTOBER THIRTY FIRST AS FOLLOWS MINIMUM OF FOUR ONE SEVEN FIVE ZERO
TONS OF MERCHANT SHIPPING AND FIFTEEN NAVAL VESSELS ARE VISABLE OF
WHICH THREE SEVEN ONE FIVE ZERO TONS OF MERCHANT SHIPPING AND ONE TWO
NAVAL VESSELS ARE IN INNER HARBOR AS FOLLOWS: ONE EACH FIVE FIVE
ZERO FOOT TRANSPORT THREE SIX ZERO FOOT CARGO TWO NINE ZERO FOOT
CARGO TWO FIVE ZERO TANKER THREE FOUR ZERO CARGO THREE FIVE ZERO
CARGO ONE SEVEN FIVE CARGO ONE SIX ZERO PROBABLE TANKER SOYE SIX
ZERO NASBABLE CARGO ONE SIX ZERO VESSEL UNDETERMINED, FOUR: ONE
TWO FIVE FOOT COLLIERS, FOUR: ONE FOUR ZERO FOOT VESSELS, ONE
COTON ONE FIVE ZERO FOOT VESSEL, TWO FLOATING CRANES ON BARGES ONE
TWO ZERO FEET BY TWO FOUR ZERO FEET, TWO SELF PROPELLING BARGES
TWO ONE ZERO FEET, MANY SMALL VESSELS LESS THAN ONE ZERO ZERO FEET.
NAVAL VESSELS AS FOLLOWS: ONE EACH TWO EILTT ZERO FOOT DESTROYER
TWO SEVEN ZERO FOOT DESTROYER TIED TO DOCK SURROUNDED BY LIGHTERS,
THREE FOUR ZERO EOFT PROBABLE NAVAL VESSEL, TWO SIX ZERO DESTROYERS
OR SUBCHASER, THREE ZERO ZERO FOOT SUBMARINE. SEVEN: ONE ZERO ZERO
BOOT PROBABLE NAVAL VESSELS IN BOAT BAGIN. IN STSFGN HARBOR ONE EACH
THREE THREE FIVE LRHT NAVAL VESSEL ENTERING HARBOR, ONE THREE FIVE
FOOT PROBABLE TANKER, ONE SIX ZERO FOOT VESSEL AND TWO NAVAL VESSELS

NOV 7 '43 AM

AS FOLLOWS THREE TWO FIVE FOOT DESTROYER UNDER WAY ENTERING HARBOR
AND ONE ZERO FIVE FOOT PROBABLE CUTTER FOLLOWING DESTROYER. WHILE
NAVAL DOCKYARDS AND PART OF REPAIR BASIN OBSCURED BY CLOUDS, OTHER
ACTIVITY REVEALS NAVAL AIR STATION THREE THREE DEGREES ZERO EIGHT

MINUTES NORTH, ONE TWO NINE DEGREES FOUR THREE MINUTES EAST AT SOUTH
END OF PENINSULA WITH NINE FOOAT PLANES WINGSPREAD FIVE ZERO FEET,
FOUR HANGARS ONE FOUR FOUR FEET BY TWO ONE FIVE FEET TO TWO ONE
FIVE FEET BY TWO FOUR ZERO FEET, TWO HANGARS SIX FIVE FEET BY TWO
ONE FIVE FEET, THREE SEAPLANE RAMPS, SHOP AND AIRCRAFT ASSEMBLY AREA
FIVE FIVE ZERO FEET BY TWO ONE ZERO ZERO FEET. ALSO INDUSTRIAL AREA
EVIDENTLY OF NEW CONSTRUCTION XBS THREE ZERO ZERO FEET BY TWO SEVEN
ZERO ZERO FEET PROBABLE SEAPLANE FACTORY. CSLWTLL AS FIELD AND
MUNITIONS DEPOT THREE THREE DEGREES ZERO NINE MINUTES NORTH BY ONE
TWO NINE DEGREES FOUR THREE MINUTES EAST CONSISTING OF SEVEN PROBABLE
BOMB PROOF BUILDINGS ONE ZERO ZERO BY ONE ZERO ZERO FEET AND ONE EIGHT
REVETTAD BUILDINGS SEVEN FIVE FEET BY ONE SEVEN FIVE FEET AND SMALLER
TEQ UNDERGROUND STORAGES, TWO CAMOUFLAGED FUEL TANKS DIAMETER ONE
THREE FIVE FEET. (NAGASAKI) THREE TWO DEGREES FOUR FOUR MINUTES NORTH
ONE TWO NINE DEGREES FIVE TWO MINUTES EAST PHOTO COVER THREE ONE
OCTOBER REVEALS IN PARTIAL COVERAGE MERCHANT SHIPPING MINIMUM OF
ONE ONE TWO FIVE ZERO TONS. ONE AIRCRAFT CARRIER RYUJO. WHILE IN
MITSUBISHI DOCKYARD NUMBER ONE DRYDOCK HAS VELLEL NUMBER THREE
DRYDOCK HAS VESSEL WITH FIFTY FOOT BEAM LENGTH UNDETERMINED
PREINDUSTRIAL AREAS IDENTIFIED MITSUIBISHI STEEL AND IRON WORKS,
NAGASAKI SPINNING MILLS, WOOD WORKING PLANT CAM FREIGHT YARDS
(ACTIVE) AS WELL AS ENGINE WORKS, DOCKYARDS DAYAGI POINT OIL STORAGE

PAGE 3.

TAKA SHIMA ISLAND COLLIERY, KOYAGI SHIMA SHIPYARD AND TWO MILITARY

AREAS ONE LOCATED ONE HALF MILE NORTH OF CITY ONE ON KAYAGI ISLAND.

DEFENSES ON KIMINO ISLAND: SIX HEAVY GUNS AT LEAST PLUS SEVERAL

BARRACKS. NOTE THIS ISLAND CONNECTED TO MAINLAND BY CAUSEWAY

WHICH FORMS EXTENTION OF QUAY ON NORTH EAST CORNER OF ISLAND.

ADDITIONAL COVERAGE SECURED THREE ONE OCTOBER INCLUDED OMURA RPT
        (naval air base)
VMURA MA AL AYR BASE THREE TWO DEGREES FIVE SIX MINUTES NORTH ONE TWO

NINE DEGREES FIVE SIX MINUTES EAST: AIRCRAFT FACTORY NOW OCCUPYING

TWO TWO ZERO ACRES AND TWO ONE ZERO ADDITIONAL ACRES ENLARGEMENT.

AIRCRAFT VISIBLE FOUR FOUR OF WHICH SEVENTEEN ALL FLOAT SINGLE ENGINE

WING SPAN FIVE ZERO FEET ARE ON DOCK BEFORE HANGARS. ONE FOUR SINGLE

ENGINE AIRCRAFT WING SPAN FOUR FIVE TO FIVE ZERO FEET IN FRONT

PROBABLE ASSEMBLY BUILDING. ONE THREE SINGLE ENGINE AIRCRAFT

ON SERVICING RAMP FACILITIES HANGAR AREA CONTAINS TWO NINE HANGARS

NINE OF WHICH ARE TWO TWO FIVE FEET BY TWO TWO FIVE FEET, BALANCE

SMALLER. ONLY PORTION OF FLYING FIELD VISIBLE THROUGH CLOUDS NO PLANES

VISIBLE. NEW CONSTRUCTION ACTIVITY NOTED AS WELL AS LARGE NUMBER OF

BARRACKS AND STORAGE BUILDINGS. ROGER ROGER STATION WITH SPURS

ENTERING FACTORY AREA FROM NORTH SIDE. TWO HEAVY DUAL PURPOSE GUNS

ON EAST SIDE OF ISLAND ONE MILE WEST OF AIRPLANE RAMP. MILITARY

CAMPONE AND ONE HALF MILES EAST OF TOKITSU THREE TWO DEGREES FIVE ONE

MINUTES NORTH ONE TWO NINE DEGREES FIVE FOUR MINUTES EAST COLON

EIGHT BOU BARRACKS FIVE ZERO FEET BY TWO ZERO FEET, FIVE LARGE

ADMINISTRATION BUILDINGS. HAIKI RPT HTIKI THREE THREE DEGREES ZERO

EIGHT MINUTES NORTH BY ONE TWO NINE DEGREES FOUR EIGHT MINUTES EAST:

ROGER ROGER TERMINAL, MILITARY CAMP OF TEN BUILDINGS NORTH OF TOWN,

TWO STORAGE AREAS EAST OF TOWN, ROGER ROGER AND HIGHWAY BRIDGES

AT SOUTH OF TOWN. KAWATANA THREE THREE DEGREES ZERO FOUR MINUTES
                        (five two)
NORTH BY ONE TWO NINE DEGREES FIRE TWT MINUTES EAST: INDUSTRIAL

PAGE 4.

AND STORAGE AREA ALONG WATERFRONT EAST OF TOWN, ROGER ROGER YARDS

ACTIVE, LARGE NUMBERS BARRACKS OR STORES ONE MILE EAST OF TOWN.

STORAGE OR BARRACKS AREA ONE MILE NORTH EAST OF TOWN. REQUEST THAT

THIS INFORMATION BE WITHHELD FROM DISTRIBUTION PENDING OPERATIONS AND

PLANS FOR FUTURE.

20,297.

RECEIVED IN ~~SECRET~~ CODE.

INCOMING RADIO: .

RECEIVED: 5 NOVEMBER 1800 Z.

FROM   :   AMMDEL

TO   :   AMMISCA

NR   :   AM 1977   FILED: 5 NOVEMBER 0422 Z.

RECEIVED
WAR DEPARTMENT
U. S. MILITARY MISSION TO CHINA
CHUNGKING, CHINA

EYES ALONE GENERAL STILWELL. LOUIS RECEIVED A REPORT
FROM HIS OWN PLANNING STAFF GIVING THEIR CONCLUSIONS AS TO THE
NATURE OF FINAL OBJECTIVES FOR THIS WINTER AND NEXT FALL (FROM
MERRILL SIGNED FERRIS.) THEY HAVE RECOMMENDED REJECTION OF THE
INDAW PLAN BECAUSE IT DOES NOT COMPLY WITH THE DIRECTIVE RECEIVED
FROM PRIME MINISTER IN ANY WAY. THEY ALSO RECOMMEND REJECTION OF
YEU RPT YEU PLAN WHICH WHILE BETTER THAN INDAW OPERATION BY REASON
OF ITS LIMITED SCOPE HAS A COMPLETE ABSENCE OF OPPORTUNITY FOR
EXPLOITATION IN EVENT OF SUCCESS. THEY RECOMMEND THE PLAN TO
ATTACK THE MANDALAY AREA AS IT IS THE MINIMUM OBJECTIVE WHICH
WILL SATISFY THE REQUIREMENTS GIVEN BY PRIME MINISTER AND IT IS
THE ONLY PLAN WHICH CAN BE QUICKLY EXPLOITED IN CASE OF SUCCESS.
ON AMPHIBIOUS OPERATIONS THEY REJECT AKYAB, STATE ANDAMANS ARE
OKEH BUT WILL CONTRIBUTE LITTLE TO OTHER OPERATIONS AND RECOMMEND
AN AMPHIBIOUS ATTACK ON THE RAMREE ~~DASH~~ TAUNGUP ~~DASH~~ SANDOWAY (mandalay)
AREA WITH SUBSEQUENT ADVANCE TOWARDS PROME. PLANNERS STATE ABOVE
COMBINATION ALONE MAKES MAXIMUM USE OF FORCES AVAILABLE AND IF
THINGS GO ALONG EASIER THAN ANTICIPATED WE ARE IN AN IDEAL POSITION
TO EXPLOIT RAPIDLY A SUCCESS IN EITHER AREA. UNCHANGED ARE XRAY

PAGE 2.

AND YOKE SOCIAL PARTY BY THIS PAPER. COMBINED GROUND AND AIR
STAFFS (LESS AMERICAN REPRESENTATIVES) WILL OFFER STRENUOUS
OBJECTIONS TO ABOVE PROPOSAL.

INCOMING RADIO

RECEIVED : 05 NOV 1900 GCT

FROM   : RELOT

TO   : AMMISCA

NR   : G 282   FILED : 05 NOV 1600 GCT

URGENT

Z Z Z Z

RECEIVED
U.S. MILITARY MISSION TO CHINA

HOLD FOR THE EYES OF GEN STILWELL ALONE TO BE
DELIVERED ZERO SEVEN ZERO ZERO HOURS SIX NOV PRD TODAY FOR THE
FIRST TIME THE THREE EIGHT DIV EVEN IN THE ABSENCE OF SUN VERY
POINTEDLY BROUGHT UP THE POINT THAT GEN SUN COMMANDED ALL CHINESE
TROOPS IN THIS SECTOR PRD TO STILWELL FROM BOATNER PRD THE POINT
INVOLVED WAS THEIR DESIRE TO MOVE THE ONE TWO ENGINEERS SO THAT
THEY WOULD BE READY FOR EITHER COMBAT OR AIR FIELD CONSTRUCTION
PRD THEY PLACED EMPHASIS ON THE FACT THAT THE TWELFTH ENGINEERS
SHOULD TAKE THEIR PLACE IN COMBAT PRD WITH TWO INFANTRY REGIMENTS
OF THREE EIGHT DIV AVAILABLE FOR COMBAT USE OF ENGINEERS WITH
THEIR DEPLETED STRENGTH FOR COMBAT IS OF COURSE ABSURD PRD EYE
BELIEVE WE CAN KEEP THE SITUATION IN HAND BUT IT IS POSSIBLE THAT
FRICTION MIGHT OCCUR THAT WOULD HINDER FUTURE COOPERATION PRD EYE
BELIEVE THE TIME HAS COME FOR A SECTOR COMMANDER OTHER THAN SUN TO
BE APPOINTED PRD ONE SOLUTION IS FOR YOU TO RESCIND THE ORDER
APPOINTING SUN COMMANDER AND PLACING ALL OUR CHINESE TROOPS THIS
SECTOR AGAIN DIRECTLY UNDER CHIH HUI PU PRD PENDING YOUR ACTION
ALL MY ORDERS TO CHINESE UNITS WILL BE IN YOUR NAME WITH ME AS
YOUR CHIEF OF STAFF

20,314

(1189)

7W-350

RECEIVED IN SECRET CODE.

<u>INCOMING RADIO:</u>

RECEIVED: 5 NOVEMBER 2030 Z.

FROM   : AMMDEL

TO   : AMMISCA

NR   : AM 1979   FILED: 5 NOVEMBER 0901 Z.

NOV 7 '43 AM

RECEIVED
WAR DEPARTMENT
U. S. MILITARY MISSION TO CHINA
CHUNGKING, CHINA

EYES ALONE STILWELL. WITH REFERENCE TO CLAIM BY LOOEY
THAT HE HAD AUTHORITY TO TEMPORARILY DIVERT TRANSPORTS FROM
HUMP TO WHICH EYE PREVIOUSLY REFERRED, BRITISH CHIEF OF STAFF
HAS REPLIED IN FOLLOWING VEIN (FROM MERRILL SIGNED FERRIS)
QUOTE WE UNDERSTAND THAT REQUESTS FOR TEMPORARY DIVERSION FOR
URGENT OPERATIONAL REQUIREMENTS WILL BE MADE TO STILWELL. IT
IS HOPED MATTER CAN BE DECIDED BETWEEN YOU BUT IF A SOLUTION IS
IMPOSSIBLE REFER IT TO US AND WE WILL GET A DECISION FROM
COMBINED CHIEFS OF STAFF. IN THIS CONNECTION THE PRESIDENT
ATTACHED MUCH IMPORTANCE TO DELIVERY OF SUPPLIES TO CHINA AND
APPOINTMENT OF STILWELL WAS INTENDED TO SAFEGUARD THIS END
PARAPHRASED QUOTE PROCEDURE TO BE FOLLOWED WHEN YOU DO NOT
CONSIDER BRITISH DEMANDS EIGHER IN PART OR IN FULL TO BE JUSTIFIED
BY THE CIRCUMSTANCES IS EXPECTED SOON. IN SHORT BRITISH ADMIT
LOSS OF ROUND ONE ON THIS ATTEMPTED GRAB.

20,322

1123

OT 34 2 - 2 - 2 - 2

E/cs
Alou

Relot for Boatner.

Come up to Chungking right away. Peanut wants to talk to you. General atmosphere
here is better.

Stilwell.

10677.

Received: 060120
Sent   : 060140

JGTB.

Nov 6 TH.

DECLASSIFIED
DOD Dir. 5200.9, Sept. 27, 1958
NCWN by ____ date 3-22-72

1124

INCOMING RADIO:

RECEIVED: 6 NOVEMBER 0606 Z.

FROM   : DRONE   U R G E N T

TO   : AMMISCA

NR   : Q 12   FILED: 6 NOVEMBER 1040 Z.

R E C E I V E D
WAR DEPARTMENT
U.S. MILITARY MISSION TO CHINA
CHUNGKING, CHINA

WHAT FOLLOWS EYES ALONE GENERAL STILWELL FROM
CHENNAULT. YOUR NUMBER ABLE FIVE ONE ZERO RECEIVED AND
WILL BE COMPLIED WITH. RE DEFENSE OF TRANSPORTS, EYE
AM MAINTAINING CONSTANT EFFORT TO THAT END AND FOURTEENTH
AF PLANES HAVE SHOT DOWN EIGHT OR MORE JAP FIGHTERS OVER
BURMA. DEFENSE OF TRANSPORTS IS GREATLY WEAKENED SINCE
THREE ZERO EIGHTH GROUP HAS SUSPENDED OPERATIONS OVER
HUMP DUE TO SHORTAGE OF AVIATION GAS IN ASSAM.

NEW SUBJECT: CHINESE HAVE LOCATED NINE JAP
REGIMENTS IN TUNHTING AREA AND REPORT CONTINUED ADVANCES
SOUTH AND WEST.

20,335.

(1190)

INCOMING RADIO

RECEIVED: 6 NOVEMBER 2345 GCT

FROM   : AMMDEL   PRIORITY

TO   : AMMISCA   AGWAR

NO   : AM 1995   AG 2659   FILED: 6 NOV. 1216 GCT

EYES ALONE GENERAL MARSHALL FROM FERRIS INFO AMMISCA.

THIS ANSWERS IN OUTLINE YOUR 4001 DATED NOVEMBER 2ND ON SUB-

JECT OF FUTURE OPERATION PLANS. SINCE PLANS MENTIONED IN YOUR

CABLE ARE THE PRIMARY CONCERN OF SEAC WE ARE SUBMITTING MAIN

FEATURES ONLY IN ORDER NOT TO INFRINGE ON PREROGATIVES OF SEAC

INDICATED TO US. WE UNDERSTAND YOU ARE ALSO IN DIRECT COMMUNICA-

TION WITH SEAC ON THIS PRD

FIRST. JUMP OFF DATE YOKE FORCE SOMETIME BETWEEN FEBRUARY

15TH AND MARCH 15TH

SENCOD. REGARDING LEDO CORPS, WE HAVE RECEIVED DIRECTIVE

FROM SEAC FOR CHINESE TO ADVANCE TO GENERAL LINE TARO-TAIPHA GA-

SHARAW. WE NOW HAVE REACHED FOLLOWING SITUATION: 1ST BATTAE

GARBLED SECTION -TWO LINES   AND IS FIGHTING IN VICINITY OF

NINGBYEN; 1 COMPANY OF SECOND BATTALION IS AT YUPBANG GA WHERE

FIGHTING IS IN PROGRESS WREN ENEMY STRENGTH ON NINGBYEN-YUPBANG GA

AREA ESTIMATED TO BE 300; 3RD BATTALION VVUQ REGIMENT REACHED

POINT 6 MILES NORTHWEST OF TARO TOWARD WHICH IT IS ADVANCING

AFTER SMALL SKIRMISH; 1ST BATTALION 114 REGIMENT MOVING FROM

SAGAP TO SHINGBWIYANG. PRESENT INDICATIONS ARE THAT SEAC WILL

ORDER ELEMENTS LEDO CKEPS   TO REACH SHADU XUP BY FEBRUARY 15TH

THIRD. LATEST TARGETS FOR LEDO ROAD CONSTRUCTION SHOW ONE

WAY ALL WEATHER ROAD TO SHINGBWIYANG BY JANUARY 1ST AND TO
MYITKYINA BY APRIL 1ST. SAME ROAD TO PAOSHAN BY OCTOBER 1ST,
WITH 6 MONTHS NEEDED TO DOUBLE TRACK GIVING 2 WAY ALL WEATHER
ROAD LEDO TO PAOSHAN BY APRIL 1ST, 1945. MCTALLING HAS NOW
REACHED MILE 53, WITH 57 TO GO TO SHINGBWIYANG

FOURTH. SEAC RECOGNIZES NEED FOR HUMP TONNAGE TO SUPPORT
14TH AIR FORCE AND YUNNAN FORCE AND IS TRYING TO ADJUST ASSAM
LOC TO MEET FULL REQUIREMENTS. SHORTAGE OF AIRCRAFT CONTINUALLY
RAISES QUESTION OF POSSIBILITY OF DIVERTING HUMP PLANES FOR
SHORT PERIODS BUT SO FAR NO SPECIFIC REQUEST HAS BEEN MADE FOR
SUCH DIVERSION. WE CONTINUE TO OPERATE WITH TARGET OF 10 THOUSAND
TONS PER MONTH

FIFTH. INDICATIONS ARE THAT GALAHAD WILL EVENTUALLY BE
USED IN ASSAM AREA IN LINE WITH OUR PLANS BUT NO DATE HAS BEEN
SET

SIXTH. ON TARZAN NO DECISION YET

SEVENTH. ORDERS WILL PROBABLY ISSUE FOR EXECUTION OF CUDGEL
IN EARLY JANUARY

EIGHTH. WE UNDERSTAND THAT ORDERS WILL BE ISSUED FOR
SAUCY TO START IN EARLY MARCH, WITH FINAL OBJECTIVES NOT YET
DETERMINED; HOWEVER THIS WILL MAKE LITTLE DIFFERENCE TO OPERATIONS
OF THAT FORCE FOR FIRST SEVERAL WEEKS

NINTH. ALL DETAILS REGARDING MNOTEBOOK SHOULD BE SECURE
FROM SEAC

TENTH. TOQEADOR IS NOW BEING CAREFULLY CONSIDERED BY SEAC
BUT PRINCIPAL DIFFICULTY APPEARS TO BE LACK OF TRANSPORT PLANES.
IF THIS CANNOT BE OVERCOME SOMEHOW A DECISION WILL PROBABLY BE
MADE BETWEEN TARZAN AND ABNORMAL

WE ARE REPRESENTED ON COMMANDERS IN CHIEF PLANNING STAFF, WHERE DETAILS OF THESE OPERATIONS ARE BEING WORKED OUT. WE HAVE NOT COMMENTED BECAUSE PRINCIPAL DECISIONS ARE STILL BEING CON- SIDERED BY SEAC. AMERICAN-CHINESE MISSIONS ARE CLEAR CUT AND OUR REQUIREMENTS REASONABLY SO, SINCE THERE IS NOT MUCH DEBATE ON THAT PART; THE MAIN DRIVE NOW IS TO WORK OUT OPERATIONS FROM THE OTHER SIDE WHICH CAN BE SUPPORTED AND HANK THE TACTICAL PUNCH REQUIRED

IF THIS ANSWER IS NOT COMPLETE ENOUGH TO MEET YOUR NEEDS WE CAN ARRANGE FOR FURTHER DETAILS, EITHER DIRECT OR THROUGH SEAC

FIRST PART IS BEING SERVICED
CMR

1128

RECEIVED IN SECRET CODE ARMY

INCOMING RADIO:

RECEIVED: 7 NOVEMBER 1225 Z.

FROM   : AMMDEL.

TO   : AMMISCA

NR   : AM 1996   FILED: 6 NOVEMBER 1217 Z.

EYES ALONE GENERAL STILWELL. DECISION REACHED TO TAKE
OVER ASSAM RAILROAD AND FOUR THOUSAND SIX HUNDRED AMERICAN RAILROAD
TROOPS HAVE BEEN REQUESTED (FROM MERRILL SIGNED FERRIS) DECISION
ON TOREADOR OPERATION WAS TO TELL BRITISH CHIEFS OF STAFF THAT THIS
OPERATION WAS FAVORED AND WOULD BE BEST POSSIBLE OPERATION BUT SHORTAGE
OF TRANSPORT PLANES AND PARACHUTE TROOPS MADE IT IMPOSSIBLE UNLESS
ADDITIONAL RESOURCES WERE PROVIDED. THEY ARE ANGLING FOR A BRITISH
PARACHUTE BRIGADE AND THE FOURTH INDIAN DIVISION FROM MIDEAST. ALSO
TRYING TO GET OUR AIRBORNE DIVISION FROM EISENHOWER IF NOT COMMITTED FOR
OVERLORD. IF TOREADOR IS NOT EXECUTED, THERE IS NO DECISION YET
BETWEEN ABNORMAL AND TARZAN FOR ALTERNATE PLAN.

LOOEY TAKING DECISION THAT HE CANNOT DIVERT TRANSPORTS
FROM HUMP WITHOUT YOUR PERMISSION WITH BAD GRACE. ASKED ME IF EYE DIDNT
THINK YOU WOULD AGREE TO LETTING HIM DECIDE WHEN IT WAS NECESSARY.
REPLIED THAT WHILE YOU DESIRED TO COOPERATE IN EVERY POSSIBLE WAY EYE
DID NOT BELIEVE YOU COULD GIVE ANY GENERAL CONSENT TO DIVERSIONS AT WILL
AND THAT A DETAILED PLAN MUST BE WORKED OUT IN EACH CASE SO THAT YOU
COULD PROTECT YOURSELF AGAINST REACTIONS. AS IT NOW STANDS WHEN YOU
DECLINE REQUESTS TO FURNISH PLANES FROM HUMP YOU MUST GIVE LOOEY YOUR
COMPLETE REASONS FOR NON COMPLIANCE WHICH EVENTUALLY GO TO COMBINED
CHIEFS WITH STORY FROM LOOEY AS WELL FOR DECISION.

REGRADED CONFIDENTIAL
ORDER SEC ARMY BY TAG/3W-350

1129

PAGE 2.

BRINK HAD A TALK WITH WINGATE IN WHICH THEY AGREED THAT IT
WAS IMPOSSIBLE TO GET GALAHAD FORCE READY PRIOR TO APRIL ONE AT
EARLIEST. THEREFORE PRESENT DECISION IS NOT TO EMPLOY GALAHAD
FORCE IN IN ITIAL LRP OPERATIONS AND SEAC HAS SO INFORMED WAR
DEPARTMENT. WAS ASKED TO PRESS YOU FOR DESIGNATION OF-BRINK AS
IN COMMAND GALAHAD. BRINK TALKED THIS OVER WITH WEDEMEYER WHO CALLED
ME IN TO LISTEN TO CONVERSATION. TOLD WEDEMEYER YOU HAD SEVERAL
IN MIND AND MEANWHILE HAD PLACED   BRINK IN CHARGE OF TRAINING
OF TRAINING. MY ONLY COMMENT IS BRINK KNEW WELL OUR DEADLINE OF ONE
FEBRUARY FOR GALAHAD TO BE READY.

RECALL YOU CONVERSATION WITH DORN AND MYSELF AT KUNMING
RELATIVE CHINESE INTENDED DEMAND FOR RELIEF OF A CERTAIN UNDESIRABLE
CHARACTER. LOOEY KNOWS A BOUT THIS AND THINKS IT IS STILL ON.
HE TOLD HURLEY WHOLE THING AND SAID MARSHALL IS BEHIND IT ALSO.
THIS INFO MAY BE USEFUL TO YOU WHEN YOU DISCUSS THINGS WITH HURLEY
DURING HIS VISIT AND WILL APPRISE YOU OF SWEET CHARACTER OUR
PLAYMATES.

20,396.

1130

854

2gwar. for Gen. Marshall, eyes alone

(For eyes alone Marshall from Stilwell)

Informational. I assume Somervell gave you full story of happenings here. Relations with CKS now excellent, better than at any time previously. Obstructions being cleared away and on surface at least war ministry getting in line. Prospects much improved. Kweilin school off to good start on Nov. first as scheduled. Unit schools reaching divisions of Y force. This will be pushed by order of CKS. Matter of replacements and improved rations now receiving full attention. Ch'en Ch'eng still sick with serious stomach trouble and will probably have to be replaced. This is bad. In India everything going smoothly. Road construction much more promising. Hope to get motorable track to Shinbwiyang by Jan. first. Ferry line operating day and night. Doing our best to cover transports in flight. Relations with Mountbatten and staff excellent. He is reasonable and open-minded, but there is obvious tendency on part of British to muscle in on us in China, and in general to submerge and absorb all American effort and participation in this area. We are co-operating to fullest extent consistent with protection of American interests.

Stilwell.

06 0320
sent 0400 TB

(1213)

Ammdel   fr   Merrill —   Eyes Alone

Reurad AM 1996. Your stand on diversion of transport planes is our policy and
we will stick to it. As to Galahad, February
first is still the dead-line. As I understand it,
Mountbatten agreed to move Galahad to
Margarita fr training after a two-weeks
stop at Gwalior to get acquainted and exchange ideas.   When will Hurley come up?
apparently he has some interesting dope.

                              Stilwell.

080420

1214

RECEIVED IN SECRET CODE

INCOMING RADIO

RECEIVED   :   06 NOVEMBER 0842 GCT

FROM   :   RELOT   URGENT

TO   :   AMMISCA

NR.   :   G 283   FILED 06 NOVEMBER 0705 GCT

      EYES ALONE OF GENERAL STILWELL PRD AM IN HOSPITAL
WITH BAD CASE MALIGNANT TYPE MALARIA PRD GENERAL STILWELL FROM
BOATNER PRD DOCTOR SAYS NEXT TUESDAY IS SOONEST I CAN TRAVEL SORRY
QUERY SHALL I COME AS SOON AS DOCTOR PERMITS PRD NEW SUBJECT A
MORE COOPERATIVE ATTITUDE WAS SUDDENLY SHOWN BY THIRTY EIGHTH
DIVISION LAST NIGHT PERIOD THEY ARE CONTINUING TO ADVANCE BUT
VERY VERY CAUTIOUSLY AND MOVING PART OF THEIR ONE ONE FOUR REGIMENT
MUCH CLOSER FORWARD.

GCV   20,341

1133

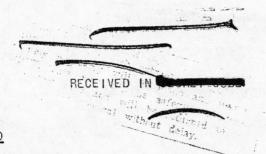

RECEIVED IN ~~SECRET CODE~~

RECEIVED
WAR DEPARTMENT
U. S. MILITARY MISSION TO CHINA
CHUNGKING, CHINA

INCOMING RADIO

RECEIVED   :   08 NOV 0920 GCT

FROM   :   WASHINGTON   PRIORITY

TO   :   AMMISCA

NR   :   3747   FILED :   07 NOV 0615 GCT

       UTMOST SECRECY MUST BE MAINTAINED CONCERNING ALL PHOTO

RECON OVER JAPAN NOTIFY ALL CONCERNED PAREN FOR HEARN SIGNED ARNOLD

PAREN REQUEST TWO SPECIAL PRINTS EACH PHOTOGRAPH SENT FASTEST SAFE METHOD

TO ACAS RPT ACAS INTELLIGENCE PD WHAT TYPE PLANE WAS USED PD WHAT WAS

DEPARTURE POINT

20,468

RECEIVED IN SECRET CODE.

INCOMING RADIO:

RECEIVED: 8 NOVEMBER 1100 Z.

FROM   : AMMDEL

TO   : AMMISCA

NR   : AM 2008   FILED: 8 NOVEMBER 0922 Z.

EYES ALONE GENERAL STILWELL. MEETING CONCERNING LRP GROUPS
WAS HOT AND HEAVY (FROM MERRILL SIGNED FERRIS) GIFFARD STATED
WINGATE VERY ANXIOUS TO USE A GROUP FROM PAOSHAN WHICH WOULD
ESTABLISH ITSELF IN KACHIN COUNTRY. ALSO THAT WINGATE OPPOSED
AMERICAN LRP GROUP BEING USED IN FRONT OF CHINESE AS BY THE TIME
THEY HAD MARCHED SUCH GREAT DISTANCES THEY WOULD NOT HAVE ENERGY
OR INITIATIVE FOR FIGHTING. LOOEY STATED THAT REPORTED SICKNESS
IN AMERICAN GROUP AND NECESSITY FOR ACCLIMATISATION MADE IT DESIRABLE
THAT THEY BE DEFERRED TO SECOND WAVE AND THERE WAS NO REASON AT ALL
FOR THEM GOING IN ON FIRST WAVE.

QUESTION OF WHAT FORCES IN CBI COME UNDER SOUTHEAST ASIA
COMMAND WILL BE RAISED VERY SOON. WEDEMEYER INFORMED ME THAT WAR
DEPARTMENT PROPOSED TO GIVE YOU SOME DOPE ON THIS BUT IT WAS STILL
IN THE MILL WHEN HE LEFT. MEANWHILE BY IMPLICATION LOOEY ASSUMES
THAT ALL FORCES UNDER YOUR COMMAND ARE AUTOMATICALLY UNDER HIS
COMMAND. ON THIS AND ALL OTHER PROBLEMS WEDEMEYER VERY COOPERATIVE
AND ON OUR SIDE AS FAR AS HE CAN.

CONCERNING OPERATIONS LOOEY STATED HE WAS VERY COLD
BLOODED I OUT FOR A VICTORY AND IF NECESSARY WOULD GIVE UP MOST
DESIRABLE STRATEGIC OPERATION TO ACHIEVE THIS END.

REGRADED CONFIDENTIAL
ORDER SEC ARMY BY TAG/JN 358 (1203)

ALTHOUGH SEAC HAS NOT GOTTEN TO FIRST BASE ON OWN PROBLEMS IT IS CASTING AN EYE NORTH. LOOEY HAS A COPY OF THE CHENNAULT AIR PLAN WHICH HE OBTAINED IN KUNMING AND HAS STATED HE WANTS TO TALK TO CHENNAULT AS SOON AS POSSIBLE CONCERNING COORDINATED ACTIVITIES FOR ONE NINE FOUR FOUR DASH FOUR FIVE OPERATIONS. EYE QUESTIONED THIS IMMEDIATELY AND WAS POLITELY INFORMED YOU KNEW ALL ABOUT THIS AND HAD GIVEN APPROVAL TO DISCUSSIONS AS INDICATED. EYE HAVE SEEN ALL PAPERS CHENNAULT GAVE LOOEY AND MUST SAY FORMER WAS CAUTIOUS AND DISCREET.

GIFFARD IS CHIEF OBSTRUCTIONIST ON GETTING ANYTHING DONE. ARRANGED A PRIVATE TALK BETWEEN SLIM AND WEDEMEYER. LATTER GREATLY IMPRESSED BY SLIM AND HIS IDEAS. WE TRIED TO GET SLIM A CHANCE TO GIVE HIS IDEAS OF WHAT COULD BE DONE TO LOOEY BUT COULDNT. GIFFARD AND HIS PLANNERS CHANGE THEIR HANDS AT LEAST THREE TIMES A DAY ON ANY GIVEN SUBJECT AND EXCEPT FOR THE GENERAL DECISIONS EYE HAVE ALREADY SENT YOU WE ARE GETTING NOWHERE FAST.

SEAC ASSUME THAT THEY WILL HAVE SOME DEFINITE RESPONSIBILITY REFERENCE OPERATION BURMA ROAD AND LOOEY MENTIONED THAT ROAD EXPERTS PROMISED BY SOMERVELL AT CHUNGKING CONFERENCE MUST BE PROVIDED AND HAS DIRECTED A STUDY BE MADE OF THIS. BRITISH DESIRE TO COLONIZE YUNNAN ON THE UP GRADE.

20,465.

THE FOREIGN SERVICE
OF THE
UNITED STATES OF AMERICA

AMERICAN EMBASSY

Chungking, November 9, 1943.

Dear General Stilwell:

    With reference to my conversation with you
yesterday afternoon on the subject of political
matters related to military affairs, I enclose
copies of the exchange of letters between the
State and War Departments.

    I suggest that, so far as concerns China, the
most convenient procedure would be by informal
conversations between us, perhaps every week or
ten days, except of course when special questions
develop requiring more frequent consultation.

                    Very sincerely,

Enclosures:
        1. To War Department,
           August 17, 1943.
        2. From War Department,
           August 28, 1943.

Lieutenant General Joseph W. Stilwell, U.S.A.,
        Commander-in-Chief, U. S. Army Forces in
              China, Burma and India,
                    Chungking.

In reply refer to
FE

August 17, 1943.

My dear Mr. Secretary:

Reference is made to the Department's letter of July 26, 1943 in which this Department informed the War Department that in pursuance of the latter's request assignments had been approved for detail to the staff of Lieutenant General Joseph W. Stilwell, Commanding General of the United States Army Forces in the China-Burma-India theater, of four Foreign Service officers named in the letter.

The Department feels that these assignments will assist General Stilwell in his theater of war in evaluating and in dealing with political aspects of military problems by providing him with the services of personnel who have had special training and experience in areas within his command.

In this connection and in view of the importance of these political questions and of the close inter-relation between political and military problems especially in the areas in question, the Department is of the opinion that all possible steps should be taken to ensure complete coordination and co-operation between the diplomatic and military establishments in political matters related to military affairs.

The Department feels that, in addition to the assigning of these officers to General Stilwell's staff, much further good can be accomplished in this direction by arranging for the direct exchange at frequent and regular intervals of views and of information between General Stilwell and the ranking political representatives of the United States in India and in China. The obvious benefits which would be derived from frank and comprehensive interchanges of the nature envisaged should be of great assistance to both establishments in discharging their respective functions in connection with the prosecution of the war and the working out of our long-range policies in that area.

The Department believes, therefore, that it is of the utmost importance that the Commanding General of United States forces in the China-Burma-India theater and the ranking American political representatives in that area should arrange for constant liaison and regular consultation one

with

The Honorable

Henry L. Stimson,

Secretary of War.

with the other to the end that coordination and cooperation be maintained between the diplomatic and military establishments in China and India of this Government in political matters relating to military affairs. For example, the Department believes that the ends in view might be well served if General Stilwell would maintain liaison and confer with the American Ambassador at Chungking in regard to matters affecting political relations with China and similarly with the Chief of the American Mission at New Delhi in regard to matters affecting political relations with India.

The Department will instruct the American Ambassador at Chungking and the Chief of the American Mission at New Delhi to take all necessary steps to work out arrangements for such liaison and conferences with General Stilwell at which all questions of mutual concern will be thoroughly explored and discussed. At the same time and for the same purpose the Department requests that the War Department issue appropriate instructions to General Stilwell in the foregoing sense.

Sincerely yours,

CORDELL HULL

August 28, 1943.

The Honorable,

    The Secretary of State.

Dear Mr. Secretary:

    Receipt is acknowledged of your letter dated August 17,
1943, indicating the desirability, in addition to the recent
assignment of four Foreign Service Officers to the Commanding
General, U.S. Army Forces, China-Burma-India Theater, of
close cooperation being arranged between the U.S. Diplomatic
and Military Establishments in China and India, and request-
ing that General Stilwell be instructed with respect there-
to.

    Cooperation between these establishments has been
common practice in the past. Nevertheless, the War Department is in accord with the views of the Department of State
that it is important that constant and regular consultation
and liaison on political matter related to military affairs
be arranged.

    Appropriate instructions are accordingly being issued
to General Stilwell so that, subject to military requirements, whatever arrangements are necessary to carry out the
intent and purpose of your letter will be put into effect.

                            Sincerely yours,

                            (Signed) ROBERT A. LOVETT

                            Acting Secretary of War.

RECEIVED IN SECRET CODE

INCOMING RADIO

RECEIVED : 09 NOV 0240 GCT

FROM   : WAR   OPERATIONAL PRIORITY

TO   : AMMISCA

NO.   : 3788   FILED 08 NOV 2245 GCT   OPERATIONAL PRIORITY

" MANY THANKS FOR YOUR MESSAGE PRD FROM THE PRESIDENT TO GENERALISSIMO CHIANG KAI SHEK CMA PERSONAL AND SECRET PRD I RPT ITEM AM LEAVING FOR NORTH AFRICA IN TWO OR THREE DAYS AND I RPT ITEM HOPE TO GET TO CAIRO ON THE TWENTY FIRST PRD CHURCHILL WILL MEET ME THERE PRD WE HOPE TO MEET MARSHAL STALIN IN PERSIA ABOUT THE TWENTY SIXTH OR TWENTY SEVENTH PRD HOWEVER I RPT ITEM WOULD PREFER THAT YOU AND CHURCHILL AND I RPT ITEM MEET BEFORE THAT PRD THEREFORE CAN YOU TRY TO REACH CAIRO BY THE TWENTY SECOND OF NOVEMBER QUERY WE WILL ARRANGE GOOD ACCOMMODATIONS AND GUARD FOR YOU AND YOUR PARTY IN OR NEAR CAIRO PRD SGD ROOSEVELT PRD PLEASE LET ME KNOW AS SOON AS YOU CAN "

Sgd. Roosevelt.

Memo for ? mo —
The following msg. has just
been received

later no. 74
11/9/43

1212

20,498

No. 74   CHUNGKING, CHINA,
                                           9 November 1943.

MEMORANDUM:

TO   : His Excellency, Generalissimo Chiang Kai Shek.

     The following message has just been received:

     "FOR GENERALISSIMO CHIANG KAI SHEK FROM THE PRESIDENT.

PERSONAL AND SECRET. MANY THANKS FOR YOUR MESSAGE. I AM

LEAVING FOR NORTH AFRICA IN TWO OR THREE DAYS AND I HOPE TO

GET TO CAIRO ON THE TWENTY FIRST. CHURCHILL WILL MEET ME

THERE. WE HOPE TO MEET MARSHAL STALIN IN PERSIA ABOUT THE

TWENTY SIXTH OR TWENTY SEVENTH. HOWEVER I WOULD PREFER THAT

YOU AND CHURCHILL AND I MEET BEFORE THAT. THEREFORE CAN YOU

TRY TO REACH CAIRO BY THE TWENTY SECOND OF NOVEMBER? WE WILL

ARRANGE GOOD ACCOMMODATIONS AND GUARD FOR YOU AND YOUR PARTY

IN OR NEAR CAIRO. PLEASE LET ME KNOW AS SOON AS YOU CAN.

                                           SIGNED:

                                                ROOSEVELT"

                              JOSEPH W. STILWELL
                              Lieutenant General, U.S.A.

HQ. U.S. ARMY FORCES

CHUNGKING, CHINA
NOVEMBER 9, 1943

CGAAF   PRIORITY

AFS

    DEPARTURE POINT WAS SUICHWAN RPT SUICHWAN PAREN ARNOLD SGD STILWELL PAREN

ONE HUNDRED FOURTEEN DEGREES THIRTY MINUTES DASH TWO SIX DEGREES TWENTY FIVE

MINUTES PRD REURAD NUMBER THREE SEVEN FOUR SEVEN NOVEMBER SEVENTH TYPE OF PLANE

DASH FOX RPT FOX FIVE RPT FIVE PRD FOR SECURITY THIS INFORMATION TREATED EYES

ALONE THIS THEATER PRD ADDRESS WHERE PHOTOS TO BE SENT NOT UNDERSTOOD CMA PLEASE

SEND MORE COMPLETE ADDRESS

OFFICIAL:

L. B. THOMPSON
MAJOR, A.G.D.
ASST. ADJUTANT GENERAL

REC'D IN CODE ROOM _ _ _ _ _ _ _ _ _ _ _ _ _ _ _ DATE & TIME _ _ _ _ _ _ _ _ _ _ _

ACTUAL TIME OF DISPATCH AND METHOD _ _ _ _ JB _ _ _ _ _ _ _ _ _ _ _ _ _

JKD/ctr/G-2.

Treat eyes alone this station.

10749

Radio to 858:

Priority

Agwar' for Gen. Marshall, eyes alone, for transmission to the president.

Following message is from Generalissimo. Quote. Mme. Chiang down with flu and dysentery. Funeral of Lin Sen (late President) scheduled for seventeenth. Provided Mme. Chiang has recovered, I intend to leave here early on the eighteenth. Otherwise I must delay my departure, in which case your conference with Stalin can take place before ours. I prefer seeing you before you see Stalin and sincerely hope our plans will work out in that way. Signed, Chiang Kai Shek. Unquote.

Stilwell.

Recd 091415
Sent 091500.

Jfm.
11/9.

Special Code

1216

10769.

1144

Urgent priority.

Agwar.   For the presi-
860   dent.

I will be in Chungking
till the twelfth unless
otherwise directed by you
Signed Hurley.

Stilwell

Rec'd   0320   11/10

RECEIVED ~~SECRET CODE~~

<u>INCOMING RADIO</u>

RECEIVED : 10 NOV 0715 GCT

FROM : WAR

TO : AMMISCA 3810 AQUILA 3689

NR : 3810   FILED : 10 NOVO955 GCT

FORMAL ORDERS WILL PROBABLY ISSUE WITH CCS RPT CCS
AUTHORITY IN THE NEAR FUTURE INITIATING AN EXTENSIVE MOBIFICATION
OF YOUR TWILIGHT PLAN PERIOD PAREN (PERSONAL TO STRATEMEYER FROM
ARNOLD) PAREN DATE OF OPERATION OF FIRST MISSIONS DEPENDS ALMOST
SOLELY UPON DATES OF WHICH FOUR BAKER TWO NINE AIRDROMES IN
CALCUTTA AREA AND FIVE BAKER TWO NINE AIRDROMES INCHANGTU AREA
CAN BE READY FOR OPERATION PERIOD I WANT YOU TO DO EVERYTHING
WITHIN YOUR POWER TO SPEED UP AIRDROME CONSTRUCTION PERIOD YOUR
REQUIREMENT FOR ADDITIONAL AVIATION ENGINEERS IS APPRECIATED COMMA
UNDERSTOOD COMMA AND ACTION IS UNDERWAY TOWARD MAKING FOUR
BATTALIONS PLUS ONE AIRBORNE BATTALION AVAILABLE TO YOU IN
CALCUTTA AREA IN JANUARY ONE NINE FOUR FOUR PERIOD OPERATIONAL USE
OF THESE AIRDROMES DEPENDS FURTHER ON PIPELINES TO THEM FROM
CALCUTTA RPT CALCUTTA PORT PERIOD TO MAKE THIS ITEM TWO PIPELINE
LAYING COMPANIES SHOULD REACH YOU IN JANUARY PERIOD I AM CONSIDERING
SENDING YOU A FORCEFUL OPERATOR TO RIDE HERD ON THIS SPECIAL
PROJECT PERIOD

INCOMING RADIO

RECEIVED: 10 NOVEMBER 0715 GCT

FROM   : AMMDEL

 **PRIORITY**

TO   : AMMISCA   PRIORITY

NO   : AM 2023 FILED: 10 NOV. 0520 GCT

EYES ALONE GENERAL STILWELL. GENERAL DECISION TO EXECUTE
TARZAN REACHED (FROM MERRILL SIGNED FERRIS) THIS AFTER A FREE
DISCUSSION IN WHICH YOUR VIEWS (WHICH WERE SUPPORTED BY SOME
OF BRITISH) WERE PRESENTED FIRMLY BY ME AND STRONGLY SUPPORT-
ED BY WEDEMEYER. OUR ONLY CONSOLATION WAS TO GET A DIRECTIVE
THAT TARZAN WOULD BE THE SECOND PHASE OF OPERATIONS FROM IMPHAL
AREA AND THAT IMMEDIATE STUDY WOULD BE MADE OF POSSIBILITY OF X
DOING SOMETHING ELSE AFTER TARZAN IS OVER. ON THE CHINDWIN
THERE WILL BE A BRIDGEHEAD OF SORTS AND A PASS MADE TOWARDS
THE OBJECTIVE FOR ABNORMAL OPERATION. WE INSISTED ON A RIDER
THAT PREPARATIONS TO EXPLOIT TO THE EXTENT OF EXECUTING ABNOR-
MAL SHOULD BE MADE AND WON ON THIS. WHICHEVER WAY WE TURN WE
EITHER RUN INTO MARKED CARDS OR LOADED DICE. THE ISSUES ARE
DECIDED PRIVATELY BEFORE THE MEETINGS AND WE ARE JUST BUMPING
OUR HEADS AGAINST STONE WALLS BY ARGUING. NEVERTHELESS WE ARE
STILL DOING WHAT WE CAN. HUMP WILL BE SERIOUSLY DISLOCATED BY
THIS DECISION AND I WILL SEND PROBABLE RESULTS LATER WHEN DE-
TAILS ARE A LITTLE CLEARER. LOOEY ASKED THAT I TELL YOU HE
RESPECTED YOUR VIEWS AND MADE HIS DECISION RELUCTANTLY BECAUSE
OF THE SAME OLD REASONS WE HAVE BEEN HEARING FOR A YEAR

CARTON DE WIART COMING UP TO TELL YOU AND THE PEANUT THE

(1225)

WONDERFUL NEWS AS SOON AS HE GETS THE PICTURE STRAIGHT. THIS
WILL MEAN HE CANT LEAVE HERE UNTIL END OF WEEK AT EARLIEST AT
RATE HE IS GOING NOW

WILSON-BRAND SENT IN A HIGHLY FAVORABLE REPORT REFERENCE
YOKE UNITS. STATED UNITS AT HIGHEST STATE OF MORALE HE HAD
EVER SEEN CHINESE TROOPS AND TRAINING AT KUNMING PRODUCING RE-
MARKABLE RESULTS

MATTER OF AN LRP GROUP FROM PAOSHAN WILL BE PRESSED ACTIVE-
LY AND I LOOK FOR A DECISION TO PUT ONE IN REGARDLESS OF YOUR
DESIRES. IF IT COMES TO A SHOWDOWN DO YOU WANT THE AMERICAN
RATHER THAN A BRITISH GROUP

Yes.

20567

1148

RECEIVED IN ~~SECRET CODE~~

INCOMING RADIO

RECEIVED: 10 NOVEMBER 1725 GCT
FROM   : WAR   URGENT
TO   : AMMISCA
NO   : 3802   FILED: 10 NOVEMBER 1535 GCT

LAST JUNE YOU RAISED THE QUESTION OF A SECOND IN COMMAND.
SOMERVELL HEN ALSO RECOMMENDED THAT YOU HAVE ASSIGNED TO YOU A
SECOND IN COMMAND OF OUTSTANDING ABILITY. (FROM MARSHALL TO
STILWELL HIS EYES ALONE). THE FOLLOWING GENERAL OFFICERS ALL
HAVE IMPORTANT ASSIGNMENTS NOW BUT IF YOU DESIRE ONE OF THEM
ASSIGNED TO YOU AS YOUR SECOND IN COMMAND IT WILL BE DONE SUBJECT
TO THE CONCURRENCE OF THEATER COMMANDER IN THE CASE OF THOSE
NOW OVERSEAS. IF YOU HAVE SOMEONE ELSE IN MIND PLEASE INFORM ME
AND WE WILL TRY AND MAKE HIM AVAILABLE. INDICATE YOUR ORDER OF
PREFERENCE: MAJOR GENERALS D I SULTAN (EIGHTH CORPS ENROUTE TO
UNIT K), J L BRADLEY, AND BRIGADIER GENERAL A V ARNOLD (DIVISION
ARTILLERY OFFICER, HAWAII). IF ARNOLD IS SENT, HE WOULD BE
PROMOTED

Ans. 11/12

(1223)

RECEIVED IN SECRET CODE

INCOMING RADIO

RECEIVED: 10 NOVEMBER 1725 GCT

FROM   : COPIR

TO   : AMMISCA

NO   : 6 FILED: 10 NOVEMBER 1340 GCT

HAVE HEARD STRONG RUMOURS THAT THE CHINESE INTEND TO INVADE INDO CHINA FROM WENSHAN. (FOLLOWING FOR STILWELL EYES ALONE FROM MOUNTBATTEN) PLEASE ENDEAVOUR TO OBTAIN IMMEDIATE CONFIRMATION AND INFORM ME. I PRESUME YOU WILL ALSO KEEP THE U S AMBASSADOR IN CHUNGKING INFORMED IF RUMOUR APPEARS LIKELY TO BE TRUE. IT SEEMS THAT POLITICAL ACTION ON THE HIGHEST LEVEL WILL BE THE ONLY WAY TO STOP THIS DISASTROUS UNILATERAL ACTION ON THE PART OF THE CHINESE, SINCE IT SEEMS CERTAIN THAT THE WHITE FRENCH TROOPS AND FRENCH LED ANNAMITES WOULD RESIST THIS, BRINGING ABOUT A STATE OF WAR BETWEEN OUR CHINESE AND FRENCH ALLIES. YOU CAN IMAGINE THE EFFECT ON OUR OWN OPERATIONS

20607

1150

INCOMING RADIO

RECEIVED: 10 NOVEMBER 2200 GCT

FROM   : WAR   PRIORITY

TO   : AMMISCA   PRIORITY

NO   : 3803   FILED: 10 NOVEMBER 1605 GCT

I AM TERRIBLY SORRY TO LEARN OF MADAME CHIANGS ILLNESS
PERSONAL AND MOST SECRET FROM THE PRESIDENT TO THE GENERALISSIMO
SIGNED ROSEVELT AND SINCERELY HOPE THAT WHE WILL BE FULLY RE-
COVERED IN TIME FOR OUR CONFERENCE .

I HAVE HAD A LONG TALK WITH GENERAL SOMERVELL AND APPRECIATE
VERY MUCH YOUR COURTESIES TO HIM. HE HAS GIVEN ME YOUR PRIVATE
MESSAGE AS I HAVE ALREADY INDICATED TO YOU.

I AGREE WITH YOU FULLY THAT WE SHOULD MEET TOGETHER BEFORE
I SEE STALIN. I WANT SO MUCH TO HAVE SOME GOOD TALKS WITH YOU
SO, NATURALLY, I AM EAGERLY LOOKING FORWARD TO SEEING YOU,

Letter #77

(1228)

Agwar - 863

Mountbatten getting idea that all U.S. forces and installations are under his command. My understanding is that only combat forces allocated for S.E.A.C. operations are under his command, which is to be exercised through me, and that troops not allocated such as port, S.O.S, and A.T.C. installations and activities are outside his jurisdiction. Since this matter may go to high levels, am reporting my views to you. Louis has already tried to split up our L R P group and scatter it among British units, and Wingate has put out opinions on who should command it. There are other moves that indicate tendency to submerge American interests. I am opposing this, but need your guidance on how far I can go.

Stilwell -

Recd msg cuts 110205
Sent TB 0230

10789

NDROE

(1234)

INCOMING RADIO

RECEIVED: 11 NOVEMBER 0720 GCT

FROM   : AMMDEL

TO   : AMMISCA

NO   : AM 2030   FILED: 11 NOVEMBER 0557 GCT

URGENT

ALONE EYES GENERAL STILWELL. THE WART DEPARTS DELHI 16 NOVEMBER FOR SHORT VISIT CHUNGKING TO DISCUSS MATTERS ON WHICH YOUR DECISIONS WILL BE VITAL (FROM MERRILL SIGNED FERRIS) WILL BE ACCOMPANIED BY KESWICK AND ONE AIDE. KESWICH HAS ACCOMMODATION ARRANGED AND THE WART IS FISHING FOR AN INVITATION FOR HIMSELF AND AIDE FROM YOU. DO YOU WISH INVITATION EXTENDED? MAIN SUBJECT WILL BE AIR TRANSPORT DIVERSION THEREFORE SUGGEST STRATEMEYER BE PRESENT AT SAME TIME WITH NECESSARY DOPE WHICH IS NOW BEING ASSEMBLED. I WILL SEND YOU FULL DETAILS PRIOR TO ARRIVAL OF THE WART AND CAN CONTRIBUTE NOTHING BY COMING UP WITH HIM BUT STRONGLY RECOMMEND PRESENCE OF STRATEMEYER WHEN YOU DISCUSS AIR TRANSPORT DIVERSIONS

answered

JWS

H

(1237)

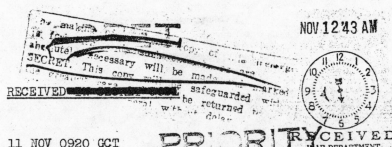

INCOMING RADIO

RECEIVED : 11 NOV 0920 GCT

FROM : WASHINGTON

TO : AMMISCA, COPIR 22, AQUILA 3696

NR : AMMISCA 3809   FILED: 10 NOV 2342 GCT

PROJECT FOR CONSTRUCTION OF FOUR VLR RPT VLR

AIRDROMES IN CALCUTTA AREA APPROVED BY JOINT US CHIEFS OF STAFF
X AQUILA 3689

PAREN FOR WHEELER SIGNED SOMERVILLE REOURAD THREE SIX EIGHT NINE TO
X 3810

NEW DELHI AND THREE EIGHT ZERO ZERO TO CHUNGKING DATED NINE NOVEMBER

FOR STRATEMEYER PAREN PD IT IS IMPERATIVE WORK ON THESE AIRFIELDS

BE INITIATED AND EXPEDITED AT ONCE TO MEET DEADLINE PD ADDITIONAL

AVIATION ENGINEERS BEING DESPATCHED BUT IN MEANTIME FULL USE SHOULD

BE MADE OF LOCAL LABOR AND MATERIAL

Treat eyes alone
C/S has seen

SECRET *Air O R ??*

JVB *21546 (eyes alone) X*

20,623

SECRET   RECEIVED and IN SECRET CODE

<u>INCOMING RADIO</u>

RECEIVED : 11 NOV, 0920 GCT

FROM : WASHINGTON

TO : AMMISCA

NR : 3808   FILED: 10 NOV, 2310 GCT

PRIORITY

RECEIVED
WAR DEPARTMENT
U. S. MILITARY MISSION TO CHINA
CHUNGKING, CHINA

IN A MEMORANDUM FROM THE BRITISH CHIEFS OF STAFF REGARDING

RESULTS OF MEETING BETWEEN GENERALISSIMO AND MOUNTBATTEN IN CHUNGKING

NINETEENTH OCTOBER CMA IT IS STATED THAT QUOTE GENERALISSIMO SAID THAT

THE YUNNAN FORCE WOULD BE READY ON FIRST JANUARY BUT THIS SEEMS TO BE
OPTIMISTIC PARTICULARLY AS THEIR DEPUTY RPT DEPUTY COMMANDER SAID AT

THE CONFERENCE THAT HIS MEN WOULD REQUIRE A THREE HUNDRED PER CENT IN-

CREASE IN THEIR DAILY RATION IF THEY ARE TO BE PHYSICALLY FIT FOR OFFEN-

SIVE OPERATIONS PERIOD UNQUOTE BRITISH CHIEFS OF STAFF REQUEST VIEWS OF

US RPT US JOINT CHIEFS OF STAFF ON THIS MATTER PERIOD (PAREN MARSHALL

FOR PERSONAL ATTENTION STILWELL PAREN) PERIOD WE SHALL AWAIT YOUR SLANT

ON READINESS YOKE FORCE PRIOR TO REPLYING PERIOD PARA WIDESPREAD MAL-

NUTRITION OF CHINESE FORCES WAS DESCRIBED TO US IN YOUR RECENT EIGHT FIVE

ONE NOVEMBER FOURTH PERIOD MEANWHILE UNDERSTAND FROM YOUR EIGHT FIVE FOUR

NOVEMBER EIGHTH THAT MATTER OF IMPROVING RATIONS IS NOW RECEIVING FULL

ATTENTION PERIOD PLEASE FURNISH WAR DEPARTMENT DETAILED INFORMATION AS

A BASIS FOR OUR REPLY TO BRITISH

Eyes alone

① 10645 (eyes alone)

REGRADED CONFIDENTIAL PARAPHRASED

DECLASSIFIED
DOD Dir. 5200.9, Sept. 27,
CEG NCWN by _____ date 3-27-72   20,626

1227

RECEIVED IN SECRET CODE

INCOMING RADIO:

RECEIVED: 11 NOVEMBER 1540 Z.

FROM   : AMMDEL

TO   : AMMISCA

NR   : AM 2036   FILED: AM 2036

EYES ALONE GENERAL STILWELL. OUTLINE PLAN FOR NEXT SEVEN
MONTHS SUBMITTED BY ADMIRAL TO BRITISH CHIEFS OF STAFF FOR APPROVAL
(FROM MERRILL SIGNED FERRIS) CURRENT OPERATIONS ARE AIR OFFENSIVE
AND ADVANCE BY BOATNER WITH COMMITMENT EI THO *OF TWO?* DIVISIONS IF REQUIRED
TO SECURE SHINGBWIYANG AND GET BRIDGEHEAD OVER CHINDWIN. IN
JANUARY SAUCY OPERATION AND OLEANDER SHOW START ON MAJOR SCALE.
SAUCY WILL HAVE THREE DIVISIONS ENGAGED AND FOUR DIVISIONS WILL MOVE
TOWARDS OLEANDER. OVERWHELMING SUPERIORITY IN THESE TWO AREAS IS
ASSURED AND SLIM STATES OBJECTIVES CAN BE TAKEN

ABOVE TWO SHOWS REACH FINAL STAGE ABOUT FEBRUARY FIFTEENTH
WHEN TWO LRP GROUPS HIT KATHA AND PAKOKKU AND, SIMULTANEOUSLY
BOATNER ADVANCES WITH THREE DIVISIONS IN HIS AREA, AND ONE NEW
DIVISION FROM SAUCY FORCE GOES ACROSS CHINDWIN AND ESTABLISHES
BRIDGEHEAD NEAR YUWA. AT SAME TIME AN LRP STARTS OUT FROM PAOSHAN
TOWARDS MAYMYO AND TEN DAYS LATER ANOTHER ONE MOVES FROM YUWA AGAINST
WUNTHO. ABOUT SAME TIME WE TAKE UTOPIA.

ABOVE OPERATIONS ASSUMED TO HAVE REACHED MAXIMUM PITCH BY
MID MARCH WHEN TARZAN WILL BE EXECUTED

ABOVE BELIEVED TO HAVE TAKEN PRESSURE AWAY FROM BOATNER WHO
CAN CONTINUE ON TO KAMAING — MYITKYINA AS CIRCUMSTANCES REQUIRE.

1236

IN MID MARCH YOKE JUMPS OFF AND XRAY FORCES MOVE AGAINST KATHA - BHAMO

TO PERMIT ABOVE OPERATIONS DIVERSION OF ATC TRANSPORTS BY MONTHS WOULD BE JANUARY TWELVE, FEBRUARY FORTY EIGHT, MARCH AND APRIL ONE FOUR SEVEN, MAY NINE FOUR AND JUNE FIFTY FOUR

WHEN ATC HAVE DELIVERED TEN THOUSAND A MONTH WHICH IS NOT INCLUSIVE OF CNAC ONE FOUR ZERO ZERO TONS A MONTH, BRITISH FIGURE WE WILL HAVE A SURPLUS OF TRANSPORTS AS FOLLOWS: JANUARY FIFTY THREE, FEBRUARY SIXTY SEVEN, MARCH EIGHT SIX, APRIL ONE ZERO SIX, MAY NINETY NINE, AND JUNE NINETY ONE.

IF ABOVE ARE DIVERTED FOR OPERATIONS THERE IS AN OVERALL DEFICIT IN THE VERY WORST CASE OF SIXTY ONE TRANSPORTS IN MARCH AND FORTY ONE FOR APRIL FROM TOTAL NUMBER REQUIRED TO DO JOB.

ASSUMING VERY WORST CASE WHICH IS THAT WE DIVERT ALL NECESSARY TRANSPORTS FOR ACTUAL NEEDS, THEY ALSO ESTIMATE HUMP TONNAGE COULD BE MAINTAINED AT TEN THOUSAND TONS EXCEPT DURING MONTHS OF FEBRUARY, MARCH AND APRIL AND THAT FEBRUARY AND MARCH COULD BE ABOUT SIX THOUSAND AND APRIL ABOUT SEVEN THOUSAND

ALL ABOVE GIVES YOU GENERAL PICTURE. EYE FEEL WE CAN GET NO MORE OUT OF THE BRITISH THAN WHAT THEY NOW PLAN. ALSO BELIEVE THAT BRITISH HAVE TWISTED SOME FIGURES GIVEN THEM BY OUR AIR STAFF AND THAT NO ALLOWANCES FOR UNFORESEEN CONTINGENCIES SUCH AS FAILURE OF AIRCRAFT TO ARRIVE, LOSSES, ETCETERA HAVE BEEN MADE WHEREAS B RITISH WITH RESPECT TO THEIR OWN AIRCRAFT HAVE PLANNED ON EVERYTHING INCLUDING POSSIBLE END OF THE WORLD. THEY HAVE BEEN ON CONSERVATIVE SIDE ON EVERYTHING EXCEPT WHEN OUR TRANSPORTS WERE CONCERNED. DE WIART WILL BRING UP ALL PAPERS AND EYE WILL SEND YOU BRIEFS PREPARED OF SAME PAPERS. FEEL YOU WILL REQUIRE STRATEMEYER WHEN TRANSPORT QUESTION COMES UP BUT THAT OTHERWISE YOU ARE FULL PREPARED. (1236)

LOOEY HAS STATED IN SUBSTANCE TO BRITISH CHIEFS OF STAFF
THAT YOU REQUIRE URGENTLY FIVE THOUSAND TONS A MONTH FOR BOTH
NOVEMBER AND DECEMBER FOR YOKE FORCES AS WELL AS FOUR SEVEN ZERO
ZERO FOR FOURTEENTH AIR FORCE AND THAT YOU HAVE INDICATED YOU
WILL NOT OPPOSE SOME DIVERSIONS FROM HUMP TRANSPORTS PROVIDED
REDUCTION IS ABSOLUTE MINIMUM REQUIRED TO MEET OPERATIONAL
REQUIREMENTS AND THAT SUFFICIENT TONNAGE LIFT IS LEFT TO KEEP
YOKE AND CHENNAULT MAINTAINED. FURTHER THAT HE WILL SEND
PROPOSALS TO YOU AS EYE HAVE INDICATED ABOVE AND WILL FORWARD
YOUR REPLY AS SOON AS POSSIBLE.

LOOEY REQUESTS URGENTLY THAT WITHIN AMERICAN FORCES YOU
AND EYE BE ONLY ONES WHO KNOW DATES AND OBJECTIVES IN OVERALL
PICTURE. FERRIS IS OF COURSE SEEING THIS MESSAGE BUT DOES NOT
UNDERSTAND ALL CODE REFERENCES. STRATEMEYER SHOULD BE KEPT IN
AAUK IF YOU HAVE HIM UP AND ONLY KNOW AIR SITE OF TARZAN.

WHATEVER DECISION YOU MAKE AND WHATEVER YOU INFORM THE
WART REQUEST DIRECT INFORMATION ON SAME LINES SO EYE CAN
STRAIGHTEN OUT THE INEVITABLE DISFORTION OF YOUR CONVERSATION
WHICH WILL RESULT ON HIS RETURN.

20,633.

No. 76   Chungking, China,
                                                11 November 1943.

MEMORANDUM:

TO   : His Excellency, Generalissimo Chiang Kai Shek.

                PROPOSALS FOR COMING CONFERENCE

        The Generalissimo's program is to bring up to effective strength,
equip, and train sixty combat divisions, in two groups of thirty each.

        1. The first group consists of the divisions in India, and those
assigned to the Y-force in Yunnan province. These divisions should be
at full strength by January 1, and by that date satisfactorily equipped
with small arms - (rifles, light and heavy machine guns, 60mm and 82mm
mortars, Boys rifles, Tommy guns, Bazookas, and five battalions of 75mm
howitzers), ammunition for four months of operations, and radio sets to
include battalions. Medical service and truck and animal transport will
be sufficient to support the operations contemplated. Training is
progressing satisfactorily. About 200 American instructors are with the
unit schools, which are set up in all divisions. The courses are for
weapons and tactics of small units.

        2. The second group of 30 divisions has been designated and a
school has been set up which takes in 200 Infantry officers a week for
a 6-weeks course. Courses are also run for Medical, Veterinary,
Engineer and Signal troops. Upon graduation these officers return to
their units and set up unit schools. It is planned to put 6,000
officers through the courses by May of 1944. By that time, this group
of divisions should be at full strength, and fairly well trained. With
a road to India open, they should be re-equipped and ready for the field
in August of 1944.

        3. A similar process can be followed, at need, to produce 60
divisions more.

        4. All resources available in China will be used to produce
effective combat units. Trained men of existing units will be made
available as fillers.

        5. China will co-operate in the recapture of Burma by attacks from
Ledo with the X-force and from Paoshan with the Yunnan force.

        6. The training program will be followed and intensified.

        7. Necessary airfields will be built and maintained.

        8. In the event that communications are reopened through Burma
and necessary equipment is supplied, an operation will be conducted
to seize the Canton-Hong Kong area and open communication by sea.

        The Generalissimo expects that:

        1. An all-out effort will be made by the Allies to re-open
communications through Burma.

2. The U. S. A. will supply the equipment for the first and second groups of 30 divisions, and for other divisions that may be required.

3. The Fourteenth U.S. Air Force will be maintained as agreed and supplied sufficiently to allow of sustained operations.

4. The Chinese Air Force will be built up promptly to 2 groups of fighters, 1 group of medium bombers, 1 reconnaissance squadron, and 1 transport squadron, and maintained at that strength. By August of 1944 a third group of fighters, and a group of heavy bombardment will be added and maintained thereafter.

5. Following the seizure of the Canton—Hong Kong area, the U. S. will put 10 Infantry divisions, 2 armored divisions and appropriate auxiliary units into South China for operations against Central and North China. Contingent upon this allocation of troops, the Generalissimo will accept American command of the combined U. S. -Chinese forces, under his general direction.

6. The U. S. will, at the earliest practicable time, put long -range bombing units in China to operate against the Japanese mainland.

7. The ferry route will be maintained at a capacity of 10,000 tons a month.

8. Training personnel will be supplied as required.

9. Medical personnel will be supplied for the second group of 30 divisions.

JOSEPH W. STILWELL,
Lt. General, U.S. Army.

1160

RECEIVED IN ~~SECRET CODE~~

PRIORITY

RECEIVED : 12 NOV 0200 GCT

FROM : WAR

TO : AMMISCA AQUILA 3700

NO. : 3815 FILED 11 NOV 1835 GCT   P R I O R I T Y

THIS IS TO KEEP YOU ABREAST SFKXOJJENT INFORMATION ON THE
USE OF VERY LONG RANGE BOMBERS AGAINST VITAL JAPANESE TARGETS PAREN
FOR STILWELL FOR ACTION AND STRATEMEYER FOR INFORMATION FROM MARSHALL
PAREN YESTERDAY THE PRESIDENT ADVISED THE GENERALISSIMO AND THE PRIME
MINISTER OF THE PLAN TO BOMB JAPAN EARLY NEXT YEAR PERIOD HE SPECIFIC-
ALLY ASKED THE PRIME MINISTER TO RENDER EVERY POSSIBLE ASSISTANCE TO
THE CONSTRUCTION OF FOUR AIR BASES IN THE CALCUTTA AREA PERIOD HE
FURTHER ADVISED THE PRIME MINISTER THAT THE NECESSARY ENGINEERS WERE
BEING PREPARED FOR EARLY MOVEMENT PERIOD IN HIS MESSAGE TO THE
GENERALISSIMO THE PRESIDENT STATED THAT FIVE LONG RANGE BOMBER AIR-
FIELDS WERE REQUIRED IN THE CHENGTU RPT CHENGTU AREA WITH LIMITED
HOUSING FACILITIES PERIOD HE ASKED FOR CLOSE SUPPORT TO ENSURE THEIR
REDINESS BY THE END OF MARCH ONE NINE FOUR FOUR PERIOD THE PRESIDENT
FURTHER STATED THAT WE WILL SUPPLY THE NECESSARY ENGINEERING SUPER-
VISION BUT MUST RELY ON THE CHINESE TO PROVIDE THE NECESSARY LABOR
AND MATERIALS SO AS NOT RPT NOT TO DRAW ON THE AIR SUPPLY LINE PERIOD
NECESSARY FUNDS THROUGH LEND LEASE APPROPRIATIONS CAN BE MADE AVAIL-
ABLE IF THIS WILL EXPEDITE AND ENSURE COMPLETION OF THE WORK THE
PRESIDENT STATED.

Tate

DECLASSIFIED
DOD Dir. 5200.9, Sept. 27, 1958
20,658 NCWN by _____ date 3-17-72   1230

Copies #4 for Mountbatten, eyes alone.

Remark 6. - This rumor is so wild and apparently groundless that I hesitate to make inquiries. There has never been the slightest indication of such a thing. It is probably the last thing the Chinese would think of doing under existing circumstances. We know positively that they are in no condition to make the move and that they have never considered anything but a defensive attitude on that front. I will try and get the dope if I can do so without being laughed out of court. I am curious to know the source of these rumors -

Stilwell -

Rec'd 120255
Sent 120310

_Re_ 1224

107.12

1239

Agwar 857 fr Gen Marshall Eyes Alone

Reurad 3802, Sultan is first choice. Believe he is only suitable candidate on your list.

Stilwell

Rec'd 120257
Sent 120320

7240

1163

AD 2??

Arundel   for   Merrill.

Very interesting dope you are sending me.
Coming down by sixteenth and can battle
with transport question down there. ~~Ask
Stratemeyer when I want you to go when
he gets there~~ Stratemeyer will have a bit
of news for you. He is on his way. Let the
wart come along. He can stay at my house
temporarily repeat temporarily. I said
temporarily.

                                        Stilwell -

Rec'd 12 0315
Sent 120330

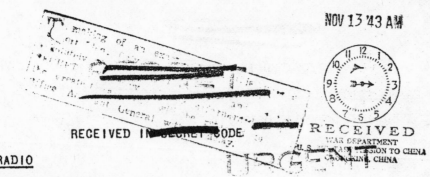

NOV 13 '43 AM

RECEIVED IN SECRET CODE

RECEIVED
WAR DEPARTMENT
U.S. ~~MISSION~~ TO CHINA
CHUNGKING, CHINA

URGENT

<u>INCOMING RADIO</u>

RECEIVED : 12 NOV 0350 GCT

FROM : ~~AMMKUN~~ COGUK

TO : AMMISCA   AMMDEL D 46 N

NR : M 45 N   FILED : 13 NOV 0226 GCT

ZZZZ

MY HEADQUARTERS ADVISED THAT DEFINITE GREEN LIGHT HAS BEEN
GIVEN TWILIGHT STOP FIVE AIRDROMES IN LAST SELECTED EASTERN AREA WILL
BE NECESSARY STOP PAREN FROM STRATEMEYER TO STILWELL FOR <u>TATE</u> INFORMA-
TION STONE PAREN SPEED ON CONSTRUCTION ESSENTIAL STOP IT IS DESIRED
TO enable us
THAT YOU COLLECT ALL POSSIBLE INFORMATION/<u>EJDBLE UL</u> TO PUT PLAN FOR
CONSTRUCTION ON AIRDROMES INTO EFFECT EARLIEST POSSIBLE DATE STOP I
WILL ADVISE CHENNAULT AND IT IS DIRECTED THAT YOU DISCUSS THOROUGHLY
WITH STILWELL PRIOR TO HIS DEPARTURE

Treat eyes alone

air off
c/s
Emc

1249

DR   20,701

1165

RECEIVED IN SECRET CODE

INCOMING RADIO

RECEIVED: 12 NOVEMBER 0613 GCT

FROM   :   AMMDEL

TO   :   AMMISCA

NO   :   SVC 154   FILED: 12 NOVEMBER 0229 GCT

    EYES ALONE GENERAL STILWELL SIGNED FERRIS. IN THE HOS-
PITAL ARE IAE [ONE] HUNDRED SEVENTY FIVE GALAHADS ACCORDING TO RE-
PORTS FROM BRINK. SEAC IS NOT IN BEING SO WE ARE COMPOSING DIRECTIVE
FOR BRINK TO BE USED IN TRAINING BUT WILL COORDINATE WITH SEAC
AND HAVE THEM CONCUR. WE HAVE SO FAR MANAGED TO PUT OFF THE
SEAC FOR A COMMANDER FOR GALAHAD BUT IT IS BELIEF THAT VERY
SOON A SMALL GROUP HEADQUARTERS AND COMMANDER MUST BE SELECTED
(THIS PARAPHRASES OUR MSG AM 2034 DATED 11TH REPLYING TO YOUR
SVC 18 FROM SIGS JGTA TO SIGS AMMISCA). MILES AND EIFFLER MAY
BE RELIEVED

    THIS ABOVE DUE TO AN EVIDENT ERROR, AS I SEE IT, IN LOCATING
THE AREA FOR TRAINING AT PRESENT

    IT IS BEING CONSIDERED THAT THIS HQ WILL BE MERGED WITH AND
UNDER SEAC; ALL OF ASIA IS WANTED BY LOOEY AND HIS MOTIVE IS
AMBITION

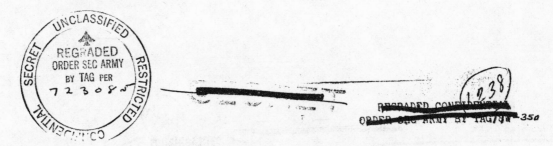

SECRET   UNCLASSIFIED   RESTRICTED   CONFIDENTIAL
REGRADED
ORDER SEC ARMY
BY TAG PER
723085

REGRADED CONFIDENTIAL
ORDER SEC ARMY BY TAG/JW 350
1238

20666

Agwar 870 ~~AAA~~ for Gen Marshall

Reurad NR 3808. There is as I have reported wide-spread malnutrition in the Chinese Army. Among the Yunnan troops it is spotty. Some are much better than others. I do not know who made the three hundred percent ration increase statement. I did not. I now have the promise of the war ministry for ~~an~~ immediate increase of the rations of the Y-force as to meat, salt, beans, and the monetary allowance for fresh vegetables, which has been doubled. ~~The increase should produce a satisfactory ration.~~ Chinese troops respond rapidly to improved diet, and my belief is that two months of the rations now promised will put these troops into ~~shape~~. ~~We~~ have been working on this matter for a long time, and I believe the agitation has already improved conditions. The new allowances should produce a satisfactory ration. Incidentally, as counter-battery, the report of Wilson-Braud, British L.O. with Y-force, might be asked for.

Stilwell

120720
Sent TB 120740

FILE
Stmts
Eyes alone

INCOMING RADIO:

RECEIVED: 12 NOVEMBER 0845 Z.

FROM   : AMMDEL

TO   : AMMISCA

NR   : AM 2038   FILED: 12 NOVEMBER 0504 Z.

ONLY FOR GEN STILWELLS EYES FROM MERRILL SIGNED FERRIS. AS EYE UNDERSTAND STRATEMEYER NOW WITH YOU. SUBMIT HEREWITH DETAILED BREAK DOWN ON TRANSPORT REQUIREMENT FOR OPERATIONS AS STATED BY MOUNTBATTEN TO BRITISH CHIEF OF STAFF CALCULATED ON BRITISH SCALE OF OPERATIONAL EFFORT REQUIREMENTS BASED ON DC THREES ARE IN MONTHS: JANUARY FIVE EIGHT [58], FEBRUARY TWO ONE THREE [123], MARCH THREE SIX ONE [361], APRIL THREE SIX ONE [361], MAY TWO EIGHT TWO [282] AND JUNE TWO TWO ONE [221]. BRITISH WILL HAVE TO PARTIALLY FILL THIS REQUIREMENT ONE FOUR ZERO [140] AIRPLANES. THIS MAKES TOTAL DEFICIENCIES BY MONTHS: JANUARY EIGHTEEN [18], FEBRUARY SEVENTY THREE [73], MARCH TWO TWO ONE [221], APRIL TWO TWO ONE [221], MAY ONE FOUR TWO [142], AND JUNE EIGHTY ONE [81]. IF ABOVE DEFICINCIES ARE MET BY AMERICAN PLANES FROM HUMP, CALCULATING ON AMERICAN SCALE OF OPERATIONAL EFFORT THE FOLLOWING NUMBER OF PLANES PER MONTH WOULD HAVE TO BE DIVERTED COLON JANUARY TWELVE [12], FEBRUARY FORTY EIGHT [48], MARCH ONE FOUR SEVEN [147], APRIL ONE FOUR SEVEN [147], MAY NINETY FOUR [94], AND JUNE FIFTY FOUR [54]. ASSUMING ATC IS LIMITED TO TEN THOUSAND TONS A MONTH OVER THE HUMP AMERICANS WILL HAVE FOLLOWING SURPLUS AIRCRAFT PER MONTH: JANUARY FIFTY THREE [53], FEBRUARY SIXTY SEVEN [67]

(1245)

MARCH EIGHTY SIX, APRIL ONE ZERO SIX , MAY NINETY NINE AND JUNE
NINETY ONE. IF THIS SURPLUS IS DIVERTED FOR OPERATIONS THE REMAINING
DEFICIT WOULD BE SIXTY ONE PLANES IN MARCH AND FORTY ONE PLANES IN
APRIL. ASSUMING AMERICANS MADE UP ENTIRE DEFICIT AND ALLOWING
TIME FOR PILOT TRAINING HUMP TONNAGE COULD STILL BE MAINTAINED AT
TEN THOUSAND TONS PER MONTH EXCEPT DURING FEBRUARY, MARCH AND APRIL
AND WOULD FALL SHORT ONLY BY TWO THOUSAND TONS IN FEBRUARY AND MARCH
AND ONE THOUSAND THREE HUNDRED TONS IN APRIL. ABOVE CALCULATIONS
ALLOWS FOR NORMAL WASTAGE NOT FOR OTHER OPERATIONAL HAZARDS. END
OF SUBSTANCE OF BRITISH FIGURES ON HUMP . EYE WAS NOT PRESENT AT ANY
DISCUSSION HELD ON THIS AND WAS NEITHER NOTIFIED OF PROPOSED DISCUSSION
NOR INVITED. ON RECEIPT OF FIGURES IMMEDIATELY NOTICED THE FIGURES
ON SURPLUS PLANES AND SUSPECTED THEY WERE GROSSLY IN ERROR. CONFIRMED
THIS WITH STRATEMEYERS STAFF AND SUBMITTED A WRITTEN PROTEST TO
LOOEY IN YOUR NAME STATING POLITELY THAT EXCEPTION WAS TAKEN TO THE
FIGURES AND WE COULD NOT ACCEPT THEM. THIS CREATED A BIG STINK AND
PRESENT INDICATION IS THAT A CORRECTION WILL BE SENT. MEANWHILE
STRATEMEYERS STAFF IS PREPARING THEIR OWN FIGURES ON SAME PROJECT WHICH
WILL BE SENT YOU WHEN READY

LRP GROUP FROM PAOSHAN IS STILL HOT AND THE WART HAS INSTRUCT+
IONS TO NEGOTIATE FOR PURCHASE OF MULES WITH BRITISH FUNDS WHILE UP
YOUR WAY. THE WART IS PRETTY MUCH OF A SOLDIER AND TOLD ME HE
DISLIKES ALL THE INTRIGUE AND HOPES HE CAN TALK OVER EVERYTHING
FRANKLY WITH YOU DURING VISIT. LOOEY TAKES OVER COMMAND OFFICIALLY
MIDNIGHT FIFTEEN DASH SIXTEEN NOVEMBER PROBABLY.

1245

20,673.

RECEIVED IN ~~SECRET CODE.~~

INCOMING RADIO:

RECEIVED: 12 NOVEMBER 1020 Z.   U R G E N T

FROM   : AMMKUN

TO   : AMMISCA

NR   : C 962   FILED: 12 NOVEMBER 0813 Z.

    WEI LI HUANG GENERAL (GEN STILWELL EYES ALONE FROM DORN) HAS DEFINITELY BEEN APPOINTED ACTING COMMANDER OF CHINESE EXPEDITIONARY FORCES ACCORDING TO CHINESE HQRS. THIS IS STRICTLY CONFIDENTIAL UNTIL OFFICIALLY RELEASED. HO YING CHIN IS BRINGING HIM TO KUNMING IN ABOUT ONE WEEK. THEY NOW ADMIT WHAT WE FEARED ABOUT CHEN CHENGS CONDITION.

FILE

20,671.

(1247)

No. 79

Chungking, China,
12 November 1943.

MEMORANDUM:

TO   : His Excellency, Generalissimo Chiang Kai Shek.

Enclosed herewith are 2 additional copies each of the
2 radios from your Excellency to President Roosevelt
together with copies of our letters numbers 63, 67, 74, 77
and 78 transmitting messages from President Roosevelt to
your Excellency.

7 Incls –   JOSEPH W. STILWELL,
   as above.   Joint Chief of Staff for Generalissimo.

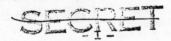

No. 77

Chungking, China,
12 November 1943.

MEMORANDUM:

TO   : His Excellency, Generalissimo Chiang Kai Shek.

The following message has just been received from President Roosevelt for transmission to your Excellency:

"I AM TERRIBLY SORRY TO LEARN OF MADAME CHIANGS ILLNESS PERSONAL AND MOST SECRET FROM THE PRESIDENT TO THE GENERALISSIMO SIGNED ROOSEVELT AND SINCERELY HOPE THAT SHE WILL BE FULLY RECOVERED IN TIME FOR OUR CONFERENCE.

"I HAVE HAD A LONG TALK WITH GENERAL SOMERVELL AND APPRECIATE VERY MUCH YOUR COURTESIES TO HIM. HE HAS GIVEN ME YOUR PRIVATE MESSAGE AS I HAVE ALREADY INDICATED TO YOU.

"I AGREE WITH YOU FULLY THAT WE SHOULD MEET TOGETHER BEFORE I SEE STALIN. I WANT SO MUCH TO HAVE SOME GOOD TALKS WITH YOU SO, NATURALLY, I AM EAGERLY LOOKING FORWARD TO SEEING YOU."

JOSEPH W. STILWELL,
Joint Chief of Staff for Generalissimo.

REGRADED CONFIDENTIAL. PARAPHRASED
VERSIONS REGRADED UNCLASSIFIED
ORDER 350 ARMY BY TAG/7 W - 250

- 1 -

SECRET

No. 78

Chungking, China,
12 November 1943.

MEMORANDUM:

TO   : His Excellency, Generalissimo Chiang Kai Shek.

The following message has just been received from President Roosevelt for transmission to your Excellency:

"PERSONAL AND SECRET FROM THE PRESIDENT TO THE GENERALISSIMO.

"WE ARE NOW ABLE TO LAUNCH HEAVY BOMBING ATTACKS UPON VITAL JAPANESE HOMELAND OBJECTIVES CONSIDERABLY EARLIER THAN PREVIOUSLY SEEMED POSSIBLE. TO ACCOMPLISH THIS WILL REQUIRE FIVE LONG RUN BOMBER AIRFIELDS FOR THE NEW AND VERY POWERFUL PLANES, WITH LIMITED HOUSING FACILITIES IN THE GENERAL CHENGTU AREA IN THE CONSTRUCTION OF WHICH WE NEED YOUR CLOSE SUPPORT TO ENSURE THEIR READINESS BY THE END OF MARCH ONE NINE FOUR FOUR. WE CAN SUPPLY THE TECHNICAL ENGINEERING SUPERVISION BUT MUST RELY ON YOU TO PROVIDE THE NECESSARY LABOR AND MATERIALS SO AS NOT TO DRAW ON THE AIR SUPPLY LINE. I WILL UNDERTAKE TO MAKE AVAILABLE THE NECESSARY FUNDS THROUGH LEND LEASE APPROPRIATIONS IF THAT WILL EXPEDITE AND HASTEN THE COMPLETION OF THE WORK ON THE DESIRED SCHEDULE. I AM PERSONALLY CONVINCED WE CAN DEAL THE JAP A TRULY CRIPPLING BLOW SO CLOSE TO BOTH OUR HEARTS BY THIS SUDDEN SURPRISE ATTACK. SIGNED ROOSEVELT."

JOSEPH W. STILWELL,
Joint Chief of Staff for Generalissimo.

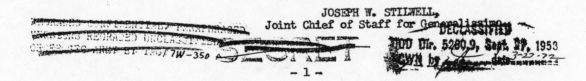

- 1 -

Eyes alone

File

INCOMING RADIO

RECEIVED: 13 NOVEMBER 0610 GCT

FROM : AMMDEL   PRIORITY

PRIORITY

TO : AMMISCA

NO : AM 2045 FILED: 13 NOVEMBER 0505 GCT

STILWELLS EYES ALONE FROM FERRIS. LEAVING HERE 14TH IS WART. CONDITIONS PERMITTING WILL GO EAST SAME DAY. MERRILL SAYS HE HAS PERSONAL MESSAGE FROM WINSTON FOR GISSIMO WHICH HE WOULD LIKE TO DISCUSS WITH YOU PRIOR TO DELIVERY. POWER POLITICS STILL APPARENT. SO FAR WE ARE OKAY BUT MUST WATCH STEP. DONOVAN EXPECTED HERE NEXT WEEK

See 1255

1252

20702

1174

HQ. U. S. ARMY FORCES

CHUNGKING, CHINA,
15 November 1943.

AMMDEL *AD 2568*

DO YOU KNOW WHAT ACTION WAS TAKEN PAREN EYES ALONE
FERRIS FOR CRESWELL FROM DICKEY SIGNED STILWELL PAREN ON
SENDING A QUOTE SPECIAL SECURITY OFFICER UNQUOTE FOR
GENERAL STILWELLS STAFF   QUERY REFERENCE SUMMARY RELAY
THIS HEADQUARTERS AUGUST ONE AND OURAD ABLE DOG ONE SEVEN
ZERO TWO ~~OCTOBER~~ *AUGUST* THIRTEEN PD   QUERY DASH IS THIS OFFICER
IN DELHI CMA ENROUTE TO THEATRE CMA OR WAS THE PROPOSAL
REJECTED PD   ASK JOE

OFFICIAL:

Edwin M. Cahill
EDWIN M. CAHILL,
Lt. Col., A.G.D.
Asst. Adjutant General.

RECEIVED IN CODE ROOM ___*OMK*___ DATE *11/13* *0720*
ACTUAL TIME OF DISPATCH AND METHOD *TB 0800.*

JKD/jjb

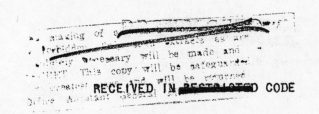

NOV 14 43 AM

R E C E I V E D
WAR DEPARTMENT
U. S. MILITARY MISSION TO CHINA
CHUNGKING, CHINA

INCOMING RADIO

RECEIVED: 13 NOV 1120 GCT

FROM : WAR

TO : AMMISCA

NR : 3828   FILED: 13 NOVEMBER 0536 GCT

COVELL WILLIAM EASY ROGER BRIGADIER GENERAL TO MAJOR GENERAL
AUS AND FRANK DOG MERRILL, MALCOLM FOX LINDSEY, REUBEN CHARLIE HOOD
JUNIOR, EUGENE HOW BEEBE, FRANK DORN AND CHARLES BAKER STONE THREE
DOG COLONELS TO BRIGADIER GENERAL AUS PAREN FROM ULIO THE ADJUTANT
GENERAL PAREN NOTIFY THEM PRESIDENT HAS SUBMITTED TO SENATE NOMINATIONS
FOR TEMPORARY APPOINTMENT TO GRADES INDICATED.

20,732

INCOMING RADIO:

RECEIVED: 13 NOVEMBER 1425 Z.   P R I O R I T Y

FROM   : WASHINGTON

TO   : AMMISCA

NR   : 3829   FILED: 13 NOVEMBER 0249 Z.

        SECRET AND PERSONAL FOR THE GENERALISSIMO FROM THE

PRESIDENT. EYE AM JUST OFF FOR FRENCH NORTH AFRICA AND OUR

MEETING PLACE WHERE EYE AM SCHEDULED TO ARRIVE BY THE TWENTY

SECOND. EYE EXPECT TO STAY THERE UNTIL THE TWENTY SIXTH WHEN

EYE WILL GO TO SEE OUR FRIEND FROM THE NORTH AND THEN RETURN

TO OUR CONFERENCE PLACE IN THREE OR FOUR DAYS. (SGD ROOSEVELT)

        EYE DO HOPE YOU CAN COME BY THE TWENTY SECOND AND

THAT MADAME CHIANG IS MUCH B ETTER. PLEASE GIVE HER MY WARM

REGARDS.

                        20,714.

No. 80   CHUNGKING, CHINA,
                                                          14 November 1943.

MEMORANDUM:

TO   : His Excellency, Generalissimo Chiang Kai Shek.

        The following message has just been received from
President Roosevelt for transmission to your Excellency:

        "SECRET AND PERSONAL FOR THE GENERALISSIMO FROM THE
PRESIDENT.

        "I AM JUST OFF FOR FRENCH NORTH AFRICA AND OUR MEETING
PLACE WHERE I AM SCHEDULED TO ARRIVE BY THE TWENTY SECOND.
I EXPECT TO STAY THERE UNTIL THE TWENTY SIXTH WHEN I WILL
GO TO SEE OUR FRIEND FROM THE NORTH AND THEN RETURN TO OUR
CONFERENCE PLACE IN THREE OR FOUR DAYS.

        "I DO HOPE YOU CAN COME BY THE TWENTY SECOND AND THAT
MADAME CHIANG IS MUCH BETTER. PLEASE GIVE HER MY WARM
REGARDS. SGD ROOSEVELT."

                                    JOSEPH W. STILWELL,
                          Joint Chief of Staff for Generalissimo.

                              - 1 -

NOV 14 '43 AM

R E C E I V E D
WAR DEPARTMENT
U. S. MILITARY MISSION TO CHINA
CHUNGKING, CHINA

OPERATIONAL PRIORITY

INCOMING RADIO

RECEIVED: 13 NOV 1620 GCT

FROM : COPIR

TO : AMMISCA

NR : 7 FILED: 13 NOV 1410 GCT

    THANK YOU FOR YOUR NO FOUR PERIOD EYE AM PASSING YOUR VIEWS ON TO THE PRIME MINISTER PERIOD (PAREN FOR STILWELL FROM MOUNTBATTEN PAREN) I HEARD THE RUMOR FROM THREE SEPARATE AND APPARENTLY RELIABLE SOURCES CMA AND WILL GIVE YOU PARTICULARS WHEN YOU COME TO DELHI PERIOD SORRY ABOUT HAVING TO CHANGE CARTON DE WIARTS MOVEMENTS BUT RECEIVED A MESSAGE FROM GENERALISSIOM SAYING HE WOULD NOT BE AVAILABLE TO RECEIVE HIM FOR ABOUT A FORTNIGHT PERIOD PAREN YOUR BEDROOM AT FARIDKOT HOUSE IS BEING GOT READY FOR YOU PERIOD LOOKING FORWARD TO SEEING YOU TUESDAY.

20,730

1256

URGENT

Agwar. 875

Gmo desires that eye
accompany him to Cairo.
Eyes also Marshell Bawa
(Stillwell). Request authority
to issue necessary orders.
He desires also that Shortinger
and Chennault accompany me.
Hearn will be in command
in my absence.

Sent TB 0255   Nov. 14

10893.

To Aquar 876 URGENT   Eyes alone
Aquila D 619 ~~SECRET~~

    Generalissimo agrees to modified twilight
plan as stated and will supply men and
materials (Marshall from Stilwell information
Stratemeyer cite War 3815 Nov. 11) He wants
technical help and engineer units started
soon as possible. Requirements technical
help to come from Uncle Sugar air priority
will follow.

red
dist + B ○ 45°
          ○ 5 10   9:14

10937

(1259)

RECEIVED IN ~~SECRET CODE~~

INCOMING RADIO

PRIORITY

RECEIVED: 1100 GCT 14 NOV

FROM : WAR

TO : AMMISCA, AMMDEL 4229

N8 : 3837   FILED: 13 NOV 2220 GCT

ALL AMERICAN TROOPS IN CHINA, BURMA, INDIA (INCLUDING GALAHAD) ARE UNDER YOUR COMMAND. (FOR STILWELLS EYES ONLY FROM MARSHALL INFORMATIONAL FERRIS FOR TRANSMITTAL AS EYES ONLY TO WEDEMEYER ANSWERING COPIR TWENTY EIGHT) AS DEPUTY SUPREME COMMANDER TO MOUNTBATTEN YOU ARE TO EMPLOY YOUR FORCES, INCLUDING CHINESE TROOPS ALLOTTED BY THE GENERALISSIMO, SO AS TO INSURE AN EFFECTIVE UNITED EFFORT BY SOUTHEAST ASIA COMMAND. GALAHAD WAS DISPATCHED TO INDIA TO TAKE PART IN LONG RANGE PENETRATION OPERATIONS. IF THESE OPERATIONS ARE TO BE COMMANDED BY WINGATE, THE AMERICAN GROUP SHOULD OPERATE IN COMBAT UNDER HIS CENTRAL DIRECTION. THE INDIVIDUAL AND UNIT TRAINING AS WELL AS ADMINISTRATION AND SUPPLY MUST REMAIN THE RESPONSIBILITY OF GENERAL STILWELL. HOWEVER, THEIR TRAINING MUST BE CLOSELY COORDINATED WITH THAT OF THE BRITISH TO THE EXTENT THAT BATTALIONS OR EVEN SMALLER UNITS CAN OPERATE WITH BRITISH UNITS OR VICE VERSA. AMERICAN UNITS OF ALL TYPES SHOULD RETAIN THEIR IDENTITY. SERVICE UNITS HAVE BEEN FURNISHED YOU TO SERVE COMBAT UNITS OR ACCOMPLISH ESSENTIAL PROJECTS. ANY DIVERSION FROM THEIR PRIME MISSION MUST BE YOUR RESPONSIBILITY CONSISTENT WITH MEETING YOUR OWN REQUIRE-MENTS AND ASSISTING TO THE UTMOST THE UNITED EFFORT. ANY DEPARTURE

DECLASSIFIED
DOD Dir. 5200.9, Sept. 27, 1958
NOWN by ___ date 3-27-72

-20,772

1257

~~REGRADED CONFIDENTIAL PARAPHRASED VERSIONS REGRADED UNCLASSIFIED ORDER SEC ARMY BY TAG# 744-354~~

(PAGE 2)

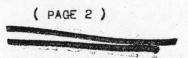

FROM THE ABOVE IN THE INTEREST OF BRINGING ABOUT A STRONGER UNITED
EFFORT SOONER WILL BE FOR YOU TO DETERMINE. WE MUST ALL EAT SOME
CROW IF WE ARE TO FIGHT THE SAME WAR TOGETHER. THE IMPACT ON THE
JAPS IS THE PAY OFF.

20,772

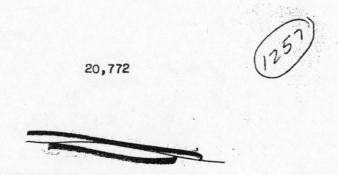

1257

No. 81

Chungking, China,
15 November 1943.

MEMORANDUM:

TO   : Her Excellency, Madame Chiang Kai Shek.

        I hesitate to discuss _over the phone_ details of the subject of our telephone conversation for secret and security reasons. You can depart, I am assured by Colonel Tate, as late as early-morning of November 19th and arrive your destination by November 22nd. In fact he says with luck you could arrive late afternoon of November 21st.

        Colonel Tate thinks it best not to attempt to settle the exact hour of departure i. e. whether 6:00 A.M., 7:00 A.M., or 8:00 A.M., and stops for gassing up, etcetra until the pilot arrives. He should reach here some time tomorrow afternoon.

        A tentative schedule could be as follows if you should so desire:

LEAVE	DATE	TIME	ARRIVE	DATE	TIME
Peishiyi	18	8:00 A.M.	Agra	18	6:00 P.M.
Agra	19	Noon	Karachi	19	5:00 P.M.
Karachi	20	8:00 A.M.	Basra	20	6:00 P.M.
Basra	21	9:00 A.M.	Cairo	21	3:00 P.M.

        I hope the above can substitute for the 5:00 P.M. telephone call which you suggested.

                        Sincerely,

                        T. G. HEARN,
                    Major General, G.S.C.
                     Chief of Staff.

INCOMING RADIO

RECEIVED : 15 NOV 151500

FROM : AMMRAM

TO : AMMISCA

NO. : AC 299 FILED 15 NOV 0900 GCT

WHEN ARMY COMMANDER INFORMED OF YOUR ORDERS PAREN
EYES OF STILWELL ALONE FROM BERGIN REURAD ROGER ABLE SIX
SEVEN ONE NOV FOURTEEN PAREN HE STATED THAT IT WAS NOT
HIS INTENTION TO MOVE HIS HQ TO LEDO BUT TO MERELY ESTAB-
LISH WHAT HE CONSIDERS A LIAISON DETACHMENT PRD HE ASKED
ME TO CLARIFY THIS AND TO ASSURE YOU/HE PERSONALLY WILL NOT
MOVE UNTIL AUTHORIZED BY YOU PRD HE WISHES TO POINT OUT
THAT SINCE TWO OF HIS DIVISIONS ARE NOW IN THE COMBAT AREA
HE CONSIDERS IT ADVISABLE TO HAVE HIS CHIEF OF STAFF AND A
SMALL DETACHMENT FROM EACH SECTION TO COOPERATE AND ASSIST
BOATNER NOW THAT CONTACT WITH THE ENEMY HAS BEEN ESTABLISH-
ED PRD SOONER OR LATER THEY WILL EXERT PRESSURE FROM HERE
AND CHUNGKING TO MOSE OUT PRD EVENTUALLY HE WILL MOVE AND
I BELIEVE THAT IF SOME DEFINITE TIME CAN BE SET FOR HIS
DEPARTURE IT WILL GO A LONG WAY TO PRESERVE THE VERY FINE
EXISTING RELATIONS WHICH WE ENJOY PARA SPECIFICALLY ARMY
COMMDR WANTS TO SEND HIS CHIEF OF STAFF TO FORWARD AREA
AND HIS REQUEST IS ACCORDINGLY TRANSMITTED FOR YOUR CON-
SIDERATION PRD FOR POLITICAL REASONS THIS MIGHT BE ADVISABLE
20,838-

1264

WITH UNDERSTANDING THAT GENERAL HSU AND PARTY WILL NOT
EXCEED TOTAL OF TEN OFFICERS AND OTHER RANKS PRD YOUR
FURTHER INSTRUCTIONS EYE AWAIT

JAHJR.

- 20. 838 -

Relayed to Arundel
for action 11/16
Urgent. Ewa

1264

RECEIVED IN ~~SECRET~~ CODE

<u>INCOMING RADIO</u>

RECEIVED   :   16 NOV 0432 GCT   PRIORITY

FROM   :   WAR

TO   :   AMMDEL 4258, AQUILA 3718, AMMISCA

NR   :   3850   FILED :   15 NOV 1709 GCT

LEAVING UNCLE SUGAR FOR CALCUTTA APPROXIMATELY FIFTEEN

DECEMBER ARE THREE ENGR AVN BNS REPEAT THREE ENGR AVN BNS AND ONE

AIR BORNE ENGR AVN BN REPEAT ONE AIRBORNE ENGR/BN WITH ASSOCIATED

SERVICES FOR CONSTRUCTION OF FIELDS IN CALCUTTA AREA PERIOD TECHNICAL

HELP REURAD EIGHT SEVEN SIX NOVEMBER FOURTEEN PAREN FOR STILWELL

INFORMATION STRATEMEYER AND FERRIS FROM MARSHALL PAREN CONTEMPLATED

FOR STAGING FIELDS IN CHINA BUT NO RPT NO ENGR UNITS WILL BE FURNISHED

PAREN CITE WAR THREE EIGHT ONE FIVE NOVEMBER ELEVEN IN WHICH NO RPT

NO ENGR UNITS ARE MENTIONED PERIOD YOUR REQUIREMENTS FOR TECHNICAL

PERSONNEL IN CONNECTION WITH STAGING FIELDS REQUESTED AT EARLIEST

POSSIBLE MOMENT

20,883

DECLASSIFIED
OD Dir. 5200.9, Sept. 27, 1958
NCWN by _____ date 3-22-72

1265

1187

INCOMING RADIO: OPERATIONAL PRIORITY

RECEIVED: 16 NOVEMBER 0800 Z.

FROM   : COGUK

TO   : AMMISCA   A QUILA A 101 NE

NR   :   M 65 NE   FILED 16 NOVEMBER 0606 Z.

        EYES ALONE STILWELL AND STRATEMEYER SGD CHENNAULT.
FIFTEEN BAKER TWO FOURS DEPARTED KUNMING TO BOMB KOWLOON DOCKS
AND SHIPPING AS DIVERSIONARY DADID, WHILE SIX LOONS EYID
TWENTY TWO MIKE THIRTEEN MIPES RD FIRST REPORTS BY OBSERVATION
MISSION VERY SUCCESSFUL. ONE BAKER TWO FOUR FORCED LANDED
FORTY MILES SOUTH KUNMING, PART OF CREW OF ONE LOON BAILED
OUT WHEN SHIP LOST AN ENGINE, PLANE LATER LANDED SAFELY.
MORE DETAILS LATER.

                        20,885.

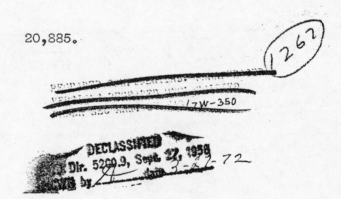

HEADQUARTERS ARMY AIR FORCES
INDIA BURMA SECTOR
CHINA BURMA INDIA THEATER

A. P. O. 885
18 November 1943

SUBJECT: Twilight Project

TO   : Major General THOMAS G. HEARN, Forward Echelon, U.S.A.F.,
          China Burma India Theater, A. P. O. 879.

    1. Colonel A. L. MOORE, AC, and Lt. Col. K. E. MADSEN, EC, are
representing my headquarters on the Twilight Project.

    2. It is requested that you assist these officers in the survey
of the Chengtu area for VLR Bombardment, Transport, and Fighter
Fields. Information must be obtained on the communication net
(air, rail, and water) and construction requirements to improve this
net to the necessary minimum standards as well as an estimate for
the complete construction requirements for the airfields.

    3. As you know, this plan is of the greatest importance to the
Army as well as to the Army Air Forces and all the assistance that
you can render these officers will be greatly appreciated.

    4. It is imperative that final agreement for airdromes and on
other engineering matter be reached at this time, and that action
be started at once toward the completion of the necessary construction
according to the target dates as given to you by Colonel MOORE.

    5. It is my desire to place under one head all the detail planning
of this project. I have appointed General OLIVER as Twilight Project
Officer. It will be appreciated if all matters pertaining to this
project be taken up through this office. General OLIVER will keep me
advised of the progress of this project.

    6. Yesterday General STILLWELL made the decision that the construction
of airdromes in China would be a responsibility of the Army Air Forces,
since China was considered as a combat zone. India was considered as a Communication Zone and the SOS would be responsible for construction in India.

                              GEORGE E. STRATEMEYER,
                              Major General, U.S.A.,
                              Commanding General.

CLASSIFICATION

~~SECRET~~

NR

No. X-434   FROM   AMMDEL   DATE 19 NOV 1943

RECEIVED 19 NOV 1943

DECODED 19 NOV 1943

FOR   AMSME

GENERAL STILWELLS EYES ONLY CMA DELIVER UPON HIS ARRIVAL AT CAIRO APPROX
NOVEMBER TWO ONE RPT TWO ONE PRD LOOEY RADIOED BRITISH CHIEFS OF STAFF
YESTERDAY A CHANGE IN HIS PREVIOUS MESSAGE ON TARZAN PLAN PAREN STILWELL
FROM STILWELL SGD FERRIS PAREN THIS TO GIVE YOU THE DOPE SINCE HE SAYS
THE CHANGES WERE MADE AFTER CONSULTATION WITH YOU AND CHENNAULT AND EYE
HAVE NO RECORD OF YOUR MEETING PRD QUOTE UNCLE SUGAR AND CHINESE AIR IN
CHINA NEED FOUR SEVEN ZERO ZERO TONS PER MONTH AND WITH YOUR OKRA HAVE
OKAY?
SET THIS UP TO SIX THOUSAND TONS PER MONTH FOR MARCH TO JUNE PRD YOKE
GETS FIVE THOUSAND FOR NOVEMBER AND DECEMBER AND THEN ONLY THREE TWO
HUNDRED RPT THIRTY TWO HUNDRED TONS PER MONTH FOR MAINTENANCE PRD THAT
THEY ARE THE ABSOLUTE MINIMUM FIGURES EYE AM CONVINCED PRD TOTAL TONNAGES
FROM JANUARY TO JUNE THUS FALL BELOW NEEDED FIGURES BY SEVEN THREE TWO
FIVE TONS AND THUS WE NEED MORE CHARLIE DASH FORTY SIXES PRD THIS COMES
TO THIRTY OF THEM FOR FOUR MONTHS OR ONE ONE SEVEN FOR ONE MONTH PRD
END PARAPHRASED QUOTES THIS TONNAGE SHORTAGE OF SEVEN THREE TWO FIVE
TONS TOTAL IS WHAT WILL BE THE RESULT TO THE LUMP TONNAGE IF THE PLANES
NEEDED FOR TARZAN ARE TAKEN FROM THE FERRY LIFT LLANFAIR RPT LLANFAIR

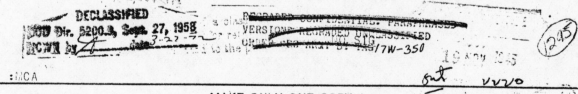

:MCA

AMMDEL AD 2637
Eyes alone Ferris from Wheeler
RVRHU AM 2100. I do not
know all back of setting up
South east Asia Theater. As
far as I know it was never
mentioned in these parts until
I discussed it with Kreuger
and afterwards sold the idea,
not too easily, to the Boss. My
conception is this. You recall
Churchills blast several months
ago, about partial demobilization
of British troops when Germany
is licked. That should be kept
in mind. As for US, as am
concerned the SEAT should
became more and more
a British Theater. That gives
them a place to pour in their
power under their own
commander. American
commitments should be kept
to the minimum and
ultimately pulled out.

1191

to make room for British
Forces. They must have a
place. repeat Place it they are
to fight when Summons is
out. When that time comes our
Show will be further East. Its
going to be tough and the
British must have a
battle ground under their own
Command in which is used
their own troops. I say let
them have it, 100 yds British. Pay.
For a time we are out
and theres a job ahead
that must be accomplished.
It is vital to our mission
in China. Our whole and
Ultimate mission lies
in China. If we dont make
a go of it, we can repeat
a long way with 50
Gynmen chasing fighting in
China. They are very friendly &
I do not think they are
to far from friendly th. Wars.
1272

RECEIVED IS SECRET CODE

RECEIVED
WAR DEPARTMENT
U. S. MILITARY MISSION TO CHINA
CHUNGKING, CHINA

INCOMING RADIO

RECEIVED	:	20 NOVEMBER 1125 GCT
FROM	:	AMMDEL
TO	:	AMMISCA, AMSME X 435
NR.	:	AM 2100 FILED 20 NOVEMBER 0751 GCT

EYES ALONE FOR STILWELL AND HEARN FROM
STILWELL SNG FERRIS PRD LECTURE TO STAFF BY LOOEY TODAY
INCLUDED STATEMENTS QUOTE WE MUST HAVE MUCH PUBLICITY IN
UNCLE SUGAR AND ENGLAND SO PEOPLE WILL KNOW WHAT WE ARE
DOING BUT FIRST WE MUST HAVE A SUCCESS TO BASE PUBLICITY
ON PRD CONCEPTION OF MODERN DIVISIONS ALL WRONG WE MUST
HAVE ONLY THREE TYPES AND FOR SOUTH EAST ASIA WE NEED A
FEW AMPHIBIOUS DIVISIONS AND SIX AIRBORNE DIVISIONS TO
TAKE THE PORTS SMCLN THEN TWENTY FOUR RPT TWO FOUR TRANSIT
DIVISIONS TO TAKE THE PLACE OF THE AMPHIBIOUS AND AIRBORNE
DIVISIONS WHILE THE LATTER GO ON TO OTHER SUCCESSES PRD
TRANSIT DIVISIONS WILL CONTAIN A HEAVY UNIT FOR TRANSPORT
BY SEA AND A LIGHT ELEMENT FOR TRANSPORT BY AIR UNQUOTE THIS
TO WARN YOU ON WHAT HE MIGHT ASK FOR IN COMING MEETINGS PRD
NEW SUBJECT YESTERDAY THEY CONSIDERED TWO PAPERS COVERING
THE FOUR INCH PIPELINE FROM CHITTAGONG TO AKHAURA TO SUPPLY
AIRFIELDS FOR TARXXN AND AIR TRANSPORT PLANE COMMITMENTS PRD

21,088

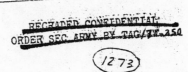

REGRADED CONFIDENTIAL
ORDER SEC ARMY BY TAG/3W-250

1273

PIPELINE RECOMMENDATION WAS TO ASK US FOR WHAT WE COULD HAVE

IN MEN AND MATERIALS FROM OUR FOUR INCH LINE TO CHINA AND AFTER

TALKING TO COXELL EYE TOLD THEM THE ANSWER RIGHT NOW AS NO

AND THAT WE HAVE HAD NO PAPERS ON IT TO STUDY PRD THE AIRPLANE

PAPER IS THAT THEY NEED ONE SQUADRON OF TRANSPORT DAKOTAS

FROM NOVEMBER TWENTY FIRST FOR LRPG RPT LRPG TRAINING PRD EYE

TALKED TO COL STONE AND HE AND EYE TOLD THEM ANSWER IS NO RPT

NO PRD THEY WILL ALSO ASK US TO TAKE CARE OF FORT HERTZ BURMA

REGIMENT INCLUDING FLYING AND MAINTENANCE.

21,088

RECEIVED IN SECRET CODE.

INCOMING RADIO:

RECEIVED: 22 NOVEMBER 0630 Z.

FROM   : AMMKUN   P R I O R I T Y

TO   : AMSME BH 131   AMMISCA

NR   : C 1029   FILED: 22 NOVEMBER 0330 Z.

PRESENTLY IN KUNMING NEGOTIATING (FOR GENERAL STILWELLS
AND GENERAL HEARNS EYES ALONE FROM DORN) WITH LUNG YUN IS
REPRESENTATIVE OF GROUP CONSISTING OF YU HAN MOU HSUEH YUEH
AND CHANG FA KTEI. PLAN OF THIS GROUP REPORTED TO BE TO TAKE OVER
IF AND WHEN CHUNGKING GOVERNMENT COLLAPSES. IF LUNG YUN JOINS
THIS GROUP, REPRESENTATIVE WILL GO TO CHENGTU TO LINE UP SZECHUAN
PROVINCIAL CLIQUE. IN THE PAST HSUEH YUEH HAS BEEN A CHEN CHENG
MAN, BUT EYE HAVE NO IDEA WHETHER OR NOT THIS FORMER CLOSE CONNECTION
IS INVOLVED NOW. IF THERE IS ANYTHING TO THIS REPORT, IT LINES
UP THE HIGHLEDSTRATEGIC FOURTH, FIFTH, AND SEVENTH WAR ZONES AS
WELL AS SZECHUAN IN THE REAR AND YUNNAN. THIS REPORTED BY
USUALLY RELIABLE POLITICAL SOURCE.   THIS GROUP REPRESENTS THE
MOST DISCONTENTED ELEMENTS IN FREE CHINA. EYE HAVE NOT DISCUSSED
IT WITH CHINESE AUTHORITIES HERE.

21,154.

RECEIVED IN SECRET CODE.

INCOMING RADIO:

RECEIVED: 22 NOVEMBER 1800 Z.

FROM : AMMDEL   P R I O R I T Y

TO : AMMISCA   AMSME X 440.

NR : AM 2112   FILED: 22 NOVEMBER 0945 Z.

       FOR THE EYES OF GENERALS STILWELL AND HEARN AND
THEIRS ALONE FROM STILWELL SGD FERRIS. LOOEYS GANG CONTINUES
TO LIST QUOTE CHARLIE BAKER ITEM (U S) UNQUOTE AS ONE OF
FORMATIONS UNDER HIS COMMAND.

       NEW SUBJECT FOR NOVEMBER AND DECEMBER YOKE GETS
FIVE THOUSAND TONS AND FOURTEENTH AIRFORCE GETS FOUR SEVEN ZERO
ZERO TONS BUT TOTAL OF NINE SEVEN ZERO ZERO PROBABLY WONT BE
REACHED THIS MONTH. TAKEN UP WITH SEAC TO GET DECISION ON
PRIORITIES ON REDUCED TONNAGE AND RESULT WAS COLON HALF OF ANY
SHORTAGE SUFFERED BY YOKE IN NOVEMBER WILL BE RETURNED TO YOKE
IN DECEMBER TO PARTIALLY MAKE UP SAID SHORTAGE EVEN IF AT THE
EXPENSE OF THE FOURTEENTH AIRFORCE TONNAGE. THIS TO BE RADIOED
TO LOOEY FOR DECISION WITH THE RECOMMENDATION THAT ALL SHORTAGES
BE ADJUSTED AND ACCEPTED AS OF END OF DECEMBER SO THAT THERE
WILL BE NO INTERFERENCE WITH TONNAGE THEREAFTER SINCE SUCH
INTERFERENCE WILL MESS UP TARZAN CALCULATIONS.

See 1280

20,190

FM MDEL AD 2 648

Eyes Alone Ferris from Tham. Do you know what is back of the shift of heavy bombers from China to India? Who is in legal command of Theater at this time and accountable for what goes on it?

w/D was informed that eye would be in command during absence of Gen Stilwell. Has there been any change? If so I desire to inform w/D

Para If I am in command it seems that I should have been informed of date of Gen Stilwells departure.

Para. Eye should be kept informed of such important matters as Movement of units from China to India, and changes of command of Theater.

1197

~~SECRET~~

PRIORITY

H.M.MDEL.

Eyes Alone Ferris from
Hearn Rec'd AM 2112 Nov. 22.

The matter of reducing 14th
A.F. tonnage in order to
give your force a better
break has been urged upon
Gmo by Chinese ministry of
War and by Gen. Stilwell
upon our WD. This over
a period of several months.
We have never gotten any
where except to be told
flatly by WD that President
himself fixed that Tonnage
at 4700 tons per month and
that it could not be reduced
except by the President himself.
If Genl Stilwell can't reduce it

11/23.

Recd 220235
Sent 220330

1/111

RECEIVED ~~IN SECRET CODE~~.

<u>INCOMING RADIO</u>:

RECEIVED: 23 NOVEMBER 0530 Z.

FROM : AMMDEL

TO : AMMISCA

NR : AM 2119 FILED: 23 NOVEMBER 0454 Z.

Z Z Z Z
RECEIVED
WAR DEPARTMENT
U. S. MILITARY MISSION TO CHI...

  EYES ALONE HEARN FROM FERRIS. MY DEAR TOM YOUR
FEELINGS FULLY APPRECIATED FOR MANY TIMES EYE AM IN SAME BOAT.
BOSS APPARENTLY APPROVED USE CHINA BOMBERS COMING TO INDIA FOR
COMBINED BRITISH AND AMERICAN EFFORT AGAINST RANGOON STARTING
SOON. EYE AM OFTEN <u>MISSIΝG</u> FROM THESE PICTURES AND HAVE TO
DIG FOR THE INFORMATION. STRAT BY PASSES ME GOING DIRECTLY
TO BOSS WITHOUT MY KNOWLEDGE ON MANY OF THESE PROJECTS. YOU
STILL COMMAND AND NONE CHANGE KNOWN TO ME. THIS BEST STORY ON
THIS SITUATION. WILL TRY TO LEARN MORE BECAUSE EYE STILL LOVE
YOU. TIME OF DEPARTURE FROM THEATER ZERO SEVEN FIVE FIVE HOURS
ONE NINE OF THIS MONTH.

     21,200.

AD 652

HAMDEL. Eyes alone Ferris Foam Hearn
Have you informed various
Hq. Concerned as to
Commander of Theater. As
eye understand it orders
issued in name of Theater
Commander, where funds
are involved, are not
legal if issued ~~issued~~
in name of any other
than actual Commander.
If this has not been
done, desire you do
so. There was no way
for us to know here
~~the~~ date. Gen Stilwell wanted
relinquished Command
so expected you to take
proper action.

(1282)

Thanks for U RAD. I never
doubted your affection.

Rcd   230920
Sent   230935 TB cK

(1282)

11119

RECEIVED IN SECRET CODE   NOV 25 '43 AM

<u>INCOMING RADIO:</u>

RECEIVED: 23 NOVEMBER 1530 Z.

FROM   : AMMDEL   <u>P R I O R I T Y</u>

TO   : AMMISCA   AMSME X 442   RECEIVED

NR   : AM 2124   FILED: 23 NOVEMBER 1141 Z.

FOR THE EYES OF GENERALS STILWELL AND HEARN AND
THEIRS ALONE FROM STILWELL SGD FERRIS. SAME SUBJECT AS MY RADIOS
XRAY DASH FOUR FOUR ZERO AND ABLE MIKE TWO ONE ONE TWO ** RE TONNAGE
TO CHINA. POWNALL CHANGED THE MINUTES OF THE MEETING SHORTLY
AFTER <u>GE</u> LEFT SO THE RADIO TO LOOEY IS CHANGED TO READ AS
FOLLOWS: HALF OF THE TONNAGE WHICH YOKE IS SHORT IN NOVEMBER,
BASED ON FIVE THOUSAND TONS, WILL BE MADE UP TO THEM AS FIRST
PRIORITY TONNAGE IN DECEMBER AND; THE REST OF THE TONNAGE
CARRIED IN DECEMBER WILL BE EQUALLY DIVIDED BETWEEN YOKE AND THE
FOURTEENTH AIR FORCE. END RADIO. THIS GIVES YOKE THE BREAKS
ON THE DEAL.

** not received
at this Hr.

* See 1277

21,256: DECLASSIFIED
         COD Dir. 5200.9 Sept. 27 1958
         DOWN by _____ date 3-27-72

1202

RECEIVED IN SECRET CODE.

INCOMING RADIO:

RECEIVED: 25 NOVEMBER 0615 Z.

FROM   : AQUILA

TO   : AMMISCA

NR   : S 44 NAOX   FILED: 25 NOVEMBER 0541 Z.

URGENT
Z Z Z Z

     FOR THE EYES GENERAL DAVISDON, GENERAL GLENN AND GENERAL HEARN ALONE : SUBJECT IS MOVEMENT OF TWO SQUADRONS AND GROUP HEADQUARTERS OF THREE FOUR FIRST BOMBARDMENT GROUP MEDIUM TO CHINA (STONE TO DAVIDSON, INFO GLENN AND HEARN EYES ALONE) INFORMATION DATED TWO FOUR NOVEMBER FROM STRATEMEYER STATES MOVEMENT IS TO BE POSTPONED REPEAT POSTPONED SINCE THERE IS POSSIBILITY THAT UNITS MAY REMAIN IN INDIA.

21,300

DECLASSIFIED
DOD Dir. 5200.9, Sept. 27, 1958
NCWN by _____ date 3-22-72

(1283)

NOV 30 40 PM

INCOMING RADIO

RECEIVED : 26 NOV 1200 GCT

FROM : RELOT

TO : AMMISCA

NR : G 322   FILED : 26 NOV 1010 GCT.

URGENT

RECEIVED
WAR DEPARTMENT
U. S. MILITARY MISSION TO CHINA
CHUNGKING, CHINA

MY RADIOS OF CRITICAL IMPORTANCE TO BOSS HAVE GONE
UNANSWERED FOR PAST FEW DAYS WHICH FROM YOUR APPOINTMENT INDICATES HIS
ABSENCE PAREN EYES OF GENERAL HEARN ALONE FROM BOATNER PAREN EYE
OF COURSE TAKE YOUR ORDERS EXPLICITLY BUT DO YOU CONSIDER YOURSELF
IN COMMAND CHINESE ARMY HERE QUERY CHINESE HAVE NOT ADVANCED IN THREE
WEEKS ON CONTRARY JAPS HAVE OUTFOUGHT THEM AND CPT BEHIND ALL THEIR
POSITIONS IN NINBYEN DASH YUBANG AREA PRD THE SITUATION IS
DEFINITELY CRITICAL PRD YESTERDAY SEN WANTED TO MAKE GENERAL WITH-
DRAWL TO LINE XHARAW DASH NINGAM DASH KANTAM BUT EYE REFUSED TO
AUTHORIZE PRD HE GAVE ME RADIO FOR BOSS TO COME HERE BUT LATER
WITHDREW PRD SUN DID NOT CONSIDER SITUATION WORSE TODAY BUT EYE DID
PRD SECURITY OF FORWARD ROAD CONSTRUCTION DEFINITELY ENDANGERED PRD
IN THE ABSENCE OF ORDERS CMA EYE WILL ACT AS MY JUDGEMENT DICTATES
PRD HAVE YOU ANY INSTRUCTIONS

- 21, 361 -

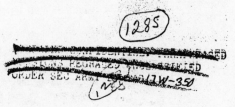

OT 56   ZZZZ

LLOT

Eyes alone Boatner from Theater 10 XT6 17D
G 322 nov 26. Eye do not consider that
eye am the Grmo's Chief of Staff
that eye Command Chinese Troops?
I know of no Chinese regulation
that prevents Gen Stilwell Commanding
Chinese troops in India when he is
not in China or India. You should
Issue orders in his name and
vigorously pursue his known policies
and directives. I know that he
is much concerned over the situation
and anxious that Chinese troops in
your sector out guess, out maneuver
and out fight any Jap troops brought
against them. The Jap aim is every
thing to lick them in order to
discredit us in eyes of Chinese.
Believe you should take Sun into
your confidence and call upon him
to exert his leadership, which we
are confident he is capable of doing.
As you know, the Grmo is asking
for Results. Your over-all Commander is Mountbatten

(1285)
See
(1290)

11,183

RE~~CEIVED IN SECRET CODE~~

<u>INCOMING RADIO</u>

RECEIVED   : 26 NOV 1600 GCT

FROM   : RELOT

TO   : AMMDEL, AMMISCA

NR   : G 323   FILED: 26 NOV 1115 GCT

URGENT

PARAPHRASE FOLLOWS OF OUR FOX FOUR SIX FIVE EYES OF GENERAL
STILWELL OR IN ABSENCE FERRIS INFORMATION HEARN EYES ONLY FROM BOAT-
NER PRD REPLY TO YOUR SERVICE THREE TWO FIVE CRYPTO JIG GEORGE TARE
ABLE BEGINS HERE PART ONE BY UNREASONABLE DEMANDS FOR SUPPLIES BY
AIR SUN HAS TRIED TO PREVENT FORWARD MOVEMENT OF HIS TROOPS PRD AS
REPORTED TO YOU BEFORE SUN HAS CONTINUED TO EMPHASISE DIFFICULTIES
OF HIS TROOPS WE FILLED SUPPLY DEMANDS AND WE BELIEVEXXXXX SUPPLY
SITUATION IS SATISFACTORY PRD PART TWO EYE AND CANNON WENT TO
THIRTY EIGHTH DIVISION HOW QUEEN AT SPECIAL REQUEST OF SUN TO
ATTEND AN IMPORTANT CONFERENCE MORNING TWENTY FIFTH NOV PRD SUN
WENT THROUGH USUAL SONG AND DANCE WITH TWO GENERALS AND SECRETARY
TAKING NOTES AGAIN EMPHASISING HIS CASUALTIES CMA LACK OF RESERVES
WHICH MADE EVEN OFFENSIVE PATROLLING IMPOSSIBLE AND SUPPLY DIF-
FICULTIES PRD ACCORDING TO HIS STATEMENTS TROOPS WERE SURROUNDED AT
YUNNANG
YUPBANQ BY FOUR HUNDRED JAP REINFORCEMENTS WHO CROSSED RIVER AND
CAME BETWEEN THAT PLACE AND <u>NFNGAM</u> AND AT NINGBYEN BY TWO HUNDRED
MORE REINFORCEMENTS AND AT BOTH PLACES HIS TROOPS HAVE ONLY SUFFICENT
AMMUNTION FOR FEW HOURS SCRAP PRD ACCORDING TO REPORT OUR LAISION
OFFICER ON SAME AREA DATED TWENTY FIFTH NOVEMBER ELEVEN HUNDRED
TWENTY FIVE HOURS THIRTY ENEMY ATTEMPTED TO CROSS RIVER AT ULUP AND
TUNGWANG
SIXTY ATTEMPTED TO CROSS SOUTH OF <u>TUNGYANG</u> PRD PART THREE HOW WOULD

EYE SUPPLY HIS TROOPS SUN ASKED ME PRD REPLY BY AIR IF NECCESSARY DIVE
BOMB BUT IF THAT IMPOSSIBLE HE WOULD HAVE TO DO LIKE JAPS AND PUSH
SUPPLIES FORWARD ON GROUND PRD SUN SAYS THIS IMPOSSIBLE PRD EYE DOD
NOT RPT NOT AUTHOIRZE NEXT REQUEST WHICH WAS TO WITHDRAW TO LINE
SHARAW DASH NINGAM SAKAN DATHYKANTBU WHICH WOULD PUT JAPS IN
FOLLOWING POCKET FOR OUR AIR FORCE TO ATTACK PART FOUR SUN THEN
SIGNED FOLLOWING RADIO WHICH HAD BEEN PREPARED PRIOR TO CONFERENCE
QUOTE SITUATION CHANGES RAPIDLY STOP ORIGINAL PLAN NEEDS MODIFICATION
STOP RESUEST COME TO LEDO IMMEDIATELY STOP REPEAT REQUEST COME TO
LEDO IMMEDIATELY SIGNED SUN UNQUOTE PART FIVE NOT REPEAT NOT MORE THAN
ONE BATTALION ENEMY STREGNTH HAVE DEVELOPED BY THIS OPERATION BUT
REPORTS INDICATE ENEMY REINFORCEMENTS MOVING NORTH IN HUKAWNG VALLEY
PRD UNDERESTIMATES EFFECT OUR AIR SUPPORT AND ENEMY SUPPLY DIFFICULTIES
DOES SUN PRD MORE CONVINCED THAN EVER AM EYE THAT SUN WILL NOT CROSS
THE TARUNO DASH TANAI AND MIGHT EVEN START WITHDRAWL UNLESS STRONG
PRESSURE IS PROMPTLY APPLIED BY GEEMO PRD IT WOULD SERIOUSLY INCREASE
OUR DIFFICULTIES IN JANUARY AND FEBRUARY TO PUT TWENTY SECOND DIVISION
IN NOW PRD AS WE CAN NOW SUPPLY IT EYE AUTHORIZED SUN FORTY EIGHT HOURS
AGOTO MOVE ONE HUNDRED AND THIRTEEN REGT FORWARD PART SIX EYE SENT
SUN OUR LIASION OFFICERS REPORTS AND REPORT THAT WE HAD PUT IN AMMUN-
ITION AND RATIONS FORWARD ON NOVEMEBER TWENTY FIFTH AND HE SENT ME
NOTE ASKING TO HOLD RADIO TO YOU FOR TIME BEING PRD EYE FEEL MY
COMMENTS REFERENCE ACTIONS THIRTY EIGHTH DIVISION STILL APPLY AND BE-
LIEVE YOU SHOULD HAVE ABOVE INFORMATION

-21, 266 -

INCOMING RADIO:

RECEIVED: 27 NOVEMBER 0605 Z.

FROM   : RELOT   Z Z Z Z

TO   : AMMISCA   AMMDEL F 474

NR   : G 324   FILED: 27 NOVEMBER 0400 Z.

SITUATION APPARENTLY EASED CONSIDERABLY PAREN
EYES ALONE HEARN INFO FERRIS FROM BOATNER PAREN BELIEVE WE ARE
OVER PRESENT CRISIS BUT WHO KNOWS.

21,400.

CHUNGKING, CHINA
NOVEMBER 27, 1943

<u>EYES ALONE</u>

AMMDEL -AD 2674

~~MESSAGE STARTS GIN~~ INFORMATION HAS BEEN RECEIVED HERE THAT A MISTER
ELLIOT REPRESENTATIVE OF THE BRITISH MINISTER OF SUPPLY IS CONTEMPLATING
MAKING THE FOLLOWING RECOMMENDATIONS TO LONDON AT THE CONCLUSION OF
HIS PRESENT TOUR PRD ONE CMA SETTING UP A JOINT BRITISH AND UNITED
STATES COMMITTEE TO CONSIDER THE REDISTRIBUTION OF CHINA DEFENSE
SUPPLIES AFTER THEIR ARRIVAL IN INDIA PAREN FERRIS SIGNED HEARN PAREN
TWO CMA PLACING CHARLIE DOG SUGAR SUPPLIES IN INDIA IN A COMMON POOL
FOR USE IN THE FAR EAST PRD PARA IT IS UNDERSTOOD THAT WHEELER HAS
OPPOSED THE IDEA STRONGLY PRD QUERY HAVE YOU BEEN APPROACHED ON THIS
SUBJECT QUERY HAS GENERAL STILWELL ANY KNOWLEDGE OF THESE PROPOSED
RECOMMENDATIONS PRD SUGGEST YOU BRING THIS TO THE ATTENTION OF GENERAL
STILWELL AND FULLY APPRAISE HIM OF THE SITUATION AND SECURE HIS OPINION
PRD ADVISE US

OFFICIAL:

L. B. THOMPSON
Lt. Col., A.G.D.
Asst. Adjutant General

REC'D MSG CEN BY ___ DATE ___ 0635.

DISPATCH TIME AND METHOD ___

G-4:WDR:efd

(4)

W-350 /// 86.

(1291)

RECEIVED ┃▅▅▅▅▅▅▅▅┃DE.

<u>INCOMING RADIO</u>:

RECEIVED: 27 NOVEMBER 0730 Z.

FROM   : AMMDEL

TO   : AMMISCA

NR   : AM 2142   FILED: 26 NOVEMBER 0020 Z.

EYES ALONE HEARN FROM FERRIS. HAVE WORD FROM BOSS WHICH HAS BEEN PASSED ON ALERTING MCCABE AND BOATNER FOR IM-PORTANT VISITOR NEXT WEEK. HAVING GROWING PAINS WITH SEAC ON VARIOUS SUBJECTS WHICH CHIEF WILL INFORM YOU. LRPS AND AIR OF COURSE PRESENT BIG QUESTIONS. SEAC IS FOR <u>INTEGRTTIP</u> AND GRABBING EVERYTHING AMERICAN. LRP MAY GO IN FROM PAOSHAN WHICH ALL ARE AGAINST BUT ONE. HAVE SEAC DIRECTIVE FOR BOSS WHICH MAKES A PEANUT OF HIM. LOOKS LIKE SEAC TRYING TO SHELF HIM. BOATNER HAVING DIFFICULTY WITH COMBAT TROOPS OF WHICH EYE AM SHORT ON ALL DETAILS. SUN FEELS THAT JAPS ARE ABOUT TO SURROUND HIM. REURAD TWO SIX FOUR NINE NOVEMBER TWO THREE, THE PRESIDENTIAL DIRECTIVE FOR FOUR SEVEN HUNDRED TONS FOR FOURTEENTH AIR FORCE ENDED WITH OCTOBER. LOC TO ASSAM NOW UNDER CONTROL OF SEAC WHICH WILL DETERMINE WHAT YOKE AND CHINA AIR WILLRECEIVE. FORTUNATELY WE HAVE RESERVE IN ASSAM WHICH WILL TIDE US OVER FOR AWHILE.

21,224.

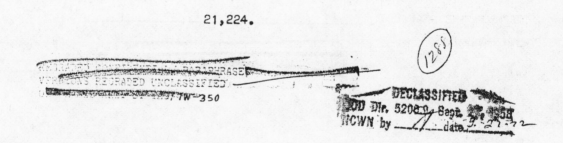

ASMF - CA 20

Eyes alone Stilwell from Hearn.

Situation in general SNAFU as usual. Informed last night that situation in Tungting lake area should begin to improve in day or two. The 14th AF giving effective assistance. Reports indicate all quiet on Salwen front. Para Boatner just reported by ZZZZ that situation has eased considerably eased. Para On th Burma front we are having the usual delays. No additional Funds yet for Burma Road. Still pending. Shra. Madame T'ung and Madame Sun expressed hope that much would be achieved this conference. I suppose they were informed. Para My program being made by State Department in regard Lend Lease. Chengtu fields being surveyed but funds will be the hitch. Para,

1282

Informed Boatner that he would
continue to issue orders in
your name.

Recd 270830
Sent 270930.

11/29.

Sent

11199

1289

1212

RECEIVED IN SECRET CODE   NOV 30 12.3 PM

INCOMING RADIO

RECEIVED   : 27 NOV 1130 GCT

FROM   : COGUK

TO   : AMMISCA

NR   : M 102 NB   FILED : 27 NOV 0937 GCT

URGENT
RECEIVED
WAR DEPARTMENT
MILITARY MISSION TO CHINA
CHUNGKING, CHINA

AT MY REQUEST THE FOLLOWING REPORT PAREN EYES ALONE GEN HEARN XX
FROM GLENN PRN REPORT ON USE OF PARATROOPS AND GAS IN CHANGTEH AREA XXX
WAS SUBMITTED BY OUR AGENT IN CHANGSHA STOP AM NOT POSITIVE BUT
BELIEVE THIS INFO ORIGNNATED FROM AGENTS LC FRILLMAN AND LILJESTRAND
RPT FRILLMAN AND KILJESTRAND WHO WRE IN CHANGTEL AT THE TIME PRD
QUOTE JUST RECEIVED YOUR LAST NIGHTS RADIO PRD FRILLMANN AND
LILJESTRAND NOW AT YIYANG PRT YIYANG AND IN CONTACT WITH CHINESE
NINE NINE ARMY PD LAST NIGHT NIPS TOOK SOME STREETS IN CHANGTEH
BUT FRAGMENTARY REPORTS STATED CHINESE FIVE SEVEN DIVISION DRIVING
THEM OUT THIS ABLE MIKE AT BAYONET POINT PRD CHINESE FROM SIXTH WAR
AREA REPORTED GAS CMA PROBABLY TEAR RPT TEAR IN USE AT CHANGTEH
CMA BUT NO PARATROOPS PAREN BIRCH TO CHENNAULT RICHARDSON AND
VINCENT PAREN UNQUOTE AND TERMINATION

EYES ALONE
           - 21, 405 -

JAH JR

(1292)

1213

INCOMING RADIO:

RECEIVED: 28 NOVEMBER 0345 Z.

FROM   : AMMKUN

TO   : AMMISCA   AMSME BH 1352

NR   : C 1058   FILED: 26 NOVEMBER 0606 Z.

P R I O R I T Y

STAFF OFFICERS OF CEF HQ SAY HO YING CHIN (EYES
ALONE FOR GEN STILWELL AND HEARN FROM DORN) MUST BE REMOVED
AS WAR MINISTER AND CHIEF OF STAFF. IF NOT DONE ALL WAR EFFORT
IN CHINA IS USELESS AS HIS INCOMPETENCE AND POLITICS HAVE WRECKED
POSSIBILITY OF OFFENSIVE ACTION. GISSIMO RECENTLY APPOINTED
KU CHU TUNG AS ACTING MINISTER OF WAR. THIS WAS MEANT AS HINT
TO HO YING CHIN TO RESIGN, BUT HO TOLD KU NOT TO ACCEPT OR ELSE.
GISSIMO DID NOT INTEND KU CHU TUNG TO TAKE OFFICE, BUT MERELY
TO BE STOOGE WHILE HE WAS GETTING RID OF HO YING CHIN. TARE
VICTOR SOOGN IS READY TO TAKE ACTIVE PART IN POLITICS. CHEN
CHENG IS NOT AS SICK AS WE THOUGHT, AND GOES TO CHUNGKING ON
MONDAY IN ORDER TO BE NEAR GISSIMO ON HIS RETURN, AND TO GIVE
ADVISE AND SUPPORT IN BREWING POLITICAL BATTLE. CEF STAFF
MEMBER STRONGLY HINTED AMERICAN SUPPORT AGAINST HO YING CHIN WILL
BE WELCOME. EYE TOLD HIM THIS WAS CHINESE POLITICS AND WE CANNOT
TAKE PART, BUT YOU MAY BE ABLE TO START BALL ROLLING AT PRESENT
CONFERENCE. SAME MAN DOES NOT ATTACH IMMEDIATE IMPORTANCE TO
POLITICAL BUILDUP IN MY RECENT EYES ALONE TO YOU, AS HE BELIEVES
HSUEH YUEH AND CHANG FA KUEI WILL STAND BY GISSIMO. THEY WANT TO
DISCUSS THIS MATTER FURTHER WITH ME. MY EARS ARE OPEN AND MY
MOUTH IS SHUT.

21,379. ORDER SEC ARMY BY TAG/JW 350

1214

INCOMING RADIO

RECEIVED : 6 DEC 0700 GCT

FROM : WAR

OPERATIONAL PRIORITY

TO : AMMISCA

NR : 3982   FILED : 6 DEC 0018 GCT

PERSONAL AND MOST SECRET FROM THE PRESIDENT TO THE

GENERALISSIMO PD SIGNED ROOSEVELT PD CONFERANCE WITH MARSHAL

STALIN INVOLVES US IN COMBINED GRAND OPERATIONS ON EUROPEAN

CONTINENT IN LATE SPRING GIVING FAIR PROSPECT OF TERMINATING WAR

WITH GERMANY BY END OF SUMMER ONE NINE FOUR FOUR PD THESE OPERATIONS

IMPOSE SO LARGE A REQUIREMENT OF HEAVY LANDING CRAFT AS TO MAKE IT

IMPRACTICABLE TO DEVOTE A SUFFICENT NUMBER TO THE AMPHIBIOUS

OPERATION IN BAY OF BENGAL SIMULTANEOUSLY WITH LAUNCHING CF THE

INDAW
ADVANCE ON I YAW KATHA AREA. OF BURMA TO INSURE SUCCESS OF OPERATION

PD THIS BEING THE CASE CLN WOULD YOU BE PREPARED TO GO AHEAD WITH

THE ICDAW KATHA OPERATION AS NOW PLANNED CMA INCLUDING COMMITMENT

TO MAINTAIN NAVAL CONTROL OF BAY OF BENGAL COUPLED WITH NAVAL

CARRIER AND COMMANDO AMPHIBIOUS RAIDING OPERATIONS SIMULTANEOUS

WITH LAUNCHING OF THE GNDAW KATHA OPERATION QUERY ALSO THERE IS

THE PROSPECT OF BAKER DASH TWO NINE BOMBING OF RAILROAD AND PORT OF

BANGKOR PD PAPA IF NOT CMA WOULD YOU PREFER TO HAVE THE INDAW KATHA

DELAYED
OPERATION DKPSUED UNTIL NOVEMBER TO INCLUDE HEAVY AMPHIBIOUS

OPERATION PD MEANWHILE CONCENTRATING ALL AIR TRANSPORT ON CARRYING

SUPPLIES OVER THE HUMP TO AIR AND GROUND FORCES IN CHINA PD PARA I

TO BE RECEIVED BY CHINA AND THE PACIFIC THROUGH THE EARLY TERMINA-
TION OF THE WAR WITH GERMANY

JAH JR

21, 826

(1501)

No. 88

Chungking, China,
7 December 1943.

MEMORANDUM:

TO   : His Excellency, The Generalissimo.

The following has been received from President Roosevelt for transmission to your Excellency:

"PERSONAL AND MOST SECRET FROM THE PRESIDENT TO THE GENERALISSIMO PD SIGNED ROOSEVELT PD CONFERENCE WITH MARSHAL STALIN INVOLVES US IN COMBINED GRAND OPERATIONS ON EUROPEAN CONTINENT IN LATE SPRING GIVING FAIR PROSPECT OF TERMINATING WAR WITH GERMANY BY END OF SUMMER ONE NINE FOUR FOUR PD THESE OPERATIONS IMPOSE SO LARGE A REQUIREMENT OF HEAVY LANDING CRAFT AS TO MAKE IT IMPRACTICABLE TO DEVOTE A SUFFICIENT NUMBER TO THE AMPHIBIOUS OPERATION IN BAY OF BENGAL SIMULTANEOUSLY WITH LAUNCHING OF THE ADVANCE ON INDAW KATHA AREA OF BURMA TO INSURE SUCCESS OF OPERATION PD THIS BEING THE CASE CIN WOULD YOU BE PREPARED TO GO AHEAD WITH THE INDAW KATHA OPERATION AS NOW PLANNED CMA INCLUDING COMMITMENT TO MAINTAIN NAVAL CONTROL OF BAY OF BENGAL COUPLED WITH NAVAL CARRIER AND COMMANDO AMPHIBIOUS RAIDING OPERATIONS SIMULTANEOUS WITH LAUNCHING OF THE INDAW KATHA OPERATION QUERY ALSO THERE IS THE PROSPECT OF B-29 BOMBING OF RAILROAD AND PORT OF BANGKOK PARA IF NOT CMA WOULD YOU PREFER TO HAVE THE INDAW KATHA OPERATION DELAYED UNTIL NOVEMBER TO INCLUDE HEAVY AMPHIBIOUS OPERATION PD MEANWHILE CONCENTRATING ALL AIR TRANSPORT ON CARRYING SUPPLIES OVER THE HUMP TO AIR AND GROUND FORCES IN CHINA PARA EYE RPT EYE AM INFLUENCED IN THIS MATTER BY THE TREMENDOUS ADVANTAGE TO BE RECEIVED BY CHINA AND THE PACIFIC THROUGH THE EARLY TERMINATION OF THE WAR WITH GERMANY".

For Lieutenant General STILWELL:

T. G. HEARN,
Major General, U. S. A.
Chief of Staff.

INCOMING RADIO:

FROM   : AMSME
                                                U R G E N T
TO   : AMMISCA

RECEIVED: 07 DECEMBER 1020 Z.

NR   : 1720 N   FILED: 7 DECEMBER 0930 Z.

        ONLY FOR EYES OF GENERAL HEARN. PRESIDENTS
MESSAGE OF FIVE DECEMBER TO GENERALISSIMO JUST MADE KNOWN TO ME
THIS MORNING (FROM STILWELL SGD ROYCE) DECISION TO POSTPOSE
OR PROCEED DEPENDENT UPON GENERALISSIMOS ANSWER. IN MY
OPINION WEAKENING OF OFFENSIVE BY REDUCTION IN SCALE OF
AMPHIBIOUS OPERATIONS IS OUTWEIGHED BY ADDED RISK TO LEDO BASE
AND FERRY ROUTE. SEE GENERALISSIMO AT ONCE. RECOMMEND TO HIM
ACCEPTANCE OF PLAN AS CHANGED. IT IS BEST THAT CAN BE GOTTEN
AND CHANCES OF SUCCESS ARE ONLY SLIGHTLY LESSENED. IT IS ONLY
PLAN ON WHICH BRITISH WILL AGREE TO USE THEIR FULL RESOURSES.

21,871.

(1502)

WAR 0919

Telegram to President Franklin D. Roosevelt:

I have received your telegram of December seventh. Upon my

Sixth

return I asked Madame Chiang to inform you of the gratifying

effect the communique of the Cairo Conference has had on the

Chinese army and people in uplifting their morale to continue

active resistance against Japan. This letter is on the way

and is being brought to you by the pilot, Captain Shelton.

First, prior to the Cairo Conference there had been disturbing

elements voicing their discontent and uncertainty of America

and Great Britain's attitude in waging a global war and at the

same time leaving China to shift as best she could against our

common enemy. At one stroke the Cairo communique decisively swept

away this suspicion in that we three had jointly and publicly

pledged to launch a joint all-out offensive in the Pacific.

Second, if it should now be known to the Chinese army and people

that a radical change of policy and strategy is being contemplated,

the repercussions would be so disheartening that I fear of the

consequences of China's inability to hold out much longer.

Third, I am aware and appreciate your being influenced by the

probable tremendous advantages to be reaped by China as well as by

the United Nations as a whole in speedily defeating Germany first.

2

For the victory of one theater of war necessarily affects all
other theaters; on the other hand, the collapse of the China
theater would have equally grave consequences on the global war.
I have therefore come to this conclusion that in order to save
this grave situation, I am inclined to accept your recommendation.
You will doubtless realize that in so doing my task in rallying
the nation to continue resistance is being made infinitely more
difficult, (1) because the danger to the China theater lies not
only in the inferiority of our military strength, but also, and
more especially, in our critical economic condition which may
seriously affect the morale of the army and people, and cause
at any moment a sudden collapse of the entire front.
Judging from the present critical situation, military as well
as economic, it would be impossible for us to hold on for
six months, and a fortiori to wait till November 1944.
In my last conversation with you I stated that China's economic
situation was more critical than the military.   The only seeming
solution is to assure the Chinese people and army of your sincere
concern in the China theater of war by assisting China to hold
on with a billion gold dollar loan to strengthen her economic
front and relieve her dire economic needs.   Simultaneously,
in order to prove our resolute determination to bring relentless
pressure on Japan, the Chinese air force and the American air
force stationed in China should be increased, as from next spring,

by at least double the number of aircraft already agreed upon,
and the total of air transportation should be increased,
as from February of next year, to at least twenty thousand tons
a month to make effective the operation of the additional planes.
(2) In this way it might be possible to bring relief to our
economic condition for the coming year, and to maintain the
morale of the army and the people who would be greatly encouraged
by America's timely assistance. What I have suggested is,
I believe, the only way of remedying the drawbacks of the strategy
concerning the China and Pacific theaters. I am sure you will
appreciate my difficult position and give me the necessary
assistance. I have instructed General Stilwell to return
immediately to Chungking and I shall discuss with him regarding
the details of the proposed changed plan and shall let you know
of my decision as to which one of your suggestions is the
more feasible. From the declaration of the Teheran Conference
Japan will rightly deduce that practically the entire weight
of the United Nations' forces will be applied to the European
front thus abandoning the China theater to the mercy of Japan's
mechanized air and land forces. It would be strategic on
Japan's part to (3) liquidate the China affair during the coming
year. It may therefore be expected that the Japanese will
before long launch an all-out offensive against China so as to
remove the threat to their rear, and thus re-capture the militarists'

waning popularity and bolster their fighting morale in the Pacific. This is the problem which I have to face. Knowing that you are a realist, and as your loyal colleague, I feel constrained to acquaint you with the above facts. Awaiting an early reply,

Chiang Kai-shek

Chungking, Szechuan
December 8, 1943

Eyes Alone still well Soam
Hearn. Th following is
paraphrase of radio girl me
for transmital to you.

Quote. Th Generalisimo
desires you come at
once to Chungking for
Conference reference the
Presidents message 17
Dec 5. End quote.

Para. Th Gmo is making
reply to presidents message
today but stating that
a definite reply can not
be made until your
return.

that he will accept one
or the other of the two
proposals but on the
contingency that China be
provided a billion dollar
gold loan and that the
air force and ferry route be doubled.
He apparently hopes to
get reply from the
president an above before
committing himself to
either one of the two
proposals. It is long, shrewd
radio which requires careful
analysis.

12/9.

Sent 090900 Z.

090810Z

11,44

1505B

921

AGWAR FROM 0034Ø2
AGNR. 11,463   AMMDEL   AD 2774 URGENT
                         and Gen. Stilwell.

For eyes alone, General Marshall, from Hearic. The following is in regard to the Generalisimos message of Dec 9 to the President.

Para. General Stilwells recommendation that the Sino accept the first of the two alternatives proposed by the President was transmitted to him personally by me. He was informed that I was free to discuss any phases of the matter with him at his convenience. The radio send by Sino to the president was drafted without any consultation with, or advice from, any member present at this hq. Thought you should know this.

Para. The best thought here is that the economic situation is not as critical as pictured.

Para. Gold will not affect the economic situation in China except possibly to the extent it is used as a medium of exchange in making purchases by Jap agents in occupied China.

Para. If the Sino accepts the first of the president's two proposals the question of an Billion dollars in gold becomes almost irrelevant. The president's first alternative is the one that will best benefit China and our war effort here.

Para. Doubling the Ferry Boat would be beneficial.

1509

HQ. U.S. ARMY FORCES

CHUNGKING, CHINA
DECEMBER 10, 1943

PRIORITY

AGWAR 922

AMDEL AD 2771

Reports here indicate that T

∧ BECAUSE OF AFFRONT RESULTING FROM EXCLUDING HIM FROM RECENT

CONFERENCES CMA FOREIGN MINISTER TARE VICTOR SOONG HAS TO THE GISSIMO TENDERED

MARSHALL
HIS RESIGNATION PRD PAREN ~~STRONG~~ SGD HEARN INFO STILWELL PAREN INFORMED CIRCLES

HERE EXPECT A POLITICAN NEAR HOW HOW KUNG TO BE APPOINTED CMA CHANG KANAI RPT

CHANG KANAI HAS BEEN MENTIONED PRD SOONG EXPECTED TO STAY HEAD OF BANK OF

CHINA CMA DIRECTOR OF NEW ORGANIZATION SIMILAR TO AMERICAN FEA RPT FEA PRD

DISSENTION KNOWN TO EXIST BETWEEN GISSIMO AND SOONG PRD BAKER DASH TWO EVALUATION.

STOP MSG BEGINS

OFFICIAL:

L. B. THOMPSON
LT. COLONEL, AGD
ASST. ADJUTANT GENERAL

REC'D IN CODE ROOM _____ DATE & TIME _100435Z_____

ACTUAL TIME OF DISPATCH AND METHOD _____

AD/ctr/G-2.

REGRADED ~~CONFIDENTIAL~~
ORDER SEC ARMY BY TAG/AW-350

~~SECRET~~

11,465
(1506)

No. 90   Chungking, China,
                                11 December 1943.

MEMORANDUM:

TO   : Her Excellency, Madame Chiang Kai Shek.

        I have been informed by the War Department
that President Chiang Kai Shek's message of December
9th to President Roosevelt has been received and that
since Mr. Roosevelt is enroute to Washington it will
be held there pending his arrival.

        General Stilwell is enroute to Chungking.
I have not yet received information of exact date of
arrival. He has reached Delhi.

                        Sincerely,

                        T. G. HEARN,
                        Major General, U. S. A.,
                        Chief of Staff.

                        -1-

SC 3/604/S

SOUTH EAST ASIA COMMAND HEADQUARTERS.

11th December, 1943.

My dear Stilwell,

A line to wish you the best of luck with the Generalissimo and to thank you for being so co-operative and helpful over the question of the integration of the British and American Air Forces.

Carton de Wiart, as I told you, was anyhow leaving for Chungking on Sunday and so will be at your disposal to help in presenting the Prime Minister's point of view to the Generalissimo if this is needed at this stage.

I feel that you would be safe in telling the Generalissimo that the Fleet that will remain behind will be good enough to ensure command of the sea in the Bay of Bengal. I am investigating now how we could use the Fleet for a sweep or demonstration by itself. As you know I am opposed to any form of Commando raid in which the soldiers have to be withdrawn, but I am examining as a matter of urgency the possibility of putting down as many soldiers as possible under shore based fighter cover, but for security reasons I hope you will not indicate to the Generalissimo when or where such an operation will take place. I fear it will be less than a tenth of the size of the original operation and I would not like to mislead him.

I am re-examining the TARZAN plan to see in what way it can be improved particularly as I fear that the original plan might possibly have been compromised in Chungking. In this respect I should be grateful if you could try to find out to what extent the plan has leaked.

I can assure you that whatever the final decision and however many resources are taken away from me I have every intention of fighting as hard as I can with whatever resources are left.

Even if you cannot get the Generalissimo to agree to the use of the Yunnan Forces I hope at least that you will get his permission for the Ledo Forces to operate against the enemy.

Best of luck.

Yours very sincerely,

Louis Mountbatten

Lieutenant General J.W. Stilwell,

P.S.   I am sending the official copy of the new directive. as soon as it is ready.

No. 380   Chungking, China,
                                           20 December 1943.

His Excellency,
General Ho Ying-chin,
Chief of General Staff,
National Military Council,
Chungking.

My dear General:

          In order to have a clear understanding of our
agreement on the movement of replacements to the Yunnan
divisions, the following is submitted for your information:

          1. The U. S. guarantees to provide all the fuel
necessary for the movement, upon notice from the War
Ministry that it has no available stocks.

          2. The War Ministry to provide 75,000 gallons
of alcohol now.

          3. The U. S. to make available all stocks on
hand in Yunnan and continue importing from India.

          4. Gasoline for return of trucks from Yunnan
to be furnished at Yunnanyi and Kunming, as available.

          5. Representatives of War Ministry and U. S. to
confer and arrange plans for transfer of gasoline and
conduct of the movement.

          I want to assure you again that we want to do
all in our power to help in getting this move completed
at the earliest possible time.

                              Sincerely yours,

                              JOSEPH W. STILWELL,
                              Lt. General, U.S. Army.

                              - 1 -

WAR DEPARTMENT
WAR DEPARTMENT GENERAL STAFF
OPERATIONS DIVISION
WASHINGTON

File

25 December 1945.

Dear General Stilwell:

The last day at Cairo I tried to see you about a memorandum you wrote the Chief in which you raised two points. I was unable to reach you before we left and only got back to Washington yesterday. I must ask you to pardon me for the delay. The points you raised and the Chief's views thereon are shown below.

<u>The future status of the C.B.I. Command.</u>
It was felt that it would be premature to determine the status of the American command in China-Burma-India in the event Burma is opened or for that matter if TARZAN should be abandoned. You know, of course, that Mountbatten has indicated his feeling that eventual separation must come. However, nothing should be done now which would hamper the job of getting together with the British for the job at hand.

<u>British activities in China.</u>
The feeling is that the points you raised should be left to the War Department in Washington. It is necessary, of course, that the War Department be kept informed of developments but any action which is required to resist this tendency should not be placed on you.

With very best wishes, I am

Sincerely yours,

THOS. T. HANDY,
Major General,
Assistant Chief of Staff.

Lieut. General Joseph W. Stilwell
Commanding General,
U.S. Army Forces,
China-Burma-India,
Chungking, China.

No. 100
Chungking, China,
24 December 1943.

MEMORANDUM:

TO   : Her Excellency, Madame Chiang Kai Shek.

1.   The following information received late yesterday afternoon is transmitted to you as it appears that there are certain recent increases which might not be known to the Generalissimo.

a.   In the North – one hundred and twenty thousand. (This includes Y-Force which is estimated to be approximately 80,000).

b.   In the South – two hundred thousand.

c.   Strength of naval, air, line of communication troops and long range penetration troops are not included in the above.

(1)   Naval and air strength available to support strong amphibious force of thirty thousand troops is said to be overwhelming. The limiting factor is landing craft.

(2)   Line of communication troops total four hundred thousand.

(3)   Long range penetration troops total twenty five thousand.

(x)   The thirty thousand amphibious troops are British. The long range penetration troops are British and American. In other operations in the South, one third of the troops are British, the remainder being Indian.

2.   Lord Mountbatten's plan of operations for the above forces is not known to me.

Sincerely,

T. G. HEARN,
Major General, G.S.C.
Chief of Staff.

No. 102

Chungking, China,
28 December 1943.

MEMORANDUM:

TO   : Her Excellency, Madame Chiang Kai Shek.

General De Wiart told me this morning of his
conference with the Generalissimo last night. The
decision given De Wiart is, to my mind, splendid.
I wonder though if Admiral Mountbatten will accept
it. May I suggest that the Generalissimo inform
President Roosevelt. It would relieve him of much
concern, and might result in pressure upon Admiral
Mountbatten, insuring his acceptance. This would
mean an overland route to China – which we all want
so badly.

                    Sincerely,

                    T. G. HEARN,
                    Major General, G. S. C.
                    Chief of Staff.

1232

No. 114.

TGH/flr.
Chungking, China
January 11, 1944.

MEMORANDUM TO: Her Excellency, Madame Chiang Kai-shek.

The memorandum which I am sending as an enclosure to this note, I am sure you will appreciate, is a personal note to me and not one addressed to the Generalissimo or yourself.

I was certain that no words of mine could paint the picture as presented by General Stilwell, hence my decision to send his note to you.

I trust that you or the Generalissimo will not take offense at this informal, unique characteristic plain language.

May I ask that it not get beyond the hands of yourself or the Generalissimo and that both the English and Chinese copies be returned to me when they have served their purpose.

Sincerely,

T. G. HEARN
Major General, G. S. C.
Chief of Staff

note delivered by Col Cleveland
Copy typed by Sgt Boyle
Proof read by Cols Cahill and Thompson.
Col Liu and the 2 civilian interpreters prepared one copy
of Chinese translation.

Col Cleveland and Gen Evans have seen - also Gen Hearn

11 Jan 44

ABOVE RETURNED BY C/S 13 JAN 44
AND BURNED EXCEPT CHINESE COPY
WHICH IS FILED HEREWITH
13 Jan 44

REGRADED CONFIDENTIAL
ORDER SEC ARMY BY TAG/JW-350

1233

MEMORANDUM FOR HEARN:

1. Mountbatten is dogging on the Burma job. His "JPS Staff", or stooges, have prepared a paper which he will endorse and send to London. It contains four recommendations:

a. Stop work on Ledo Road after it reaches Myitkyina, because it won't be finished in time and will be of little use even then. Divert the engineers and equipment to airfields so as to raise hump tonnage to maximum. It is necessary to take the road to Myitkyina in order to "protect the ferry route".

b. The recapture of Burma is <u>not worthwhile</u>. Do a little skirmishing in the Chin Hills and of course attack Akyab (that valuable metropolis) but nothing else.

c. Attack Sumatra this fall, and then work north. (Presumably to prevent construction of the Kra canal.)

d. Include Hong Kong in the South East Asia Command boundary. ¶ ¦ ¦

The limies have now shown their hand. This pusillanimous and double-crossing program amply confirms all our suspicions. They are determined to keep China blockaded and powerless. They aim to go to Singapore, but that is the limit of their contribution. Louis at first thought he could take command in China, but ran into much opposition, so now he is out to keep any help from reaching her. The argument that it is <u>not worthwhile</u> to retake Burma is a hot one. If made in good faith, <u>why attack Akyab</u>? The attack on Sumatra is of course aimed at getting Malaya, and incidentally at controlling the Kra isthmus, so that Singapore will remain important. But the pay-off is Hong Kong! That must be put in the South East Asia Command boundary so that China cannot possibly take it back.

You can see how we must be hated; we are diametrically opposed to all this improper "thinking", and I am surprised that Louis hasn't had me relieved. I aired myself in Delhi on the 1st, and he didn't like it at all — maybe it will come unannounced.

Whether to tell the Generalissimo or not, I don't know. I am afraid he would just say "to hell with everything", and call off the dogs. On the other hand, he could squawk to high heaven that he was deserted and get President Roosevelt to put pressure on the limies. The limies couldn't make much of a case out of leaving us holding the sack out here in the jungle while they sat back and did nothing. If they would fight, and if Ho would send replacements over, we could do something. I mean we have good chances of pushing it through, but all alone we would be sunk.

- 1 -

REGRADED CONFIDENTIAL
ORDER SEC ARMY BY TAG/JN-350

1234

You may have had this dope already, but I am writing on
the chance that you haven't. If the Generalissimo had agreed to fight,
the limies could not have welshed. Now they will point the finger of
scorn at him and say it's his fault. Tell him what's cooking, and urge
him to let the Y-Force loose, or he's lost. The limies will certainly
follow some such program unless the Y-Force cooperates, and even though
now the Generalissimo will get poorer terms than he could have, it's the
only recourse left him. Tell him the case is urgent, and that if he
doesn't assist, he will be played up as the quitter, and all sympathy
for the Chinese cause will be lost. The British will get all the
CDS stuff in India, our special troops will all be pulled out or given
to the British, the Chinese will NOT get Hong Kong, and China will be
left blockaded. And not just till next fall, either; more likely at
least two years.

2.   If the Generalissimo does not help the X and Y Forces to
get going, the Japs can put at least three (3) divisions against
Paoshan. The Chinese will have to meet them alone without any help
from the British. There will be nothing to divert Japs in north and
west Burma to prevent Japs concentrating against Chinese of Y-Force.
If Kunming falls, it will be a very serious blow to China.

    Also Japs could attack Kunming from Indo-China and, feeling
secure in Burma, would probably try both from Burma and Indo-China.

3.   Filler replacement requirements: Units at Ramgarh are short
11,000 men, and we are having casualties. The 30th Division was
promised complete last May, and is still short 8,500 men. Already too
late to put them in unless we use them half trained. This matter must
be expedited in some way. Impress this upon General Ho Ying Chin, and
keep after Madame to do what she can. Your answer reference 200th
Division may be on the way but not received yet. Our communications
are very slow.

                    Yours etc.,

                    J.W.S.

致賀安參謀長之備忘錄

(一)蒙巴頓對於攻擊緬甸事極為固執。彼之軍事參謀『或不良助手已準備妥當一

個計劃，蒙巴頓當予以簽字，並送至倫敦。其中包含四個建議：

(甲)待力多公路修至米支那後，即予以停止前進，因時機一到路恐不能完成，並屆時其

用途亦極小。將工程師及器材轉移至飛機場，使飛中國之物資數量增至最高點。

公路應修至米支那因其重要性在『保護航線』也。

(乙)收復緬甸，並不值價。在泰山(Gin Hiii)之區域祇與敵小戰，在阿卡布(Akyab)那個大城

市)區域當然要大為攻擊，除此之外別無用意。

(丙)本年秋季反攻蘇門答拉(Sumatra)，然後佝比出擊。(推測其用意在阻止克若

（六○ ） 運河之建築。

（丁）包括香港在東南亞洲統帥部之內！！！

英人之手腕已極明顯。此種畏縮及陷害之計劃，證實吾等所懷疑者。彼等所

決定者乃是要將中國封鎖並使中國無力。彼等之目的地為新嘉坡，其貢獻

亦即止於此矣。先是路易斯（即蒙巴頓）以為彼可在中國境內得有指揮權，但彼

到處受挫。因是彼亦出來設法對於任何援助中國之事加以阻止。其關緬甸不能收

復之點因其無重要性，實為一最可笑之雄辯也。如對緬甸收復計劃忠實相信，

為何攻擊阿卡布？出擊蘇門答拉之用意，在收復馬來亞，其最巧者，亦即控

制克斯馬斯（Christmas）為使新嘉坡終為一重要城市也。但其最可憂慮者即為

香港。故該地區必須劃在東南亞洲邊境之內，以期致使中國而不能收復也。

由是君可視之吾等如何被恨，因吾等對彼等之不合理之『思想』加以反對。予

極為驚奇，因路易斯未能將予去職。予在一號時曾在德里放此空氣，彼極不

喜悅。其或去職之事，在不公開發表之範圍內光臨乎。

以上之事是否告知　委員長予不得而知。予畏　委座或言『管他那些事呢』然

後停止一切。其他一方面思之，彼可以最大之聲音何高天呼喊，因彼已被雜棄並

請羅斯福以方壓制英人。英人使予等在森林中拼命，彼等在後方閒坐無事，

此一點英人似不可能戰勝也。如彼等（華人）決意作戰，如何總長能將補充，兵運

印，吾等或可有所成就。予意吾等有相當良好機會本原有計劃而求得戰勝。

但如吾等單獨作戰定必失敗也。

或者君對於此等消息早有所聞，但予書此完全以君對此而不知也。如彼同意作

戰，英人或不至如此而行。現時英人將用手指彼並言為彼之過錯。轉告彼現時之

狀況，並請其特遠征軍放鬆，否則彼將丟失矣。遠征軍如真不合作，英人絕採取此

種計劃），委座雖不能得到較為更妥善之合作援助，但所餘者祇此矣。告知彼

此事極為迫切。如彼不予以協助彼將被稱為不合作者，其對中國人之同情心盡

將失去矣。英人當將所有在印之國防供應公司之物品盡行取去。吾等（美人）之

特種部隊恐亦將被調開或撥與英人使用，中國人恐仍不能將香港取回，中國

仍將被為封鎖。其時間不祗止限於明秋，其最可能者亦恐至少二年以後矣。

（二）委座不允使用遠征軍及駐印軍，日人至少可使用三個師團攻擊保山。屆時中

方將單獨作戰，而不能得到英人之協助也。是時緬北及緬西亦將無人牽制敵人兵

方而使其不能集中攻擊遠征軍。昆明一失，將予中國一極大之打擊。

日人仍可由安南方面攻擊，緬甸敵人覺得安全以後，彼等定從緬甸及安南雙方進攻中國也。

(三) 其關補充房之缺額，在蘭伽之部隊單位，短火一萬一千人。吾等亦有作戰之傷亡。第卅師於去年五月即允補充全軍，現仍缺火八千五百人。現在使用該師已較遲，即或使用，皆為半訓者。此事必須設法催促。轉告何應欽。追告蔣夫人看彼有何辦法。第二百師或者正在途中，仍未接到。吾等之交通電信極為遲緩。

美國駐中緬印軍總司令史迪威

Ammisca for Hearn.

"1. Mountbatten is dogging on the Burma job. His "war staff", or stooges, have prepared a paper which he will endorse & send to London. It contains four recommendations.

  I. Stop work on Ledo Road after it reaches Myitkyina, because it won't be finished in time and will be of little use even then. Divert the engineers and equipment to air-fields so as to raise hump tonnage to max imum. It is necessary to take the road to Myitkyina in order to "protect the ferry route."

  II. The re-capture of Burma is not worthwhile. Do a little skirmishing in the Chin Hills and of course attack Akyab (that valuable metropolis-) but nothing else.

  III Attack Sumatra this fall, and then work north. (Presumably to prevent construction of the Kra canal.

IV. Include Hong Kong in the S.E.A.C. boundary.   !!!

The limies have now shown their hand. This pusillanimous and double-crossing program amply confirms all our suspicions. They are determined to keep China blockaded and powerless. They aim to go to Singapore, but that is the limit of their contribution. Louis at first thought he could take command in China, but ran into too much opposition, so now he is out to keep any help from reaching her. The argument that it is not worth while to retake Burma is a hot one. If made in good faith, why attack Akyab? The attack on Sumatra is of course aimed at getting Malaya, and incidentally at controlling the Kra isthmus, so that Singapore will

1242

remain important. But the pay-
off is Hong Kong! That must be
put in the S.E.A.C. boundary
so that China cannot possibly
take it back.

You can see how we must
be hated; we are diametrically
opposed to all this ~~compulsory~~ improper "thinking", and I am surprised that
Louis hasn't had me relieved. I
aired myself in Delhi on the 1st,
and he didn't like it at all. —
Maybe it will come unannounced.

Whether to tell the G-mo or
not, I don't know. I am afraid
he could just say "to hell with
everything", and call off the dogs.
On the other hand he could squawk
to high heaven that he was deserted and get F. D. R. to put
pressure on the limies. The
limies couldn't make much
of a case out of leaving us hold-

ing the pack out here in the jungle while they sat back & did nothing. If they ~~bastards~~ would fight, and if ~~they wouldn't~~ ~~do anything~~ Ho would send re-placements over, we could do something. I mean we have good chances of pushing it through But all alone we'd be sunk.

You may have had this dope already, but I am writing on the chance that you haven't. ~~It would~~ ~~give us a chance~~. If the field had agreed to fight, the limies could not have welshed. Now they will point the finger of scorn at him & say it's his fault. ~~May-~~ ~~be this letter is going have is too~~ ~~late by the time you get it.~~ Tell him what's cooking, and urge him to let the y-force loose, or he's lost. The limies will certainly follow some such program unless the y-force co-operates, and even though now

the G-mo will get poorer terms
than he could have; it's the only
recourse left him. Tell him
the case is urgent, and that if
he doesn't assist, he will be played
up ~~in the~~ as the quitter, and
all sympathy for the Chinese
cause will be lost. The British
will get all the C.D.S. stuff in
India, our special troops will
all be pulled out or given to the
British, *the chinese will NOT get Hong Kong,* and China will be left
blockaded. And not just till
next fall, either; more likely at
least two years —

Well you know the words &
music. ~~Try if this will scare him~~
as much as the japs do.

yrs etc.
J.W.S.

2.

P.S. ~~We are pushing to get another action set up which may~~
or may not get us forward.

1245

2. If the G-mo does not help the X & y Forces to get going, the Japs can put at least three (3) Divisions against Paoshan. The Chinese will have to meet them alone without any help from the British. There will be nothing to divert Japs in North and west Burma to prevent Japs concentrating against Chinese of Y-Force. If Kunming falls, it will be the finish of the G-mo. a very serious blow to China.

Also Japs could attack Kunming from Indo-China and, feeling secure in Burma, would probably try both from Burma and Indo-China.

3. REPLACEMENT REQUIREMENTS: PAREN STILWELL ~~PAREN~~ UNITS AT RAMGARH ~~ARE~~ EIGHT ELEVEN THOUSAND REPEAT ONE ONE ~~ZERO ZERO ZERO MEN~~ CMA AND WE ARE HAVING ~~DIFFICULTIES~~ PRD THIRTIETH ~~RPT THREE ZERO~~ DIVISION WAS ~~PROMISED~~ COMPLETE LAST MAY ~~REPEAT MAY~~ CMA AND ~~WAS~~ IS STILL SHORT EIGHTY FIVE HUNDRED ~~FIVE ZERO ZERO~~ MEN PRD ALREADY TOO LATE TO PUT THEM IN UNLESS WE USE THEM
TRAINED
~~HALF~~ IN SOME WAY PRD ~~I MPRESS THIS UPON AGAIN WITH~~
Para
~~TO~~ ~~DO YING REPEAT DYS~~ CHIN ~~REPEAT CHIN~~ CMA AND KEEP AFTER MADAME TO DO WHAT
Para
SHE CAN PRD YOUR ANSWER REFERENCE TWO HUNDREDTH DIVISION MAY BE ON THE WAY BUT NOT RECEIVED YET PRD OUR COMMUNICATIONS ARE VERY SLOW PRD ~~WE ARE PECKING AWAY HERE~~

JWS